The Wines of Rioja

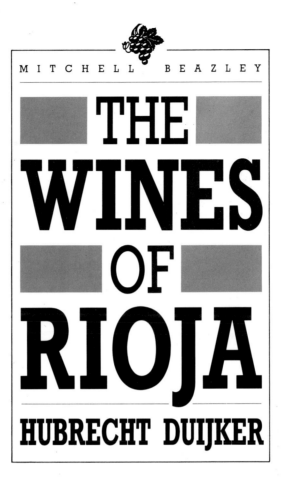

MITCHELL BEAZLEY

THE WINES OF RIOJA

HUBRECHT DUIJKER

Design by Will van Sambeek & Cie, Amsterdam
Photography by Peter van der Velde, with additional
photographs by the author
Maps by Gieb van Encevort
English translation by Raymond Kaye
Edited by Carrie Segrave Associates
First published in the UK by Mitchell Beazley London,
Artists House, 14–15 Manette Street,
London, W1V 5LB
© 1985 by Het Spectrum B.V., Holland
English translation © Mitchell Beazley Publishers 1987
ISBN 08533 680 3
Typeset by J&L Composition, Ltd., Filey, N. Yorkshire
Printed by Egedsa, Sabadell
Depósito legal: B.19.350-87
Printed in Spain

For Tineke and Eugène,
good friends whose great hospitality
is of Riojan quality.

Acknowledgments

This book could not have been written
without the splendid cooperation not only of
the bodegas, but also of various
organisations and individuals. The author
and the publishers are greatly indebted
to:

—Instituto Nacional de Fomento de la
Exportación (INFE)
—Grupo de Exportadores de Vinos 'Rioja'
and its chairman Fernando Salamero
Laorden; also Carlos García-Ogara Wright,
its dynamic director, and his staff
—Manuel Ruiz Hernandez of the Estación
de Viticultura y Enología in Haro
—Gabriel Chinchetru García of the Casa
del Vino in Laguardia
—Consejo Regulador de la Denominación
de Origen 'Rioja' and its president Santiago
Coello Cuadrado
—Instituto Nacional de Investigaciones
Agrarias (INIA), and in particular Julio
Fernandez Sevilla
—Tom Wesel of the Rioja Wijn
Informatiecentrum in the Netherlands,
together with his splendid colleagues
Marianne Nuberg and Nelly Ordelman.

Contents

Spanish Surnames
In Spain it is customary, and a more or less official usage, to add your mother's maiden name after your own surname. Wherever the maternal surnames of people referred to in this book were known to me I have generally given them at one or two points in the text.

Figures and Labels
Statistics concerning vineyards, vine planting, wine production, the capacities of bodegas and many other topics are given in this book. Obviously these figures are subject to alteration and the reader should bear this in mind; the same applies to label designs.

Opposite page:
Rioja Alavesa landscape, near the village of Elciego. In the background is the Sierra Cantabria, which shelters the area from north winds.

Right:
Comportas, wooden tubs used by grape pickers, in front of one of the small bodegas in Laguardia after being washed in the village street. The grape harvest can begin.

Foreword

I would like to begin by thanking Hubrecht Duijker for inviting me, as President of the Consejo Regulador de la Denominación de Origen 'Rioja', to write a foreword to his book on the wines of my region.

For a Riojan it is a source of satisfaction that a writer like Hubrecht Duijker, already well known for his books on other regions such as Bordeaux and Burgundy, has now turned his attention to Rioja and its wines — wines to which, without any fear of exaggeration, I can attribute the same quality as the products of these French districts.

Rioja is a Spanish region with a thousand years of wine tradition: Latin and Romance texts from the Middle Ages confirm this. Today this tradition is upheld by a company of men of worth and merit who harvest the fruits of this unique soil by methods both old and well tried and modern, and make the famous Rioja wines, now appreciated by connoisseurs throughout the whole world.

The quality control exercised by the Consejo Regulador over which I preside is, to the best of my knowledge, one of the strictest in the world. In this book, which I most sincerely welcome, you will find this and many other interesting topics dealt with in an agreeably readable and stimulating way. I anticipate that this book will become a classic as far as the wines of Rioja are concerned, the more so since it has been — and of this I am quite certain — so thoroughly and conscientiously researched.

I hope that readers will enjoy this book and that it will help them discover all the excellent qualities of our Rioja wines.

Santiago Coello
President of the Consejo Regulador de la Denominación de Origen 'Rioja'

Introduction

It was a long time before I really discovered Rioja. My first acquaintance dates from the 1960s, when I used to pick up the occasional bottle of cheap Rioja from the supermarket. Since then this wine and I have gradually grown closer. My taste has developed, and so has that of the Rioja. My regard for this Spanish wine increased steadily, but even so I did not make my first visit to Rioja until 1983. That first visit occupied just a few days, but it was followed some months later by a longer stay. These visits were very enlightening. Like every Rioja drinker who has never been there, I had been harbouring a number of prejudices and misconceptions. Thus for example I had expected a rather primitive, rural area, but I found many large bodegas with up-to-date equipment, as well as a bustling modern provincial capital. I had also imagined that the interpretation of the wine laws here would be somewhat loose — but I learned that they are among the most stringent in the world. I had regarded Rioja as always strongly influenced by wood, yet a good deal of the production consists of wines that have not been aged in barrel. I had entertained the idea that Rioja wines were fairly uniform in character, but I came across many variations in taste and style.

These and other discoveries made the Rioja so interesting that I decided to devote a book to the region, and so there were further visits.

Just as the Champagne district in France is dominated by its shippers, so the bodegas hold sway in Rioja; they handle about 95% of all the wine. It was therefore essential that I should visit all the bodegas of any importance — around 55 of them — both exporting and non-exporting firms. It will be clear from the Acknowledgements opposite that this was facilitated by the support of various individuals and bodies. My programme of visits was exhausting (not least because of constantly having to switch languages, sometimes using French, now English, and then Spanish) but at the same time incredibly instructive and very fascinating. I tasted whole series of wines that were unknown to me, gathered great quantities of facts, and discovered many

striking contrasts among the bodegas of Rioja. There is, for example, a world of difference between houses such as Lopéz de Heredia and Bodegas Olarra. And the same is true of Bodegas Carlos Serres and La Granja Remélluri; of the Santa Daría cooperative and Bodegas Gurpegui; and of Bodegas Campo Viejo and the Sociedad Vinícola Laserna. The world of Riojan wine is a very varied one.

In this book practically every bodega visited is given a separate chapter, with a descriptive text and the labels of the best wines illustrated. There is also a wealth of photographs — Peter van der Velde went around all the selected bodegas after me. Luck was on his side, for whereas I had concluded my schedule of visits under grey skies and in pouring rain, he arrived two weeks later in brilliant autumn weather. This, combined with Peter's great talents as a photographer, has provided a unique collection of pictures of the region's landscape, villages, bodegas and people.

Riojan hospitality is proverbial. We were cordially welcomed virtually everywhere; people provided us with all the information we sought and gave us freely of their time.

My endeavour has been to make *Wines of Rioja* the most detailed and comprehensive book, both in its text and its illustrations, so far dedicated to the region and its bodegas; a book the reader will take with him through the various districts, that outlines and explains the growing, making and maturing of Rioja, that in straightforward fashion describes the bodegas, critically examines hundreds of wines, picks out the specialities, and names the people. In short, a book that will chart all the aspects of the Rioja wine region.

I believe Rioja has a right to such a book, for anyone who comes to know this area and its wines really well must reach the conclusion that it deserves a secure place among the foremost regions in the world of wine.

Hubrecht Duijker
Abcoude, Netherlands

La Rioja

La Rioja, the region, is the birthplace of *el Rioja*, the wine. The area lies in northern Spain about 60 miles from Bilbao, San Sebastián, the Atlantic coast and the French border. Madrid is more than 180 miles to the south. Despite the nearness of the ocean, Rioja does not have a markedly maritime climate, for to the north a wide, deep succession of mountain chains forms a natural shield against cold sea winds and rain showers. Clouds can often been seen piling up high against the nearest mountain ridge, the Sierra de Cantabria, so that while one side of the range is damp and misty, Rioja basks in bright sunshine under an intensely blue sky. Sometimes in June there is snow on the northern slopes of the mountains while summer temperatures prevail on the southern side. A marked change in the vegetation can also be seen: on the Rioja side of the mountains it suddenly becomes more abundant, more Mediterranean in character, with lavender and olive trees. Because of this many Basques come here in summer. Their children acquire better appetites and more colour. La Rioja is a Mediterranean oasis in the cool Spanish north.

The rivers

The peaks of the Sierra de Cantabria rise to nearly 5,000 feet, which is high, but not quite high enough to keep all oceanic influences out of Rioga. This is a good thing as far as wine growing is concerned. The best wines always come from areas with a mild climate that is not too dry and without extremes of temperature. As well as being protected on the north side against too much cold and damp, Rioja has a barrier on its opposite flank against the sometimes searing heat and violent storms of the Spanish plateau, for to the south lies the Sierra de la Demanda massif with peaks of over 7,200 feet.

The river Ebro flows across the Rioja, fed here by a number of tributaries. The most important, from west to east, are: Río Tirón, Río Oja, Río Najerilla, Río Iregua, Río Leza, Río Cedacos and Río Alhama. For hundreds of thousands of years a great deal of fertile river silt has been deposited in this basin, which is why Rioja produces large quantities of vegetables and fruit as well as wines.

Origin of the name

The name Rioja is probably derived from Río Oja, but there is no certainty about this. It could be that the region was named after a pre-Roman tribe that lived here, the Ruccones, later called the Riugones. Equally the name could derive from *roja*, Spanish for 'red', for the soil here has a pinkish colour in parts. Another possible origin is the Basque Ería-ogia (corrupted to Errioja): this means something like 'land of bread', a reference to the cornfields that were here. Whatever the truth of the matter may be, the earliest document in which the Rioja is mentioned – as Rioxa – dates from 1092: and there it is clear that the name meant the area around the Río Oja.

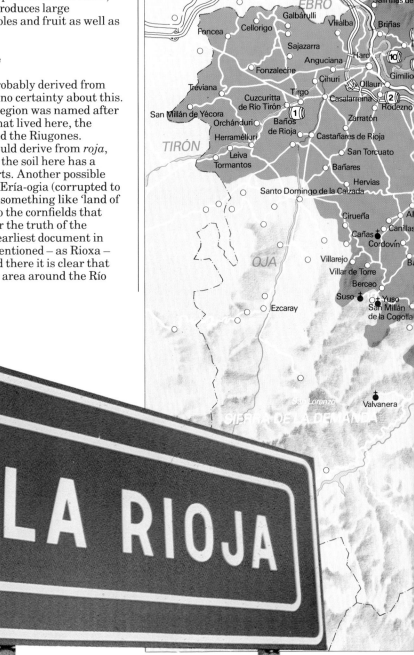

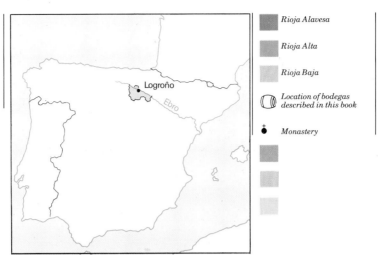

	Rioja Alavesa
	Rioja Alta
	Rioja Baja
	Location of bodegas described in this book
	Monastery

La Rioja

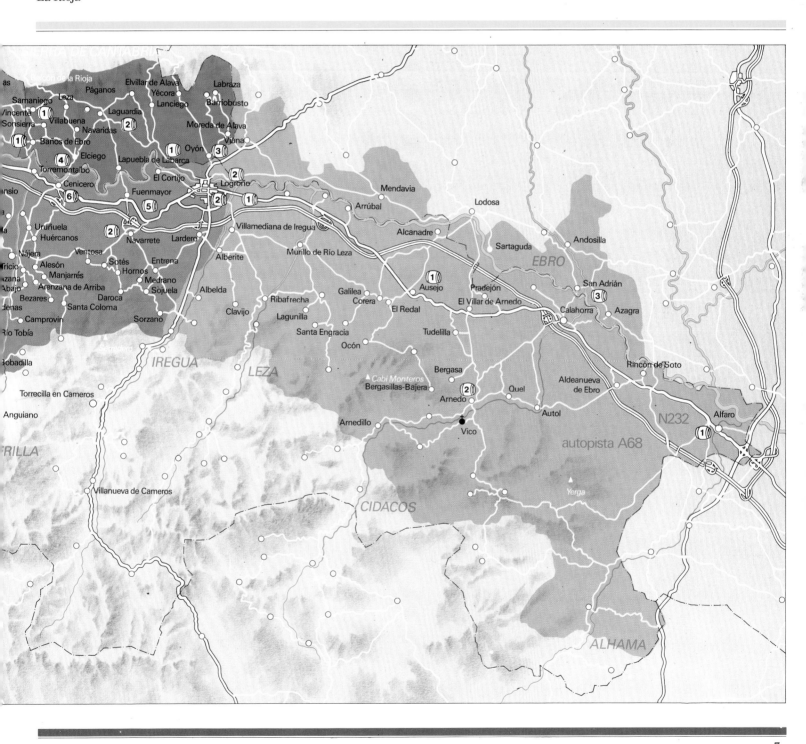

La Rioja

Parts of three provinces

Geographically there are two Riojas: the administrative and the wine-growing region. Once the administrative area was called Logroño, after its capital. The administrative and the wine-growing Riojas do not entirely correspond. The roughly 1,900 square miles of the former include terrain (mountains for example) that does not lend itself to growing grapes. In addition, two small sections of other provinces, Alava and Navarre, belong in the wine-producing area. The two border on the Rioja in the north. The Alava communities involved lie between the Sierra de Cantabria and the Ebro and in fact have always produced Rioja. Indeed, the calcareous soils there often give the finest wines of the whole region. The Navarran villages joined the Rioja by request. When in the 1930s it became necessary to give Rioja wine a more precise territorial definition it appeared that a number of Navarre communities traditionally made their wine as Rioja. These villages were given the choice of either joining Rioja or Navarre. If they chose Rioja, the condition was that there could be no 'islands' of Rioja within the Navarre region. Each of the applicant communities had either to border on Rioja directly, or via a neighbouring village that also wanted to belong to Rioja. In this way half a dozen villages were included in the Rioja *denominación de origen*.

Tranquil and unspoiled

The wine district of Rioja stretches for about 75 miles, following the Ebro from north-west to south-east. It is some 30 miles across at its widest. Not many people live there: only about 250,000, nearly half of them in Logroño. Mass tourism has not been developed here so that large parts of the area are still quiet and unspoiled. There are vineyards everywhere, and peaceful hill villages marked out by the silhouettes of their churches. It is a

landscape of steep slopes that offers the visitor distant views that are often unexpected and strikingly beautiful. The summer days are sunny, with pleasantly cool evenings. Autumn can be mild, with showers, and winter does not last long here as a rule, with snow and frost usually only in the west of the region. The mild, long springs are often announced by a warm southerly wind called the *solano* or *bochorno*. And the inhabitants are almost proverbially friendly and very hospitable.

Rioja Alavesa

The Rioja wine region has been divided into three districts: Rioja Alavesa, Rioja Alta and Rioja Baja. The first two cover the western portion, the third district the whole of the eastern part of the region. As its name indicates, *Rioja Alavesa* belongs to the province of Alava (Araba in Basque, a form which also appears on the provincial border signs). Its vineyards run from the foot of the Sierra de Cantabria practically to the Ebro, which has a very steep northern bank in places. The district comprises 18 villages with about 1,700 acres of vineyards, practically all on clay and limestone. The westernmost vineyards begin just past the ravine where the Ebro flows into Rioja and the easternmost are in Oyón, a village a few miles north of Logroño and its bridges over the great river.

Rioja Alta

While Rioja Alavesa follows the winding northern bank of the Ebro, Rioja Alta runs parallel to it on the southern side. At least for the most part: there is a remarkable Rioja Alta enclave in Rioja Alavesa territory. This has come about for political and administrative reasons: the boundary follows the administrative border. The two most important of these Alta communities on the north bank are San Vicente de la Sonsierra and Abalos. Altogether Rioja Alta ('Upper Rioja') has 77 wine villages and 40,800 acres of vineyards. Geologically there are clay and limestone, clay and iron, and soils of alluvial origin. The district starts at the Rioja border in the west and stretches to just past Logroño. It is very hilly and in the south the vineyards go up to about 2,000 to 2,300 feet above sea level.

Rioja Baja

Rioja Baja ('Lower Rioja') starts east of

La Rioja

the Logroño–Oyón line. It is in fact lower-lying than the other two districts. The mountain ranges are further apart here, the river valley broader and the landscape flatter. Alluvial clay is the most common type of soil (there are also considerable areas of ferruginous clay). Not only vines but many kinds of vegetables and fruit thrive here. One reason for this is that the Rioja Baja climate is warmer and drier than that of the other two districts. Warm Mediterranean winds are drawn in here by the broad valley of the Ebro. The vineyards cover 37,000 acres, distributed over 37 communities. However, fruit and vegetable growing is more important for this district, where there is a flourishing and extensive canning industry. This spends an annual 7 thousand million pesetas on packaging materials (metal cans and glass jars). In addition Rioja Baja is an important supplier of fresh vegetables and fruit. Here are cultivated – mostly on the irrigated valley soils – potatoes, artichokes, asparagus, beans, peppers, peaches, sprouts, sugar beet, tomatoes, onions and carrots. The area on which these and other crops are grown has been doubled since the 1960s – quite often at the expense of vineyards.

History

Finding reminders of Rioja's earliest inhabitants poses no problems for the present-day visitor to the region. At the foot of the Sierra de Cantabria, between San Vicente de la Sonsierra and Elvillar there are seven dolmens, burial places and monuments built by early peoples. They were constructed from massive stones and are situated between 1,900 and 2,230 feet. It has been established scientifically that these dolmens are more than 4,000 years old. Other traces of inhabitants from the distant past have been discovered. In 1935 the archaeologist Alejandro Sanpedro Martínez found the remains of a very ancient village near Laguardia. It was given the name La Hoya and excavations have been going on right up to the present day. Under the topmost layer the remains of two other levels of habitation and culture have been discovered. The earliest occupants lived in the 15th century BC; they were followed two centuries later by a new population. It became apparent from the construction of the dwellings, the materials used and the objects found on the site that a Celtic tribe was settled here in the 4th century BC. These were undoubtedly the Berones who had established themselves in this fertile valley several centuries earlier. The territory they controlled was called Beronia and took in most of present-day Rioja. Only the eastern part did not belong to them: that was the property of the Basques.

The Roman era

The Roman advance into the Iberian peninsula began in the 2nd century BC and their conquests included the Ebro valley. Their long presence left its indelible mark on the region. Calagurris (the present Calahorra) lay on the Roman road that led from Tarragona to the west coast and became one of the most important towns of the empire. It therefore obtained the right to issue its own coins. The many excavations carried out in and around the town have brought to light not only the remains of walls and pillars, but an artificial lake and all kinds of art objects –

including the Dama de Calahorra, a female head in marble from the 1st century. Calahorra also became well known as the birthplace of the Roman orator Marus Fabius Quintian and the poet Aurelius Prudentius Clemente. There are further reminders of Roman times in other parts of Rioja, among them the remains of a large bridge near El Cortijo, just west of Logroño. The Romans also practised viticulture. At Funes, a village $7\frac{1}{2}$ miles as the crow flies from Calahorra, the remains of a large Roman winery have been found. In the west of the region, in the Rioja Alavesa district, many old pressing vats have been discovered in the countryside.

The struggle against the Moors

After the fall of the Roman Empire barbarian tribes invaded Spain. The first were the Vandals and Suevi, in AD 409, later followed by the Alani. The Visigothic state established in this period was attacked in 711 by the Arabs, who penetrated north as far as the Ebro valley. Rioja became a frontier region and the kings of Navarre built fortresses on hilltops north of the river, Laguardia and Labastida being the best-known examples. According to tradition one of the battles between the Christians and the Moors took place in 844 at the foot of the Clavijo, a clifftop stronghold south of Logroño. The Christians are said to have won the bloody encounter through the intervention of St James (Santo Jacobo – Santiago in the vernacular), who appeared on a white horse. This apostle had been martyred eight centuries before; his bones had been brought to Spain and buried there. They were discovered, according to the legend, thanks to a falling star. King Alfonso II had a church built on this field of the star (*campus stellae*); later one of the most important Christian places of pilgrimage grew up around it: Santiago de Compostela. It is hard to separate fact from fiction in the stories about St James, and historians are doubtful whether the battle at Clavijo ever took place. However that may be, the Muslims were finally

expelled from the Rioja by Sancho the Great in 923.

A wine-loving monk

In the succeeding centuries it was the kings of Castile, Aragon, the Basque country and Navarre who repeatedly disputed possession of Rioja. At the same time religious life flourished there. Existing monasteries increased their power and new ones were built. Thanks to the monks, wine

History

growing on a significant scale developed once more. It was probably a bishop, called Abilio, who drew up the first wine laws for the region in the 9th century. That grapes were already being grown here in the early Middle Ages is also apparent from a 10th-century document in which the king of Navarre and his queen donated Lucronia (Logroño) and Asa with all their lands, including *vineis* (vineyards), to the monastery of San Millán de la Cogolla. It was in the 10th and 11th centuries that the development of modern Spanish, or Castilian, took place. From being a local, spoken idiom – alongside Latin, the official medium of communication – it evolved into a national language. The first man known to have written in Castilian, thereby helping its spread, was the Riojan monk Gonzalo de Berceo (1180–1246). In the monastery of San Millán he wrote a four-line verse that ends with the words '*un vaso de bon vino*' – a glass of good wine. A monument dedicated to Gonzalo de Berceo was unveiled in Logroño in 1977.

Pilgrim's way

Clerical influence also increased through the development of the pilgrim route to Santiago de Compostela. The importance of this destination was greatly enhanced in the 11th century because the Turks had made the pilgrimage to Jerusalem too dangerous. One of the roads to Santiago de Compostela, in the far north-west of Spain, ran through Rioja. This was the *camino frances*, so-called because of the large numbers of French pilgrims who used it.

Poblado protohistórico

Right:
An association of Rioja wine growers was set up in 1560. To guarantee the authenticity of their wines they devised this monogram from their initials. This they branded on the pellejos (wineskins made from the whole hide of a goat) in which the wine was transported. At that time Rioja was already exported to Flanders, France, Italy and elsewhere. The monogram is still used today in the seal of the modern Riojan wine fraternity, and by one firm – Bodegas Alavesas (see page 118).

Far right:
A fine tapestry from Bodegas Montecillo in Fuenmayor.

Opposite page, above left:
By the Ebro – a grower cleaning harvesting equipment.

Opposite page, above right:
Clavijo castle, at the foot of which a legendary battle between Christians and Moors is said to have taken place in 844.

Opposite page, below:
View over Rioja Alavesa from Laguardia with the church of Elvillar in the centre.

Logroño, Nájera and Santo Domingo de la Calzada became the familiar stopping places, where the pilgrims could cross the Ebro, the Najerilla and the Oja, and this was where many churches were built, as well as monasteries and hospitals. Santiago de Compostela declined in importance after its relics were hidden in 1589 for fear of plunder by Sir Francis Drake; they were not rediscovered until 1879.

Regulation

The name Rioja, in the form Rioxa, first appeared in writing in a local statute (*fuero*) of Miranda de Ebro in 1092. Probably this just referred to lands in the river basin itself. Later the name was applied to the whole of the region as we know it today. Gradually the regional wine also came to be known by the same name. In 1621, for example, *vino de clarete de Rioxa* was sold in Vitorio. Wine growing had already brought prosperity to a village like Haro by the beginning of the 14th century and thereafter the economic importance of wine continued to increase. In the 16th century this led to much new planting and all kinds of activity. In 1560 the first league of wine growers was set up, and a decree was promulgated forbidding the import of wines from Arnedo and elsewhere. At the same time a precise statement of vintage was prescribed which had to record the weight and type of grapes used. League members also marked their barrels with a monogram devised to guarantee the authenticity of their wines. Despite these and other measures there was fraud and corruption concerning wine. And when in 1592 Philip II visited Rioja the wine did not appeal to him. It was mainly white wine that was produced at that time; it was only at the end of the 17th century that the red began to predominate.

Hesitant cooperation

The growing production of Rioja meant that the wine had to be sold outside its own region. This proved to be far from simple, for communications with the towns of the north-west and the Basque country were poor. At the end of the 18th century the Junta General de Cosecheros de Vino de Logroño looked into the possibility of improving the roads to the north. The Junta came to the conclusion, however, that the wine growers of Logroño could not manage the necessary investment by themselves. It was therefore decided to broaden the social and economic basis of the association. In 1787 the Real Sociedad Económica de la Rioja Castellana came into being, representing the interests of 52 wine communities. The first meeting was held in Fuenmayor in 1790. The proposed plan for improving the road from Logroño to Santander was not approved because the remoter villages did not expect to profit from it. After a great deal of time had been lost the Real Sociedad undertook only a few such works, between 1808 and 1815. It was only from the 1830s that the society became really active in improving communications.

The start of barrel-ageing

Not long before the setting up of the Real Sociedad wooden barrels were used for the first time in Rioja for maturing the wine. It was Manuel Quintano who, inspired by Bordeaux, began the practice in 1780 in his native village of Labastida. He used large barrels of 210 (255 US) gallons. Proof that the wine in them would remain good without the usual addition of pitch, alcohol or resin was convincingly provided in 1795, when Quintano shipped 10 barrels of Catalan wine and 1,500 bottles of Rioja across the Atlantic from Santander in *La Natividad*. All the wine arrived in good condition. Although Quintano's idea was imitated on a modest scale, it encountered criticism. He was not given permission to sell his better, and more expensively produced, wines at a higher price than other Riojas from his village. Protests were of no avail. The decision taken by the mayor in 1802 was confirmed once more in 1806. Two years later Napoleon's French troops invaded Spain and the innovative idea of ageing in wood was shelved for the time being.

Luciano de Murrieta

In 1850 the idea was taken up again by Luciano de Murrieta, later the Marqués de Murrieta. As can be read in the chapter on Bodegas Marqués de Murrieta, this remarkable man brought in some hundred wooden casks from Bilbao to Logroño. These casks had a capacity of 16 (19 US) gallons and in 1852 they were successfully used for shipping Rioja wine to Cuba. The characteristic Bordeaux barrel of 225 litres – 50 (60 US) gallons – came into fashion a decade later: apparently the Marqués de Riscal was the first to use these in his bodega, which was opened in Elciego in 1860. Since then the region could not be imagined without its *barricas bordelesas*.

The coming of the French

In the year that Luciano de Murrieta was shipping out his first consignment of wine in barrels the Bordeaux region was affected by oidium or mildew. As a result of this parasitic fungus, which shows its presence by white powder on the vineleaves, Bordeaux had to contend with a series of difficult vintages between 1852 and 1862, the more so since no effective remedy could at first be found. Bordeaux mixture, made from copper sulphate and lime, was discovered later. To obtain an adequate supply of wine the French merchant houses therefore sent buyers out to various Spanish regions, including Rioja. French interest faded when the oidium had been conquered, but intensified again just a few years later when Bordeaux, along with the other French wine regions, began to suffer from *Phylloxera vastatrix*. This grape louse went on to destroy the greater part of the French vineyards. The parasite was first reported in Bordeaux in 1867 and shortly afterwards a golden age dawned for Rioja. Because of increased demand from France the Diputación Foral de Alava had earlier contacted a Bordeaux man, Jean Pineau, who had arrived in 1862. He lived in Elciego and was given the task of teaching French techniques to the wine growers. Whether his ideas met with any response

among the conservative Riojans may be doubted, but after his contract had ended in 1868 he was engaged by the Marqués de Riscal, for whom he did excellent work for many more years.

Fiesta

Year after year the French *comisionados* arrived in Rioja in large numbers to sample and buy the still young wines; after the railway connection between Haro and Bilbao had been opened in 1880 French orders rose sharply. In a single month as much as 11 (over 13 US) million gallons could be sent back over the frontier. This trade was further stimulated by the Franco-Spanish agreement of 1882 which reduced the import duties.

The agents usually travelled to Haro in February and their arrival was a real fiesta. The trains were met by musicians and the French were showered with confetti. A particular kind of confetti is still called *parúse* in Haro, allegedly after the '*Pas rouge!*' of the Frenchmen who were afraid that their clothes would be stained. A number of the French remained in Haro either on their own initiative or that of their employers. They founded bodegas on the French model. Famous 'immigrant' names were Anglade, Blondeau, Boisot, Heff, Kruger, Leenhardt, Sauvignon, Serres and Viguier. Many Spanish bodegas were also established, again often on French lines. And in the space of a generation the total vineyard area of about 84,000 acres grew to around 128,000 acres: the biggest ever known in the Rioja.

Disastrous decline

Although bodegas continued to be built in good numbers up to the turn of the century, French purchases had already begun to drop off. In 1887 a remedy for the phylloxera had at last been found – grafting European vines on to American rootstocks

Right:
The Bordeaux connection is clear from this old wall painting on the little bodega of Martinez de Ayala at Labastida.

Far right:
The splendid tower of the cathedral in Santo Domingo de la Calzada, once a famous place of pilgrimage. In the foreground is the parador nacional, a comfortable state-owned hotel in a former pilgrim hostel.

Centre:
Old picture from the time when horse ploughs were still used in the Marqués de Riscal's vineyards.

Bottom:
In Elciego, where the Marqués de Riscal began establishing his vineyards and cellars around 1860, the modern Domecq bodega was built about a century later.

In 1609 the planting of new vineyards was banned in order to limit production. Tradition has it that the driving of carts through the streets of Logroño was prohibited from 1635, so that the wine could mature undisturbed. And in 1635 the city council is said to have been excommunicated for allowing grapes to be picked without adherence to the strict rules then in force.

During the 'French' period at the end of the last century 80 to 100% of all Rioja was shipped to France.

– and this was applied on a large scale. Coincidentally the Rioja had to contend with mildew in that same year, which demanded a lot of extra work out in the fields. Wine prices therefore had to rise. In order to remain competitive many bodegas had recourse to fraud. Water and colouring matter were added, as well as alcohol from molasses, of which 22 (26 US) million gallons were imported from Germany. The last big export year was 1891. After this, French purchases dwindled to a quarter of the volume in two years. The enormous French vintage of 1893 was partly to blame for this. In Haro the euphoria subsided; frugal times were coming. Most of the French sold up their bodegas and returned to their homeland. The early years of this century were disastrous for Rioja. In 1900 France greatly increased the import duty on wine; in 1901 the phylloxera finally reached Rioja and within seven years it had destroyed 70% of the vineyards. In addition colonial export markets such as the Philippines and Cuba were lost.

New prosperity

It was a long time before the region recovered from these setbacks. During World War I it succeeded in gaining an entry into America and elsewhere for its wines, when France was unable to export, and by 1935 the vineyard area amounted to 86,000 acres. Then the Spanish Civil war broke out (1936–39), which meant another reverse. It was not until the 1960s and 1970s that Rioja experienced considerable growth again. World demand was rising, Bordeaux had had a number of poor grape harvests and a consequent increase in prices, and in Spain itself the economy was revitalized, with a resultant steep rise in the home market for quality bottled wine. Banks, drinks firms, industrialists, wealthy individuals and multinationals all poured into Rioja to buy or set up wineries. Home sales rose steadily and in 1972 9 million (11 million US) gallons of wine were exported, an unheard-of amount before this century and a third of the total vintage of that year. This boom, too, has passed, but not without

some beneficial consequences. Through the inflow of capital and expertise Rioja was able in a short space of time to catch up with wine regions elsewhere in the world. New, up-to-date bodegas were established, and many existing ones were drastically modernized. Better vinification methods were adopted, for reds, whites and rosés, as

well as the whole concept of marketing. There can be no doubt that Rioja now has the means of securing for its wines their well-earned place in the world market.

Visitor's Rioja

Ancient villages, fine churches, imposing monasteries, splendid art treasures, variety of landscape – Rioja offers the visitor many sights worth the seeing. This chapter will give an impression of these, via three possible routes: the first leads through the Rioja Alta and its upland terrain south of the Ebro; the second runs through the Rioja Alavesa; and the third through the Rioja Baja. All three circuits start and end in Logroño.

The Rioja Alta route

From Logroño you drive along the N 232, already going uphill, to Navarrete, where the Corral bodega is the first important building you come to. Like many villages in the area, Navarrete is built on a hill. It has a 15th-century church, the tower of which has recently been restored. A specifically local craft here is pottery. Various potteries are established in the narrow streets at the foot of the church. Navarrete also has the remains of a Romanesque chapel, and if you are leaving the village in the direction of Nájera you can pause by the churchyard. Its gates came from a hospital that centuries ago cared for pilgrims to Santiago de Compostela (*see also* Bodegas Corral, page 150); there are a number of wine motifs in the carved stonework.

Town of kings

The road, offering some beautiful distant views in places, leads on to Nájera, also known as 'Nájera of the Kings'. This was where the kings of Navarre had their second court and, after 1076, when Rioja had become part of Castile, the town was also very important to the monarchs of that kingdom. Consequently the abbey of Santa María la Real has a whole pantheon of kings, queens, princes and princesses of Navarre, Castile and León. This abbey stands on the west bank of the Najerilla, in the centre of an old part of the town. It was founded in 1032 but the original Romanesque buildings have entirely disappeared. The present abbey dates from the 15th and 16th centuries. The Gothic cloisters and the sculptured tomb of Doña Blanca de Navarra are just two of its treasures. The monks are said once to have cultivated 'mysterious' plants for the making of Benedictine liqueur. Nájera, like Navarrete, was well known as a stopping place for pilgrims. Its population holds fiestas at least four times a year: at the end of April, in the last week of June, in mid-September and at the beginning of October.

Rugged mountain landscape

From Nájera you can follow the valley of the Najerilla southwards. Deciduous trees and fertile fields give way to pinewoods and the grey, rugged mountains of the Sierra de la Demanda. The winding road climbs gradually and one of the places it passes through is Anguiano, a village that around 22 July and on the last Sunday in September holds a fiesta that features dancers on stilts. At 3,300 feet in a side valley stands the Benedictine abbey of Valvanera, Rioja's patron saint. As well as a 15th-century church and an 11th-century statue of the Virgin, this remote foundation has its own hotel, restaurant, cafeteria and bar.

A visual and spiritual experience

As the crow flies the distance from Valvanera abbey to San Millán de la Cogolla is only 7½ miles. However, there is no direct road connection between the two and you have to drive double the distance, part of it back through the Najerilla valley. San Millán de la Cogolla is named after the saint who lived here between 473 and the mid-6th century. The village has two remarkable monasteries. That of San Millán de Suso stands high up on a wooded hillside and dates from the 10th century: its austere interior shows clear Moorish influence. San Millán, patron saint of the whole of Christian Spain, lies buried here in a 12th-century Romanesque tomb. It was at Suso that the first recorded words in Castilian, i.e. modern Spanish, are known to have been written down. At the foot of the hill on which the Suso monastery is situated stands the abbey of San Millán de Yuso. Because of its impressive size and brilliant interior it has been dubbed the Escorial of Rioja (after the vast palace Philip II built north-west of Madrid). A visit to Yuso is both a visual and a spiritual experience, with the sublimely decorated sacristy and the abbey church with its treasures as the highpoints. Nothing is left of the original 11th-century abbey. The existing structures were built in the 15th to the 17th centuries.

Chickens in church

From San Millán de la Cogolla it is not far to Cañas, the site of a convent. This was consecrated in 1170 and was later extended. Outstanding features of this Cistercian house include the 13th-century carved tomb of the Abbess Urraca López de Haro and an 18th-century crib. The present-day nuns do embroidery and paint porcelain. The next stop is Santo Domingo de la Calzada. This village was founded in the second half of the 11th century by the saint of that name who built bridges and improved the roads to aid the pilgrims. It was also through him that a hospital came into being. Today this is a *parador*, a luxurious state-owned hotel. Near by rises the 13th-century cathedral, built in several styles and with a free-standing Baroque tower. Inside the cathedral there is a cage containing a white cock and a hen. Their presence is explained by a legend. A young pilgrim was wrongfully accused of theft and sentenced by the judge to be hanged. When his parents returned after four weeks they found that their son was still alive. They pleaded with the judge to cut him down but the latter, at table, said that after four weeks a hanged man would be about as much alive as the roast chicken in front of him – whereupon the fowl suddenly grew feathers, cackled and began to run about.

Storks

From Santo Domingo de la Calzada a road runs into the Tirón valley. In the village of Cuzcurrita de Río Tirón there is a tastefully restored castle where a bodega has been established (*see* Castillo de Cuzcurrita, page 58). Another, larger bastion stands in Sajazarra. If you go on from there to cross the Tirón at Cihuri you will pass a Roman bridge. Haro, the wine capital of Rioja, is not far from here; a separate chapter is devoted to this town. From Haro the route continues in the direction of Logroño – not, of course, on the motorway but along the N 232. The road climbs steeply into Briones, a

village at the top of a high hill. What is said to be the oldest house in Rioja stands on a corner of the square here and may be the work of a Dutch builder. The church near by with its tall tower, a national monument, is visited every year by storks. According to the local growers the day they arrive there to nest will indicate the quality of the year's vintage. In good and abundant years like 1920, 1925, 1934, 1935, 1942, 1947, 1954, 1961, 1964, 1968, 1970, 1973 and 1976 the storks apparently flew in on exactly the right day. Behind the church there is a view out over the peaceful, smiling valley. Briones, too, contains castle ruins, and many wine cellars dug out of the hill.

Mortar made with wine

The next village of importance is Cenicero, where there are bodegas (including Berberana, Marqués de Cáceres, Riojanas, Velazquez and a cooperative), modern flats and an old centre with the customary large church in the middle. Along the main street there is a public garden with a monument to the fallen and a small replica of the American Statue of Liberty. Cenicero also has a cooper's workshop and on sunny afternoons women can be seen in the street making *alambrados*, the metal meshes for Rioja bottles.

By crossing a ridge, a broad valley, and then another ridge you reach Fuenmayor. It is said that in periods of drought the mortar for the clock tower was mixed with wine. Once back in Logroño you could take a drive out to El Cortijo, a hamlet high up on the slope above the south bank of the Ebro. It offers a tremendous view across the Rioja Alavesa. From El Cortijo you take an unsurfaced road, uneven throughout, to the remains of the *puente Mantible*, once a large Roman bridge over the Ebro. Another short excursion can be made south from Logroño, to the mountain village of Clavijo and its large, ruined castle, below which the legendary battle between Christians and Moors took place. Logroño itself is dealt with in a separate chapter.

The Rioja Alavesa route

After crossing the Ebro in Logroño, Oyón is soon within your view, a village in the province of Alava (Araba in Basque). In its

old centre this growing commuter village has a beautifully decorated old church. The road to Laguardia from Oyón leads through vineyards on broken ground, mostly planted on pale-coloured limestone soils. Laguardia was formerly an important strongpoint, defending Navarre against persistent Arab attacks. In fact this hill village is still largely walled: the western wall is particularly impressive. Behind one of the gateways stands the church of San Juan with its round chapel, but this is surpassed in terms of beauty by Santa María de los Reyes with its magnificent porch. The village of Laguardia forms a narrow oblong and so its three most important streets run parallel to one another. Motor traffic is banned – and largely impossible – and so the pedestrian can enjoy the many old houses undisturbed. There are traditional wine cellars behind some of the façades where the grapes, with their skins and stalks, ferment in open concrete vats.

The Spanish fabulist Félix de Samaniego lived in Laguardia. His former house now serves as a *casa del vino* for Rioja Alavesa, and a bust of the famous villager has been placed in an open cupola in a small park, against the mighty backdrop of the nearby mountains. During the celebrations that Laguardia holds in the last week of June there are enthusiastic *encierros* in which young bulls are let loose in the narrow streets. San Blas (3 February) is also celebrated, when specialities including *hojaldre*, a sort of crumbly pastry, and *vino rojo*, red wine sugared and heated against the winter cold. Not far from Laguardia the prehistoric village of La Hoya has been excavated (*see* the previous chapter).

Mountain balcony

In the neighbourhood of Laguardia there are a number of dolmens, burial chambers from the Bronze Age and earlier. They are signposted. A total of seven has been found in the Rioja Alavesa running across country from Elvillar to the road from San Vicente de la Sonsierra to Peciña. Several have also been found north of the Sierra de Cantabria. The biggest dolmen, the one at Eguílaz, is covered by a stone weighing more than 10 tons. A small detour from Laguardia will take you to Navaridas; of its 1,750 acres, some 1,235 acres are planted with vines, or about 70% of all the land here. This is more than in any other village of the Rioja Alavesa. As well as a lot of wine and atmosphere, the village also has an old church. On leaving Navaridas you can take the mountain road to Balcón de la Rioja, a viewing point 3,600 feet up. In clear weather you can look down on a view that includes Samaniego, once a fortified outpost for Laguardia. A visit to this little place will show you that even the sturdy church had towers built for defence.

Summer retreat

As you drive through this lovely wine country the outlines of Labastida come into view, an ancient village that grew up in the 8th century around a castle, since disappeared. It nestles against a large hill, but unfortunately the view from the east is spoiled by an enormous white-painted sangria and table wine factory (belonging to Sant' Yago), while around the village centre all kinds of new building is being carried out. This is where many Basques come in summer. On the western side you come into the centre through a splendidly restored gateway. In addition to a beautiful 18th-century village council hall there is a large church with one of the most valued

Visitor's Rioja

organs in Rioja. On the hill above the church stands the chapel of Nuestra Señora de la Piscina, built to mark the capture of Jerusalem on one of the Crusades. Distant views in different directions can be enjoyed from around this chapel and to this end the local authority has placed public benches there.

Gateway to Rioja

Briñas is a short distance away and at a crossroads here stands the hotel restaurant El Portal de la Rioja, a hexagonal building with a small wine museum next to it. A couple of hundred yards away the Ebro winds into Rioja through a narrow ravine; this rock formation is called the Conchas de Haro. On the way there you should not miss the opportunity of seeing the once rich village of Salinillas de Buradón which derived its prosperity from a salt mine (still in existence). Note the gateway here and the gallery behind it supported on wooden posts. The church here is also worth seeing.

Open air festivals

The way back to Logroño lies through places that are situated closer to the Ebro. The first of these is San Vicente de la Sonsierra, where a hill towers over the roofs, with a castle and a church built on its top. As in many other Riojan villages a fiesta is held in September – and lasts for a week. *Encierros* take place every day and the main street becomes the domain of the young bulls. The high point comes on the last day when the inhabitants dine out of doors on meat from the bulls slain in a *corrida*. After the meal they all go down into the village again where there is dancing – and practically everyone ends up in the fountain. At Easter the atmosphere is entirely different. Penitants go in procession through the village, wearing tall pointed hats and beating themselves on their bare shoulders.

Village of two churches

The route continues in the direction of Elciego, with the chance of turning off to Villabuena and its big houses built for the gentry. Elciego, independent since the 16th century, numbers a good many bodegas, large and small. That of Marqués de Riscal was one of the first. The village is built on a hill with two churches at the top. The larger one has a pair of dissimilar towers flanking the main door, over which is a striking six-arch gallery. On a number of the houses here the family crests of the owners are carved in the stone façades or on the corners. Elciego concludes the Rioja Alavesa route.

The Rioja Baja route

The busy N 232 runs along the south bank of the Ebro in the direction of Zaragoza, and your route through Rioja Baja starts on this road. On the right-hand side of the road a few miles out of Logroño an elegant white gateway gives access to the Marqués de Murrieta bodega. the next winery is the Ausejo cooperative, located at the lower end of this village, which rises steeply. Passing Tudelilla, with its more than 1,350 acres of vineyards, you come to Arnedo. The most striking part of this town is the 330-foot hill with the ruins of a Moorish fort. Doves have nested in the steep slope of this hill for a great many years. Arnedo has three important churches, including Santa Eulalia, which dates from the first half of the 16th century, and a number of shoe factories. During the fiesta here at the end of September a 'Golden Shoe' trophy is awarded.

The Town of Three Lies

The monastery of Vico is near Arnedo, where painted porcelain is displayed and sold. It is possible also to drive from here to Arnedillo, a spa whose waters are said to have a therapeutic effect on rheumatism,

Left:
Church of San Miguel, Alfaro.
Pigeons and storks nest on and
around the building.

Far left:
Calahorra cathedral. Bunches of
grapes can be seen in the carving
above the pillars.

Below:
Distant view from the Balcón de
la Rioja, about 3,600 feet up in
the Sierra de Cantabria.

Visitor's Rioja

sciatica and bone disorders. One of the Rioja's first wine cooperatives was founded in Quel. Through this village and on through Autol the road leads to Aldeanueva de Ebro – also known as the Town of Three Lies. This place is no *aldea* (hamlet), still less *nueva* (new), and is not on the Ebro. What it does do is produce a lot of wine.

The town of fighting bulls

The next place, Alfaro, is one of the most spread-out communities in Spain, covering some 75 square miles. At the same time it is one of the biggest wine-growing districts in Rioja for it has more than 5,500 acres planted with vines. In the middle of the town stands the church of San Miguel with its unusual 17th-century brick façade. Bulls play an important part in the fiestas here in mid-August and the beginning of September. The Alfaro *corridas* are famous, not least because of the breeding station for fighting bulls near the town. Cortès, the

Spanish *conquistador*, is said to have taken bulls from Alfaro with him to Mexico. The *encierros* in the narrow Calle García Escamez are also very popular; the municipality hires the young bulls for these. Quite often, however, the inhabitants so get the taste for them that they collect money for a repeat performance the following day.

Diocesan museum

Alfaro is the turning point for this tour, which now heads back through Calahorra. With a population of 18,000 this is the biggest town in Rioja Baja. In the previous chapter mention has been made of the fact that the town was well known in Roman times. It has been the seat of a bishop since the 5th century and there is a museum devoted to the bishopric. Calahorra's Gothic cathedral stands at the top of a hill; its building lasted, with interruptions, from the 12th to the 18th century. It has a number of splendid chapels. Other religious

buildings worth seeing are the churches of San Andrés and Santiago. Around the town the remains of its defensive walls still stand. Like Santo Domingo de la Calzada, Calahorra has its *parador* or state-owned hotel, situated on the edge of the central area. Objects from Roman times have been assembled in its garden, including the remains of columns and ornamental carving. The *parador* gives a charming view out over the Ebro valley, broad and fertile here. The vegetables and fruit grown here are largely processed by the big local canning industry. From Calahorra the *autopista* can be taken back to Logroño, but a pleasanter route is along the north bank of the Ebro, via San Adrián, Lodosa and Mendavia.

Logroño

Logroño, capital of Rioja, is probably the only wine community in the world that can be recognized as such from its pavements: they are inset in many places with tiles with a grape motif, symbolizing the importance that wine has for centuries had for this town. In present-day Logroño, with its 110,000 inhabitants, wine companies are, however, quite hard to find. They have left the centre for industrial estates or outlying districts. The visitor will also be struck by the fact that Logroño bears no resemblance at all to the dull, sleepy provincial town he had perhaps imagined. The first impression is of a go-ahead no-nonsense place with wide *vias* and *avenidas*

busy with traffic. It all looks very modern and prosperous – but is somewhat lacking in character and atmosphere. This first impression, however, is far from complete or truly representative, for in the midst of the new districts there still lies Logroño's old centre, bubbling with life and flowing with wine.

A fortified town

This centre with its narrow streets extends to the south bank of the Ebro. It was here that the Romans founded a settlement which they called Vera, later changing the name to Lucronio. All that now remains of the fortifications of this central nucleus is the Carlos V gate, a memorial to the French siege that Logroño lived through in 1521. The lifting of the siege, on 11 June, is celebrated every year in the Fiesta de San Barnabé. It was not only the French who fought over Logroño. The Muslims occupied it from the 8th to the 10th century and subsequently the possession was disputed

by the kings of Aragon, Navarre and Castile, and others. A more peaceful role was that of stopping place for pilgrims on the way to Santiago de Compostela. The pilgrims crossed the Ebro here on a stone bridge with three defensive towers. Today there are two bridges: an iron one of 1882 and a stone structure that replaced the old bridge in 1884.

Impressive churches

It is partly because of these pilgrims that the old part of Logroño has some striking churches. The 165-foot spire of Santa María de Palacio can be seen from a long way off;

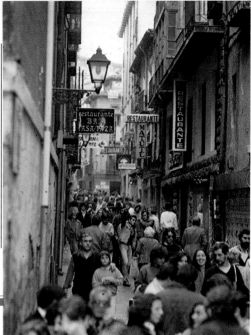

Logroño

the earliest parts of this church date from the 12th and 13th centuries and it has been declared a national monument. Also imposing is the cathedral of Santa María de la Redonda (15th, 16th and 17th century), with a Gothic nave and two splendid Baroque towers – they are called the San Pedro and the San Paulo. There is fine Gothic carving – unfortunately worn and damaged – around the door of the church of San Bartolomé. There are other ancient churches in Logroño, and some have disappeared. Treasures from former churches, and from the whole of the Rioja, have been assembled in the provincial museum here, an 18th-century building where the famous General Baldomero Espartero lived in the last century. Almost opposite the museum is Logroño's fine post office building, the foundation stone of which was laid in 1932.

Paseo del Espolón

People walking through the centre of Logroño are bound sooner or later to come to the Paseo del Espolón, the main square, a wide, green oasis between the old and the new parts of the town. This square achieved its present extent around the middle of the 19th century. It is rectangular, paved and provided with many kinds of trees as well as flower beds. The wooden benches here

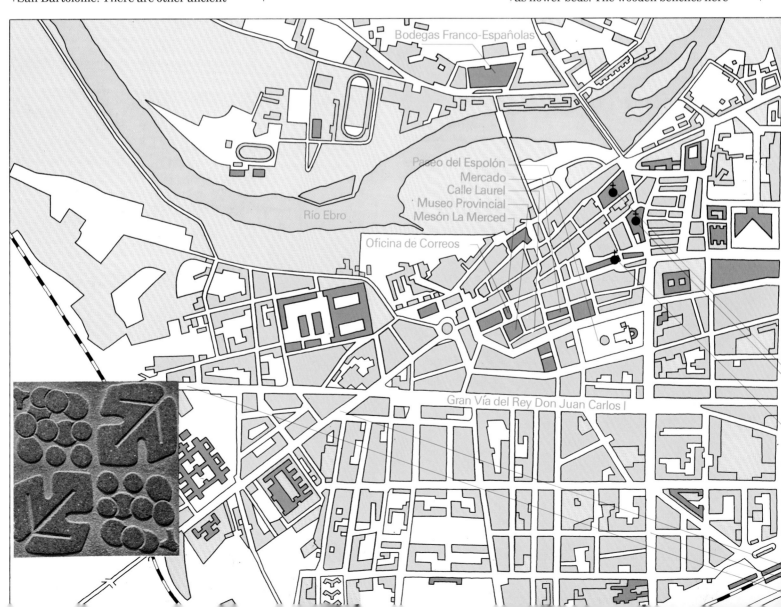

Logroño

are well used, for this is the town's meeting place. It begins to fill up in the late afternoon. Mothers exchange items of news while their children play. The ice cream stalls do a brisk trade, as do the terrace cafés. The buzz of voices almost drowns the sound of the traffic. The statue of Espartero (a Riojan) proudly seated on a horse forms a centre point of the square. It is mounted on a high stone plinth and is surrounded by fountains and recumbent lions. This bronze monument was completed in 1895 and weighs about 11 tons. There used to be statues of six Spanish kings in the square, but these were pulled down in 1931. Open air music performances are given in the Espolón – an auditorium was built here in 1954. Many activities take place in this square during the week-long Fiesta de la Vendimia (or Fiesta de San Mateo) starting around 20 September.

Talking, drinking, playing

Although in the modern residential districts it grows quiet after eight o'clock in the evening, many places in the old town stay crowded and bustling, with the dozens of cafés doing good business. Most of them are small, plainly furnished establishments where a male clientele stands at the bars and drinks glasses of *tinto*, the simple red wine of the district. There are other, more sophisticated, establishments however, such as the well-known Café Moderno in the Calle Francisco Martínez Zaporta. It stands in a small square with houses and small shops all round, where children play tag and where tables and chairs are put out in summer. Light globes hang from the ceiling in the Café Moderno, the floor is tiled and the tabletops are of marble. Games of chance are played intensively here every afternoon and evening. Married couples sit together playing cards (on green baize) and there is much throwing of dice. In fact you can hear the click of the dice all through the room, despite the sound from the television, which nobody watches. On the long bar with its brass rail there are glass display cases with *tapas*, always there to assuage the least pang of hunger. On the walls hangs a collection of photographs of former days.

A street of bars

Evenings in the Calle Laurel, a little street not far from the Espolón, are even livelier, for young people make their way there in large numbers. While ten yards away from this street – which is at most 170 yards long – peace may reign, the Calle Laurel itself will be quite incredibly busy and teeming with people, for once in it you stay there. People do not go there just to chat but also to fortify themselves internally, for the Calle Laurel has a great number of bars: at least 25 within this short distance, bars with names like Angel, Torrecilla, Simpatía, Daniel, El Soledad de Tudelilla, Páganos, Blanco y Negro, Cid, Universidad, Charly – or with no name at all. Along with the wine and the beer some places make a speciality of fried mushrooms. But should your hunger become too great you can always turn to one of the six restaurants.

Splendid restaurant

The best-known restaurant in the Calle Laurel is El Cachetero, a nicely lit room with about a dozen tables. Like many of the Logroño restaurants it is strictly regional in orientation, and has simple furnishings, informal service and low prices. Other – random – examples of the type are Asados Gonzalez, El Fogón, Asador Zubillaga and San Remo (known particularly for its magnificent Entrecôte Avion). You can, however, eat at a more exalted level in Logroño, for in tall, stately premises in the middle of the old centre there is the Mesón la Merced. From the outside it does not make a particularly hospitable impression, but once inside you are in an exceptionally tasteful, even sublime interior which even many French three-star restaurants could not equal. In addition the owner, Lorenzo Cañas, has assembled here a brilliant collection of paintings, with work by local artists. He has also brought together an impressive collection of old Rioja wines and exhibits them in a separate area. And so Logroño is continually surprising; it is a town that demands time to be explored, but rewards the patient visitor in all kinds of ways.

Avenida del General Franco

Santa María de Palacio
San Bartolomé
Santa María de la Redonda

Calle del Marqués de Murrieta
Calle General Vara de Rey
Avenida de Gonzalo de Berceo

Haro

Logroño is the administrative centre of the Rioja but Haro, 27 miles to the west, is its wine capital. There are fourteen bodegas and a cooperative here. By reason of its strategic position on a hill at the north-western entrance to the Ebro valley and at the confluence of the Ebro and its tributary the Tirón, the origins of Haro go back into the dim past. The Romans certainly settled here, but the first written reference to the place dates from 1040. The relevant document records the name 'Faro'. About half a century later Haro was given to Don Diego I, who thereafter adopted the surname López de Haro. His successor, Lope IV, was chased out of Haro by Aragonese troops in 1124, but regained the town ten years later. He acquired the title

of Conde de Haro, which his descendants were to bear for many centuries. The rule of the Counts of Haro did not end until the Napoleonic occupation: the nobility was abolished in Spain in 1812 and Haro was given a mayor.

Wine and prosperity

Wine has played a significant rôle in the rich history of Haro. We read for example that in the early 14th century, when the town was still completely walled, that it enjoyed a period of prosperity thanks to wine. Wine production was already the most important source of income for this *Ciudad de Jarreros* (City of Jar Makers). It was here that an association of wine

growers came into being in the 18th century whose activities included improving access to the vineyards. But the town's greatest flowering came at the end of the 19th century: the French were buying a lot of wine in Rioja at this time; and in addition Haro's railway station was opened. This linked Haro with the line to Bilbao and its port – and exporting on a large scale could begin.

The opening of the railway

The station was located just outside the town, across the Río Tirón. The opening took place in 1880 and brought a hitherto unknown level of prosperity to the community. In 1881 the water supply was

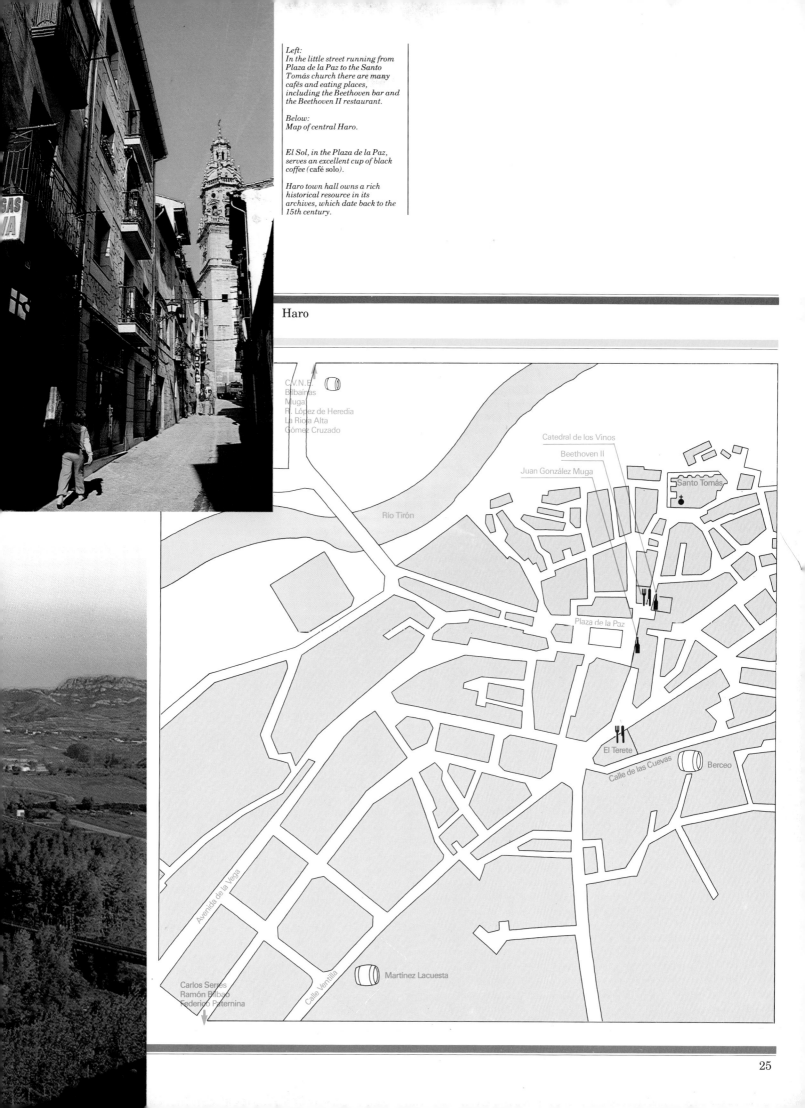

Left:
In the little street running from Plaza de la Paz to the Santo Tomás church there are many cafés and eating places, including the Beethoven bar and the Beethoven II restaurant.

Below:
Map of central Haro.

El Sol, in the Plaza de la Paz, serves an excellent cup of black coffee (café solo).

Haro town hall owns a rich historical resource in its archives, which date back to the 15th century.

Haro

C.V.N.E.
Bilbaínas
Muga
R. López de Heredia
La Rioja Alta
Gómez Cruzado

Río Tirón

Catedral de los Vinos
Beethoven II
Juan González Muga
Santo Tomás
Plaza de la Paz
El Terete
Calle de las Cuevas
Berceo

Avenida de la Vega
Carlos Serres
Ramón Bilbao
Federico Paternina
Calle Ventilla
Martínez Lacuesta

Haro

improved; in 1882 there were plans for a theatre and in the same year Haro received its first telephone; in 1884 the first wine fair was held; in 1886 the bullring was renovated; and electric light arrived in 1890. Not long after this Haro was given full municipal rights and privileges. Another memorable year was 1892, when the Estación de Viticultura y Enología opened its doors. This institute continues to play a most important role today, performing a great range of tasks, including the testing of some 13,000 wine samples annually (each of them undergoes eight to ten analyses). The old Haro bodegas were mostly in their traditional quarter in the Calle de las Cuevas (Street of Cellars), on a steep slope a few dozen yards from the centre. As a result of the arrival of the railway, however, new bodegas were built in the immediate neighbourhood of the station. The Barrio de la Estación grew into the district for the ageing and shipping of Rioja wine. The importance of the railway for the transportation of wine has of course declined over the years, but a good number of bodegas large and small are still to be found in this quarteer, among them Bilbaínas, CVNE, López de Heredia, Muga, La Rioja Alta and Rioja Santiago.

Palaces

A number of grandiose dwellings to be found in Haro are evidence of the prosperity that wine brought. These *palacios* carry the family crests carved in stone of the people who lived in them. Three splendid examples are the Palacio de Paternina, the Palacio de la Cruz and the Palacio de los Condes de Haro (now a municipal cultural centre). Handsome later examples are provided by the *fin de siècle* buildings to be found around the main square, the Plaza de la Paz, and elsewhere. Nor does Haro lack for fine churches and of these the Santo Tomás is the most impressive. Around its two doors this Gothic church has splendid 16th-century sculptures. Haro's late 18th-century town hall is also worthy of note. It stands on the Plaza de la Paz and a road runs underneath one of its arched gateways.

Festive weeks

The inhabitants of Haro are hospitable and enjoy life, so fiestas are celebrated here with commitment. In the last week of June there are festivities that conclude with the famous Batalla del Vino in which people drench one another with *botas* of wine. It is said that this wine battle represents the disputes and legal skirmishing that took place between Haro and Miranda de Ebro just to the north over this part of the Rioja. There is also a fiesta in the second week of September, that of the Virgen de la Vega, the town's patron saint. The population, young and old, takes part in many events, culminating in the day on which Nuestra Señora de la Vega is honoured. At midday the townspeople dressed in their Sunday best gather in the small park around the basilica of their patroness. The local band plays and long lines of children (many in traditional costume) lay bunches of flowers at the foot of a statue of the Virgen de la Vega mounted on a high platform. There are songs and recitations. Those who bring this floral tribute are each given an inscribed earthenware mug which is filled with must from large barrels; after this official issue, everyone present is entitled to a mugful – but the pourers often run out of supplies rather quickly. Everyone then strolls back to the Plaza de la Paz and the band leaves for the same destination. Subsequntly the bars, cafés and restaurants do excellent business all day.

At the Beethoven

In the Café Beethoven, for example (so-called because its founder, like the composer, was deaf), there will be quite a throng at the long bar. Dozens of people come here before starting on their extensive dinners to drink a glass or two of *tinto* and eat *tapas*. Waiters go back and forth with plates filled with all kinds of tempting snacks, including pieces of ham, fresh crayfish, bread rolls with omelettes, skewers with crayfish, olives and egg, various sorts of fish, and so on. The plates go back empty in an amazingly short space of time.

But it is not just on high days and holidays that they enjoy life in Haro. Throughout the rest of the year, too, the bars and eating places can reckon on plenty of customers. Haro's best-known restaurant is Terete, which dates from 1867 and is famous for its roast leg of lamb. People like to spend time in Beethoven II, a few doors down from Café Beethoven, where the cooking is expert, and lovingly done.

Wine shops

Haro attracts many tourists, particularly from the Basque province (Vizcaya in Spanish, Euskadi in Basque) and Alava (Araba in Basque), and a lot of them are interested in wine. This is why there are two notable and flourishing wine shops on the Plaza de la Paz. Both have a large selection of wines from Rioja and some other Spanish regions. Next to the town hall there is La Catédral de los Vinos and to the right, on the square itself and in an arcade is Juan Conzález Muga's business. The latter has a charming shop where besides wines (including Riojas with his own label, which Muga selects from the bodegas), regional preserves and wine literature are sold. Behind the shop there is a room fitted out as a museum, mainly with old bottles of Rioja. When I visited it there were a good number of wines from the 1940s, 1950s and 1960s, but I also saw a bottle of Marqués de Riscal from 1880. Muga has many more bottles in stock at his bodega in the Calle de las Cuevas – bottles that are sold all through Spain. The conclusion is obvious: if you visit Haro you are going to come across wine on every hand. It is present in its history, in its economy, in its bodegas, in its shops, bars and restaurants. Haro lives by and for wine.

Soil and climate

Although the Rioja is not an especially large wine region, a number of different soil types and climatic zones are found there. The soils can be divided into three main categories: clay and limestone (about 25% of the total vineyard area); clay and ferruginous (also 25%); and alluvial (50%). Generally they are easy to recognize. Areas of clay and limestone soil show a yellowish colour (varying from white to brownish), clay and ferruginous soils appear reddish, and those of alluvial origin have a range of brown shades. The last-named type also represents the flattest terrains as it is formed from river silts.

Clay and limestone soil

The biggest concentration of calcareous clay soils is in the Rioja Alavesa district in the north-west corner of the Rioja. This type of soil is found around practically all the wine communities there. The terrain has a terraced structure, rising from just above the bank of the Ebro (about 1,280 feet above sea level) to the foothills of the Sierra de Cantabria (with a highest point at 2,625 feet). The Rioja Alta in the west of the region, but mainly south of the Ebro, also has considerable areas of clay and limestone. Their distribution is somewhat

freakish and they are bounded roughly by the communities of Villalba, Haro Galbárruli, Sajazarra, Fonzaleche, Cuzcurrita del Río Tirón, Tirgo, Briones, Gimileo, Ollauri, San Asensio, Cenicero and Fuenmayor. There can be no doubt that in the Rioja this type of soil yields the best wines: wines rich in extracts and glycerine and often – where reds are concerned – with a good colour.

Clay and ferruginous soils

In some places soils containing clay and iron are contiguous with areas of clay and limestone. Generally, however, they form enclaves of higher ground in alluvial terrains. The biggest area is in the eastern part of the region, in the Rioja Baja, but this type of soil also occurs in the Rioja Alta, mainly south-west of San Asencio,

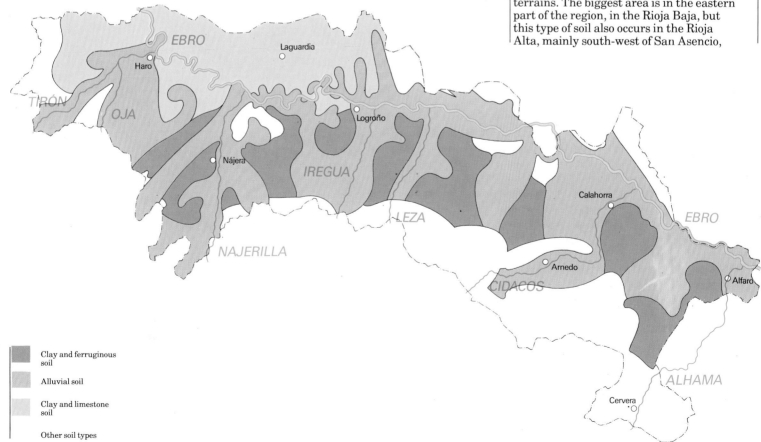

Clay and ferruginous soil

Alluvial soil

Clay and limestone soil

Other soil types

Soil and climate

Left:
October colours at the foot of the
Sierra de Cantabria.

Soil and climate

Nájera, Fuenmayor and Logroño. Garnacha grapes are sometimes grown on it, from which fragrant, fresh rosés can be made. In the Rioja Baja the clay and ferruginous soils are distributed over five zones, and partly because of the warmer climate there they produce mostly sturdy wines, rich in alcohol and iron.

Alluvial soils

Quite obviously many of the alluvial areas occur in and around the river valleys. This soil type predominates in the Rioja Baja, but also covers quite a few acres in the Rioja Alta. In the Rioja Alavesa, on the other hand, alluvial soil is only sporadically encountered. The treatment of this type of terrain under the Rioja system of classification may be regarded as controversial. Elsewhere in the world (in Bordeaux and Burgundy for example) wine from alluvial soil goes into a lower category than that from clay and limestone. The Rioja does not make this distinction – and it may be wondered why not. One of the reasons could be that wine from alluvial soils here is nearly always mixed with wine from the other two types. Wines from Riojan alluvial soils have high alcohol levels as their most important quality and so are used to strengthen lighter types. They are not very reliable in terms of colour, they are poor in extracts and prone to oxidation.

Temperature differences

The Riojan terrain slopes gradually down from west to east – Haro is at 1,575 feet above sea level, Alfaro at 920 feet – and there is also a change of climate. In Haro annual rainfall is roughly 20 in (500 mm) with nearly 2,000 hours of sunshine a year are measured. The figures for Alfaro are 15½ in (390 mm) and 2,300 hours respectively. Consequently there are also differences of average temperature between the two places: it is 12.7°C in Haro, 14.4°C in Alfaro. The city of Logroño, roughly in the middle of Rioja, has an annual average of 13.1°C. These differences are caused partly by the prevailing winds. Those blowing from the Atlantic bring moisture and freshness to the Rioja Alavesa and Rioja Alta; those from the south-east carry dry heat to the Rioja Baja. Typically, great Rioja years nearly always occur under the influence of north-west winds, moderate vintages when south-easterlies prevail. The region also has various microclimates, produced by the rugged character of the landscape.

Frost and drought

It could be said that the western part of the Rioja comes under the influence of a 'semi-moist' climate, with a 'semi-dry' type dominating the eastern part. In practice this means that summers in the Rioja Alavesa and Rioja Alta are less hot and dry than those in the Rioja Baja, while winters are colder with even some frost and snow. The Tempranillo grape is very much at home here. Unfortunately, however, there is a danger of frost in both spring and autumn in these two districts, particularly in the Rioja Alta valleys. Near Haro in the beginning of May 1984 the temperature fell to 4° below zero for just two hours, but the result was a large number of vines 'scorched' by frost. It has been calculated that in mid-April the risk of night frost can be put at 16%, at the end of April at 8%, and 3% at the beginning of May. Normally the vines begin to show shoots between 12 and 20 April. Hailstorms can be another problem in Rioja Alavesa and Rioja Alta: on 1 October 1984, for example, vineyards near Nájera were struck by a devastating shower, and hail was also an affliction in 1983. In the Rioja Baja they have to contend mainly with drought, and sometimes with excesssively high temperatures.

A shift to the Tempranillo

The Granacha grape has few problems in the Mediterranean climate of Rioja Baja. However, this variety does not produce particularly interesting wines and for this reason the Consejo Regulador advises that replantings in this district should include at least 25% Tempranillo vines – advice that is being widely followed. The San Adrián cooperative has even made this percentage mandatory for its members. The Tempranillo, however, needs more moisture than the Garnacha. Consequently there are growers who argue for irrigation: not on a grand scale via sprinklers (as in California) but more modestly by means of devices that drip water on the plants. Although such devices have been installed here and there, so far there is no legislation in sight that would make them legal, let alone compulsory. Some growers are seeking to give their Tempranillos somewhat cooler temperatures by planting at higher altitudes. The most spectacular example is provided by the Monte Yerga estate, at the foot of the mountain of that name to the south-west of Aldeanueva de Ebro and Alfaro. This estate rises to about 2,100 feet above sea level and will eventually extend over some 2,000 to 2,500 acres, with more than 60% of its vines Tempranillos. Several hundreds of acres are already planted and the area is growing steadily. Bodegas Berberana was originally involved in this gigantic project, but now it is a public limited company.

The Rioja Baja is also distinguished by a change of attitude and outlook that has taken place there. A few decades ago wine makers here were entirely geared to producing wines of high alcoholic content. Managing one with 18% alcohol was regarded as a great achievement. Today, however, growers are increasingly striving to produce balanced Riojas with other characteristics than alcohol alone.

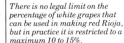

Wine legislation

Decrees were issued and regulations drawn up centuries ago in the Rioja to protect the quality and authenticity of its wines. This was done mostly at community level, or by groups of growers. In the course of the 1920s the name 'Rioja' was given protection at the local level in a phased process. Rioja was legally recognized as simply a region of origin in 1920, and then in 1925 Spain's first actual *denominación de origen* was created for it. The setting up of the Consejo Regulador de la Denominación de Origen 'Rioja' followed in 1926. The zone within which Rioja wines could be made was precisely defined for the first time by this supervisory council in 1928. This was subsequently confirmed by the national wine legislation passed in 1933. The Consejo Regulador, however, was not as yet very effective: in fact it practically dropped out of sight for many years. An attempt to breathe new life into it in 1945 did not succeed. Not until 1953 did the Consejo Regulador assume real significance again – and this is now regarded as its official year of foundation.

Important role

A great deal has changed in the Rioja since the 1950s, including the role of the Consejo Regulador. Supported *inter alia* by the new Estatuto de la Viña (replacing the 1933 legislation) and the decree of 1976, the Consejo Regulador has grown into a powerful institution that regulates the Riojan wine world in a most effective manner, administering, supervising, advising and advertising. The council is housed in a modern building in Logroño and consists of fourteen members. The president is appointed by the Ministry of Agriculture on the advice of the Instituto Nacional de Denominacione de Origen (INDO) and others. The vice-president is appointed by the Ministry of Trade. The council has five representatives of the wine growers, five from the bodegas, an independent specialist in the field of viticulture and an independent oenologist.

Legal criteria

Of all the tasks the Consejo Regulador undertakes, that of supervision is undoubtedly the most important. The council sees to it that the decree (*reglamento*) of 1976 is strictly adhered to. Matters dealt with in this voluminous enactment include:

The production zone, divided into the districts of Rioja Alta, Rioja Baja and Rioja Alavesa.

Methods of planting and pruning.

Grape varieties, Tempranillo, Garnacha, Graciano and Mazuelo being the only black varieties permitted, and Viura, Malvasía and Garnacha Blanca the only white. The Tempranillo is the most important kind for red wines, and Viura for whites.

Yield, which may not exceed 6,000 kg per ha (5,030 lb per acre) for black grapes or 9,000 kg per ha (8,030 lb per acre) for white. From every 100 kg (220 lb) of grapes not more than 70 litres (15.5, or 18.5 US, gallons) of must may be processed. To convert to the more familiar French figures, the maximum yields are 42 hl/ha (black grapes) and 63 hl/ha (white grapes).

Vinification – chaptalization (adding sugar to the must to increase the alcohol content) is not permitted.

Minimum percentages of alcohol, which are stipulated by district:

	%
Rioja Alta red, white, rosé	10
Rioja Alavesa red	11.5
white and rosé	11
Rioja Baja red	12.5
white and rosé	12

Volatile acids content – this can vary from 0.6 g per litre to 1.2 g per litre, depending on the alcohol content and other factors.

Ageing the wine. There are different standards according to the type of wine (*see* 'The Categories of Wine'). For maturing in the wood, oak vats of the Bordeaux type, with a capacity of 225 litres (about 50, or 69 US, gallons), are obligatory. In addition since 1976 the places where ageing in the wood may be carried out have been designated.

Computer control

To control these and other aspects of Rioja wine the Consejo Regulador not only has registers of all the vineyards and bodegas, and full-time inspectors, but also a very efficient computer system. This came into service at the time of the 1981 vintage – after it had long been urged by a group of quality-conscious bodegas. From that moment it became impossible to give the term 'vintage' a looser interpretation than was desirable. Thereafter if a Rioja was sold with a date on the label no more than 15% of its content could be wine from another vintage. The system works through what is called a *cartilla del viticultor*, a form that follows every litre of wine from its creation to its consumption. Every year each wine grower receives a *cartilla* on which is indicated the quantity of grapes he may pick in relation to the size of his vineyard, the varieties planted and the expected yield. When the grapes are sold the bodega takes the documentation over. After the grape harvest the Consejo Regulador calculates, with reference to the *cartillas*, how many bottles can be made and issues numbered back labels for this quantity. Since 1982 every bottle of Rioja has had to carry one of these back labels – and in fact may not be sold without one. The Consejo Regulador also keeps track of the ageing process that the wine undergoes and also its movement (between various bodegas, for example). The chapter 'The Categories of Wine' gives the rules that apply to the use of such terms as *crianza, reserva* and *gran reserva*. Their use is carefully controlled today.

Two oenological stations

The Consejo Regulador also concerns itself with protecting the qualify of the wine. To this end there is continuous chemical analysis and organoleptic testing, particularly where Riojas for export are concerned. The wines of Rioja Alta and Rioja Baja are investigated in the Estación de Viticultura y Enología in Haro. This dates from 1892 and although its buildings look fairly elderly on the outside, inside they are equipped with the most modern apparatus. Every year here some 13,000

wines are submitted to eight to ten different analyses. In order to acquire an export licence Riojas must not only be chemically correct, but aroma and taste must also be right. A committee of five to seven persons therefore carries out blind tastings of all wines for export. A licence is granted only if there is a majority decision in favour. One of the eminent directors of the Estación de Viticultura y Enología was Antonio Larrea Redondo, author of various works on the Rioja. The present director is Manuel Ruiz Hernandez, another great expert.

The Casa del Vino in Laguardia dates from 1982 and was created by the Diputación Foral de Alava, with the support of the ruling body of the autonomous Basque region. Here wines from the 1,200 growers in Rioja Alavesa are analysed and approved. The cosecheros (growers) can also come here for advice, for the improvement of the quality of the wine is one of the aims of the Casa del Vino. Promotion is also one of its functions. The centuries-old building is tastefully furnished and serves as an exhibition area for items that include an 18th-century press, old wine-related articles and information literature. Under the management of the dynamic director Gabriel Chinchetru a unique photo library of wine technology has also been created and a number of publications devoted to the Rioja Alavesa are displayed.

Districts with more than 4 million vines are Aldeanueva de Ebro, Alfaro, Ausejo, Autol, Cenicero, San Asensio and Tudelilla. Alcanadre, Briones, Elciego, Haro, Labastida, Lapuebla and San Vicente de la Sonsierra each have about 3 million in their areas.

Around the turn of the century the Rioja had some 128,000 acres of vineyards, about one third more than today.

Vines must be at least three years old before the wine from them can be sold as Rioja.

Vineyards and wine growing

The *denominación de origen 'Rioja'* covers about 40,300 acres in Rioja Alta, 33,400 acres in Rioja Baja and 19,000 acres in Rioja Alavesa: some 92,700 acres in all. This is considerably less than, for example, the 190,000 acres of Bordeaux. The difference in production is even greater. Bordeaux produces an annual average of 77 million (92 million US) gallons, Rioja 27.6 million (33 million US) gallons. From this comparison – which could also be made with other French regions – it is clear that the yield per acre is relatively modest in the Rioja: the average is around 730 (870 US) gallons (33 hl/ha), whereas Bordeaux achieves more than 990 (1,190 US) gallons (45 hl/ha). This brings us to a central problem of the Rioja. The low yield of the vineyards here is in fact a structural problem that has various causes. One of the most important is the fragmented state of land ownership.

Small properties

Of the grapes used for Rioja wine 85% is produced by some 14,000 growers, the rest coming from a few dozen bodegas. A simple calculation shows that the average holding is therefore around 7½ acres. This figure in fact gives a flattering picture, for a relatively large vineyard area is owned by that small group of bodegas. The average area of the private holdings is around 5 acres (and only ¾ of an acre in Rioja

Vineyards and wine growing

Alavesa). This fragmentation has arisen largely because of the way the land has been inherited over many generations. In addition many growers pursue this activity only as a sideline so that they would never be able to work more land. There are an estimated 8,000 in this latter group. The fact that most plots are small has all kinds of consequences. Their owners not only lack the money to buy modern equipment, but often the means, manpower and time to replant as well. There is a lot of uneconomic working of vineyards that are mainly planted with old, not very productive vines. With many growers the yield does not rise above 135 to 270 gallons per acre (15–30 hl/ha).

Threats

The situation appears even more dire if you remember that the growers themselves are an ageing group: because these small plots are not very profitable, many young people are leaving the land. At the same time there is now talk of a real threat to the vineyard acreage coming from the canning industry. Land in Rioja Baja, and in Rioja Alta, has been lost to grape growing because owners can earn more by raising asparagus or fruit – and sometimes with less trouble. The canning industry uses contracts whereby practically all the work is taken out of the grower's hands. Given this background it is easy to guess why quite a few bodegas have invested in their own vineyards. Domecq, with its relatively new Rioja bodega, has amassed about 990 acres, with some additional land for possible planting. These are the bodegas with more than 250 acres planted with vines:

CVNE (Haro)	1,160 acres
Domecq (Elciego)	985 acres
Faustino Martínez (Oyón)	865 acres
Campo Viejo (Logroño)	640 acres
Bilbaínas (Haro)	620 acres
Marqués de Riscal (Elciego)	495 acres
Riojanas (Cenicero)	495 acres
Gurpegui (San Adrián)	495 acres
Martínez Bujanda (Oyón)	495 acres
López de Heredia (Haro)	420 acres
Marqués de Murrieta (Logroño)	365 acres
La Rioja Alta (Haro)	310 acres
El Coto (Oyón)	300 acres

In addition quite a number of bodegas rent vineyard land. In the vineyards owned by bodegas the yield per acre is considerably higher than in the bulk of the private holdings.

Vineyards and wine growing

Growth necessary

As Rioja production is in fact dominated by a large group of small, not very progressive growers, the bodegas are anxious about the future of the region. If sales rise by 5% a year, as was the case from 1979 to 1982, then big problems are expected – unless there is further planting on a large scale. Mindful of EEC agreements, however, the Spanish government will give only meagre support here. An association of quality bodegas (*see* the chapter 'The Bodegas') has calculated that if demand goes on rising steadily and there is no new planting, the Rioja will be more than 54,000 acres short of the necessary vineyard area by 1993. But that is not all. The average age of the vines in this region is between 35 and 40 years (with a good many plants from 50 to 60 years old). This means that replanting, too, is needed, for the yield from a vine falls dramatically after its 40th year. It is foreseen that half the existing vines will have to be replaced before 1993, representing an area of nearly 50,000 acres. If the Rioja is to go on growing and prospering then an enormous effort will be required: 105,000 acres will have to be either planted or replanted within seven years or so.

Pruning and mechanisation

At the same time the size of holdings will have to be increased. Only larger vineyards will allow the efficient use of tractors and other mechanical aids, which would make more profitable working possible. The method of planting constitutes a separate problem. Vines in Rioja are grown *en vaso*, as free-standing bushes that are pruned by what is known in France as the *goblet* method. In this you end up with twelve axils to a vine with one shoot, capable of bearing two bunches of grapes, growing from each axil. The traditional method of planting was to have the vines about 6' to 6' 3" apart, with the same distance between the rows. With tractors in mind the latter distance has been increased (and that between the plants reduced so as to keep

sufficient vines to a given area), resulting in measurements such as 4' 3" between vines and about 9' between rows, or 3' 6" and just under 10' respectively. The number of vines per acre normally varies between about 1,000 and a maximum 1,500 (2,500–3,600/ha).

The free-standing, low-growing vines make mechanical harvesting a problem. This is one of the reasons why some estates are now experimenting with a quite different method of planting and pruning in which the vines are trained along wires in broad bands. The author has seen examples at estates including Domecq, Marqués de Riscal, Viña Salceda (all in Elciego) and at an independent grape supplier's vineyard in Alfaro, Rioja Baja. This Guyot method, as it is called, is essential for anyone growing French varieties such as the Cabernet Sauvignon; various concerns are working, or experimenting, in this area (*see* the 'Grape Varieties' chapter). However, the Guyot method is not (as yet) legal and is allowed only under special dispensation. Irrigation, too, is prohibited. Nevertheless, at least two growers (Domecq and the Rioja Baja supplier mentioned above) have already installed drip irrigation systems – principally, they say, to protect the vines in periods of heat or drought.

Abuses past

The legally permitted yield for Rioja black grapes is 5,350 lb per acre, and 8,030 lb for white. Since no more than 70 litres – $15\frac{1}{2}$ (16 US) gallons – of must may be fermented from 1 kg (2.2 lb) of grapes, this represents a yield of 375 (450 US) gallons per acre for black grapes (42 hl/ha) and 560 (670 US) gallons per acre (63 hl/ha) for white. From what has already been said it will be clear that these amounts are seldom achieved. In the past this led to abuses. For example, a grower might seek, and be granted, permission to harvest 5,000 kg per ha (4,460 lb per acre), but in actual fact pick only 4,000 kg per ha (3,570 lb per acre). This left the bodega in a position to make up the 1,000 kg difference by bringing in cheaper grapes from elsewhere, with the

result that incredibly low-priced Riojas could suddenly appear on the market. The much more stringent legislation brought in in the early 1980s has put an end to this practice (*see also* the chapter 'Wine Legislation').

Late harvests

Harvest time generally comes later in Rioja than north of the Pyrenees in Bordeaux – just the reverse of what might be expected. The usual starting date is 10 October. Picking starts in Rioja Baja and the harvesting of white grapes begins shortly afterwards in the other two districts. Recruiting pickers is hardly ever a problem. Gypsies come streaming into the region weeks before the harvest, and the local population is also intensively involved. Picking generally lasts from 30 to 40 days, which means that in some places the helpers are busy right into November. The pickers work with *corquetes*, curved knives or small sickles. The grapes are picked into large, 35 to 45 lb wicker baskets (*cestos*), collected in 175 to 265 lb wooden tubs or boxes (*comportas*), and then tipped into tractor trailers, although some growers still use donkey carts. Some large bodegas have gone over to plastic crates holding 33–38 lb. These can be stacked when full so that the grapes remain largely undamaged and the juice does not oxidize. Intact grapes are essential for *macération carbonique*.

The power of the bodegas

The bodegas vinify about one quarter of the total grape harvest. Roughly half of this amount comes from their own land and the rest is bought in from growers. Another quarter is made into wine by individual growers, the *cosecheros*. Most of the remaining half of the grapes goes to the cooperatives. The Rioja has about 30 of these, and 9,000–10,000 growers are associated with them. Although the cooperatives receive about 45% of the grapes, they are responsible for only 2% of all the Rioja on the market. Practically all their production is sold in must or wine

Right:
One of the best Riojan cooperatives is that at Labastida. It exports on its own account – which is rare among cooperatives.

Below:
Grape harvest in former times on the Marqués de Riscal estate. On the cart is a man with a comporta, a tall wooden tub for collecting grapes.

Bottom:
Comportas are still used by many growers, as can be seen from this picture taken near Elciego.

Chozas, small stone cabins for the field workers, can be seen in the Riojan vineyards. Bodegas Faustino Martínez (Oyón) has built a more lavish version for receiving visitors.

Vineyards and wine growing

form to the bodegas. Most cooperatives do not even have their own bottling line, still less vats for ageing the wine. Most of the *cosecheros* also sell the wine they make to the bodegas. Less than 1% of them take the wine through all stages and then sell it on their own account. To sum up, the bodegas vinify around 25% of all the grapes and in addition buy in some 70% of all the wine the Rioja produces. Thus they control 95% of the total. Despite this there are limits to the power of the bodegas: since there is a free market in grapes and wines in the Rioja the bodegas could not prevent an explosive rise in grape prices in 1982, 1983 and 1984, with increases from 30 to 35 pesetas per kilogram up to 70 pesetas and more.

Grape varieties

Although some 40 different grape varieties may be encountered in Rioja, the Consejo Regulador at present allows only seven: the Tempranillo, Garnacha Tinta, Mazuelo and Graciano black grapes; and the Viura, Malvasía and Garnacha Blanca whites. All Rioja wines come from these. The use of other, unauthorized varieties is restricted to old vineyards where, following earlier traditions all manner of types are planted together. This kind of vineyard is disappearing, however – there is now a legal obligation to plant the varieties in such a way that they can be picked separately – and with it the last vines of Calagraño, Maturana (black and white), Miguel del Arco, Monastrel, Moscatel, Turrentés and other grapes from former times that are now prohibited. Of the permitted varieties, black grapes are in a strong majority with 76% of the total, and it is with these that the following descriptions begin.

Tempranillo

The Tempranillo is the most characteristic black grape of the region. It represents more than half the grape content of nearly all the better red wines and in some cases it is the only variety present. Most experts regard the Tempranillo as native to Rioja, although it is just possible that monks brought it from Burgundy on their pilgrimages to Santiago de Compostela. The name itself means 'early' or 'early-ripe'. In theory this grape does in fact reach maturity relatively early, about mid-September. Riojan practice, however, indicates fairly late picking, from 10 or 12 October. The reason for this is the comparatively cool climate in the districts where this grape is prinicpally planted, Rioja Alta and Rioja Alavesa. The Tempranillo does in fact thrive best in a cool, rather wet climate and it resists cold well. Limestone favours it, which is not the case for many black varieties (the Cabernet Sauvignon, for example, gives much less successful wines in this type of soil). Its yield per acre can be considerable, but in the Rioja this is limited by the low density of planting and the age of some of the vines. Wine from the Tempranillo possesses a straightforward, not strikingly aromatic taste with good fruit, relatively low acidity; it usually – but not always – has sufficient alcohol, a strong, stable colour, and less tannin than Bordeaux grapes. The juice of the Tempranillo lends itself to the processing both of Riojas that require long maturing and to supple wines for drinking within the year. Other grapes are often added to give the wines a little more acid, aroma and tannin. In the Rioja the Tempranillo accounts for 40% of all vines, a percentage that is still increasing because in the Rioja Baja a lot of Garnacha Tinta is being replaced by Tempranillo. The Tempranillo occurs in other Spanish regions besides Rioja. It appears as the Cencibel in La Mancha, the Ull de Llebre in Penedés, the Tinto Fino in Ribera del Duero. In addition it is reported that experiments are being conducted with the Tempranillo in the United States and Australia.

Garnacha Tinta

The official name of this grape variety is Garnach*a* Tint*a*, although in common parlance it is often treated as masculine – Garnach*o* Tint*o*. This book will stick to the first, correct variant. Whereas most of the Tempranillo vines grow in Rioja Alta and Rioja Alavesa, the Garnacha Tinta holds sway in Rioja Baja, where it represents some 70% of plantings. It is hard to give the exact percentage because preference goes to the Tempranillo when replanting is carried out in this district; new vineyards, too, are mostly planted with Tempranillo. The Garnacha Tinta (also called the Tinto Aragones) is identical to the Grenache Noir of the South of France and it is also encountered in other hot countries and regions: this grape likes the sun and drought is no problem for it. In addition it is very resistant to mildew. Its rather light-coloured, abundant juice has a good deal of sugar so that the wine acquires a lot of alcohol. Colour on the other hand is not its strongest point, and acid even less so. Wine from the Garnacha Tinta does not usually have very much character or aroma and it oxidizes easily. A pure Garnacha wine is therefore not very suitable for long maturing in wood.

In the Rioja the Garnacha Tinta is used mainly to add strength to Tempranillo wines – or for making rosés, for it offers fruit in plenty. Although there are some good Garnacha Tinta rosés produced in the Rioja Baja, for the author's taste the most attractive come from the Rioja Alta. In this district you find a modest proportion of the vines (about 15%) growing on south-facing higher slopes. Because of the cooler microclimate there the grapes often produce too little colour for red wine but lend themselves perfectly to rosé.

For a long time the Garnacha Tinta was the most prevalent grape in the Rioja, but today the proportion (about 33%) lies well below that of the Tempranillo, and even this will undoubtedly be further reduced.

Mazuelo

The name Mazuelo is believed to be derived from *mats*, the Basque word for grape. This variety is related to the Carignan found in the South of France and elsewhere, and identical to the Crujillón of Cariñena. A Mazuelo vine can bear a lot of grapes, but this does not always come about because the plant is prone to all kinds of diseases. This is why the numbers of this vine have fallen to about 1.5% of the total. Most Mazuelo vines are found in the Rioja Alta, where they represent an estimated 2% of plantings. A pure Mazuelo wine (which the author has sampled – from a vat at Bodegas Lan) has a colour that is not really deep, but very stable, which it does not lose with ageing. Its aroma rather suggests ripe fruit and it is generous in structure. The Mazuelo makes a wine with a lot of tannin and fairly high acidity, a wine, too, with a good ageing potential. Knowing the characteristics of the Tempranillo it can be imagined how excellently the Mazuelo complements it – and various bodegas compete every year to obtain sufficient of this variety.

Grape varieties

Graciano

The Graciano is of obscure origin, but it is very typical of this north Spanish region. In 1790 it was apparently the most important variety here. At that time it was concentrated in the Rioja Alta and the western part of the Rioja Alavesa. Nothing now remains of this pre-eminence. Indeed, the Graciano has practically dropped out of sight and accounts for only 0.3% of vines (355 acres in Rioja Alta, 190 in Baja and 40 in Alavesa). This decline is due to its low yield per acre, which makes it unprofitable. The aroma of Graciano wine is fresh, rather in a vegetable way, and evolves into something suggesting brushwood. It is added to Tempranillo chiefly because of this particular aroma. The colour starts as ruby red, but it is not very stable. In addition the wine tends to oxidize. In order to preserve the Graciano, and its fragrance, for Rioja, Bodegas Faustino Martínez in Oyón has decided to plant 15% of its own vineyard area with this variety: an example that may be followed.

Viura

The most widely distributed white grape in the Rioja (at 19%) is the Viura. It is probably related to the Macabéo (the Maccabeu of the South of France). The name Viura may be derived from Basque terms such as *zuri* (white), *ori* (yellow) and *urín* (juice). The grape was brought here from Aragon around 1850. The Viura grows best in deep, well-exposed soil containing clay and lime. These conditions exist in Rioja Alta and Rioja Alavesa and that is where the greatest concentration is found (about 26% and 15% of the total respectively, against some 12% in Rioja Baja). For generations Viura wines were treated in the same way as reds and were left to mature for long periods in the wood. This presented no difficulties for Riojas made from the Viura are not prone to oxidation, partly because of their high degree of acidity. This characteristic is in fact the main reason why wine from the Viura is added to many Rioja reds (15 to 20%

The Tempranillo generally forms its leaves late in spring. One characteristic of Garnacha vines is that they are resistant to oidium (mildew).

The Viura has a higher yield of grapes than the Malvasía, which is one reason why growers prefer it.

The Mazuelo is liable to oidium and requires a lot of treatment on this account. This used to make it an expensive variety, but now that vineyard spraying has been largely mechanized this grape is making a hesitant come-back: on the Monte Yerga estate for instance.

In Rioja the Tempranillo is also called the Tinto de Rioja.

The Garnacha is usually the first black variety picked.

Must from the Graciano, a fairly disease-resistant grape, is generally rather difficult to clarify.

The Viura is sensitive to spring frosts.

The most recent figures of the percentages of the different grape varieties used in Rioja are:

	%
Tempranillo	*38.5*
Garnacha Tinta	*32.5*
Mazuelo	*1.5*
Graciano	*0.3*
Viura	*19.3*
Malvasía	*0.35*
Garnacha Blanca	*0.25*
Mixed; and other varieties	*7.3*
	100.0

sometimes), and also to quite a few rosés. Led by Bodegas Marqués de Cáceres, however, a new style of pure Viura white wine has been created which ferments at a low temperature and no longer comes into contact with wood. It is only in this type of Rioja that the true class of the Viura can be tasted, which in addition to its acidity is aromatic, juicy and fruity in a refined kind of way.

Malvasía

The Malvasía is known in France as the Malvoisie and on Madeira as Malmsey. This grape also occurs in Yugoslavia and other countries around the Mediterranean. However, scholars doubt whether the Riojan Malvasía is identical to its namesakes in Spain and elsewhere. In any case its nickname in the region is *rojal* as the grapes have a pinkish tinge (*rojo* is Spanish for 'red'). This variety of white grape does best on dry, well-ventilated soils high up, as it is very susceptible to rot. This will be one reason why this vine is restricted to less than 0.5% of the total in Rioja – especially in Rioja Alta and Alavesa. The Malvasía gives a wine that is fairly heavy, oxidizes easily, and tends to be yellow in colour and limited in alcohol, but has good aromatic qualities and is very low in acids. It is mostly blended with Viura.

Garnacha Blanca

The Garnacha Blanca is closely related to the Garnacha Tinta and it, too, gives strength and plenty of alcohol, little acidity and only a moderate nose. It is also liable to oxidation. These represent qualities that are not very desirable in today's white wines and so there is no reason to regret the fact that this variety (the Grenache Gris of France) accounts for only 0.25% of all Rioja vines. That it is still grown is probably due to its resistance to disease and its vigorous, productive growth.

Other varieties

In practically all the wine regions of the world growers experiment with other grapes besides the officially permitted varieties, and the Rioja is no exception. Quite a few bodegas have undertaken such trials, sometimes in collaboration with oenological institutes or the authorities, sometimes not. Campo Viejo, for example, is experimenting with the Cabernet Sauvignon, Pinot Noir, Gamay, Merlot, Chenin Blanc, Sémillon and Chardonnay vines. One supplier to José Palacios is growing Cabernet Sauvignon. Martínez Bujanda vinifies small quantities of Cabernet Sauvignon, Riesling and Müller-Thurgau. And there are others. In addition a bodega such as Marqués de Riscal is allowed to go on including Cabernet Sauvignon, Cabernet Franc, Malbec and Pinot Noir in its wines for the simple reason that the firm has been doing this since the 19th century and the style of its Riojas is partly determined by these grapes.

The Bodegas

The Spanish word *bodega* means literally 'wine cellar', but it is also understood as 'wine company' and it is in this latter sense that the term will be used in this book. The Consejo Regulador distinguishes four different types of bodega and these are listed in four separate registers:

Bodegas de elaboración where grapes are made into Rioja wines.

Bodegas de almacenamiento which store wine already made: *see* the *Cooperatives and wholesalers* section below.

Bodegas de crianza where the ageing of Rioja wines is permitted. These firms must be located in one of the 34 communities selected for this purpose and hold a stock of

at least 49,500 (58,500 US) gallons of wine, with a minimum 50% of this in 500 barrels of 50 (59 US) gallons (225 litres) capacity. There are also requirements regarding the storage areas, which have, for example, to be vibration-free.

Bodegas de exportadores which comprise companies in the previous category with a minimum storage capacity of 165,000 (195,000 US) gallons capacity (see also the *Export* section below).

Nearly all the bodegas to be described belong to the third or fourth of the above categories. Only a few cooperatives and small private concerns are listed as *bodegas de elaboración*. This does not mean that you

will encounter no barrel-aged wines there, only that their stock of wine is small.

A number of functions

In the same way the *bodegas de crianza* should not be seen purely and simply as firms that mature wines. They often process grapes as well, frequently from their own vineyards. And there are other areas where the *crianza* bodegas can be active. Six possible functions can be distinguished:

Producing wine from their own vineyards.

Buying in grapes and/or must from other producers for processing.

Buying in made wine from other producers or holders of wine stocks.

The storing, selecting, blending and maturing of wine.

The treatment and bottling of wine.

Selling and distributing wine.

The last three functions are common to all *bodegas de crianza*; the first three vary from company to company. There are, for

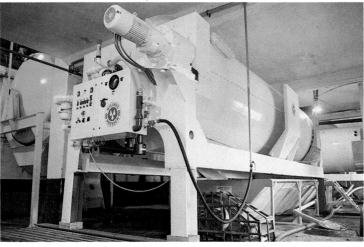

The bodegas

example, bodegas that handle only their own grapes, while others use nothing but wine bought elsewhere. Whichever way they work, the Riojan *bodegas de crianza* have a multiple function, both technologically and economically. They are the motors that propel the region and keep it moving forward – and they handle 95% of all its wine.

The first wave

As we saw in the 'History' chapter, the first bodegas of any importance date from the second half of the 19th century. The oldest still in existence is Marqués de Murrieta, which started operating before 1860; the exact year of its foundation is not known. The first still extant wine firm to begin to market Rioja was that of Marqués de Riscal, which opened its doors in 1860. In the following decades many new bodegas were established under the influence of the explosion in the French demand for Riojas. The list below gives the bodegas described in this book that date from this first period of growth and prosperity:

185? Marqués de Murrieta
1860 Marqués de Riscal
1861 Faustino Martínez
1870 Rioja Santiago
1874 Montecillo
1877 López de Heredia
1877 Berberana
1879 CVNE
1880 Martinez de Ayala
1881 del Romeral (now the AGE group)
1882 Muerza
1885 Lagunilla
1886 Gómez Cruzado
188? SMS
1890 La Rioja Alta
1890 Franco-Españolas
1890 Martínez Bujanda
1890 Riojanas
1894 Palacio
1895 Martínez Lacuesta
1895 De la Torre y Lapuerta (Campo Burgo)
1896 Carlos Serres
1898 Federico Paternina
1898 Corral
1901 Bilbaínas

The bodegas are given with their present names; quite a few of them bore different ones then. Many of them have also changed their location since they were founded, to say nothing of their scope and structure.

A second period of growth

Not many more new bodegas came into being until the 1970s. People were far too busy surviving a series of crises. Among the bodegas that were founded in this intervening period were Faustino Rivero Ulecia (1903), Señorio de Arana (1905), Navajas (1918), Gurpegui (1921), Ramón Bilbao (1924), Las Veras (1926; now with AGE), Muga (1932), José Palacios (1947) and Campo Viejo (1959). The setting up of this last concern actually ushered in a new period of prosperity for Rioja. Increasing demand, a series of good, large harvests and rising wine prices meant there was a great deal of interest in the region in the course of the 1960s, not least from banks or other institutions or persons with plenty of capital. Thus by the end of this decade the formation of a series of new bodegas was planned or under way, a trend that continued in the early 1970s. This new generation included:
1970 Marqués de Cáceres
1970 Lan

Left:
Old casks, mildewed and dusty, at Martinez de Ayala in Labastida.

Below, centre:
At some of the smaller bodegas the wine is still filtered by vine twigs tied in bundles. This is done when the wine is transferred from the fermentation tanks to the barrels. In the picture: Julio Cañas Caballero, cellarman at Bodegas La Primicia, Elciego.

Below right:
Still life in the cellars of La Rioja Alta.

The bodegas

1970	El Coto
1970	Bodegas y Viñedos
1972	Marqués del Puerto
1972	La Real Divisa
1973	Olarra
1973	Beronia
1973	Alavesas
1973	Viña Salceda
1973	Domecq
1973	Velázquez
1974	Laserna

Take-overs

At about the same time a number of existing bodegas changed owners. large drinks companies bought up bodegas, or acquired considerable interests in them. The American drinks firm Schenley acquired 49% of AGE in the period 1972–3, and in 1973 Montecillo was taken over by the brandy and sherry producer Osborne. Another sherry house, Croft (originally port shippers) became the new owners of Lagunilla in 1974. Pepsi-Cola bought up the shares of Rioja Santiago in two stages (1970 and 1975). The most spectacular take-overs, however, came about through the Rumasa group and involved Federico Paternina in 1972, Franco-Españolas in 1973, Berberana in 1981 and Lan in 1982. The Rumasa group, created in 1961 and named after its founder and owner Ruiz Mateos, controlled more than 300 firms in many different businesses when at its height, among them important sherry firms, accounting for 40% of all the wines from that region. In 1983 the Rumasa group was nationalized by the Socialist government. The former Rumasa

The bodegas

bodegas came temporarily under state
control.

Great contrasts

As a result of the startling growth – and, in
many cases, renewal – of the Riojan
bodegas, great contrasts developed between
them. On the one hand you come across big-
scale firms with up-to-date equipment, and
on the other strictly traditional houses of
very modest size – and all possible
variations in between. There is, for
example, a world of difference between
Lan's cool, tautly efficient complex and the
very old-fashioned family firm of Martinez
de Ayala in an untidy old house. Naturally
these contrasts are not confined to
buildings and equipment; they also occur in
the wine. Using exactly the same grape
variety the Marqués de Cáceres bodega
with its modern plant produces a white
Rioja that is totally different from the one
made by the conservative Marqués de
Murrieta concern. In fact this is a good
thing, for nothing would be more boring
than uniformity. One of the charms of the
Rioja is the diversity of styles of wine you
find there.

Cooperatives and wholesalers

Besides the ordinary bodegas of the Rioja
there are the wine cooperatives, the
bodegas cooperativas. These market very
little wine themselves – about 2% of total
production – as they function primarily as
suppliers to the bigger bodegas. They are of
great importance in this area as they vinify
some 45% of all grapes. The cooperative
phenomenon did not manifest itself in the
Rioja until 1943, when the first of these
collective enterprises was set up. A second
followed in 1947, but the breakthrough did
not come until 1953. Before the 1960s all
the cooperatives except two (San Asensio
and San Vicente de la Sonsierra) were in
Rioja Baja. Subsequently the movement
shifted to Rioja Alta with cooperatives
opened at Huércanos (1961), Tirgo (1961),
Nájera (1962), Cenicero (1963), Haro (1965)
and Alesanco (1966) and elsewhere. At

present the Rioja has 30 cooperatives with
9,000–10,000 *socios* or members. Many of
these concerns have permanent contacts, if
not contracts, with large bodegas. The
collaboration can be so close that the
bodega tells the cooperative members when
they should start picking.

The *almacenistas* occupy a place apart in
the Riojan wine world. They function
principally as wholesalers, collecting wine
from cooperatives, individual producers
and their own vineyards and then holding
it in stock for the large bodegas – who are
then often able to order a particular style of
wine to measure, as it were. The *bodegas de
almacenamiento* supply about 4% of total

Rioja production to the big bodegas. In
addition they market wine on their own
account, representing some 2% of the total:
the same percentage as the cooperatives,
double that produced by the independent
growers and only a tiny fraction of the 95%
handled by the bodegas.

Differences

The position of power occupied by the
bodegas also entails responsibilities. These
are the firms that determine the image of
quality presented by Rioja. The Consejo
Regulador has of course laid down
standards of quality for all types of Rioja.

The bodegas

But these are only minimum standards and they leave plenty of scope for wines that are barely worthy of the name of Rioja. Although the region numbers firms that are very quality conscious there are others that seem to specialize in characterless wines of only mediocre standard. This is one of the reasons why a group of bodegas is working together as an association, with the aim of using all possible means to protect and improve the quality of Rioja, including combined pressure on the Consejo Regulador and other bodies. It is not only the wine itself that attracts their attention but also, for instance, policy with regard to new planting. The members of this association are, in alphabetical order, Beronia, Castillo de Cuzcurrita, Corral, CVNE, Granja de Remélluri, Laserna, Marqués de Cáceres, Montecillo, Muga and La Rioja Alta.

Export

Not all bodegas are allowed to export. Before it can be considered as a potential exporter a firm has to have a storage capacity of at least 165,000 (195,000 US) gallons, of which 49,500 (58,500 US) gallons has to mature (half of it in wooden barrels) just as in the *bodegas de crianza*. In addition the bodega has to join the Grupo de Exportadores de Vinos Rioja, set up in 1968 to further the interests of exporting

bodegas. The usual entry fee for this Grupo is high, some millions of pesetas, and its requirements make it difficult for the smaller bodegas to become members. Despite this it numbers some smaller firms among its more than 40 members, as well as a few cooperatives – not as a rule the most prosperous kind of producer. When, after the late 19th-century boom and the subsequent decline, Rioja exports at last picked up again in the 1960s, they were principally in bulk form. In 1962, for example, 3.5 million (4 million US) gallons were exported, of which only 15.3%, or roughly 530,000 (625,000 US) gallons were bottled. Today the situation is entirely reversed. More than 90% of exported Rioja is sold in bottled form. Among the biggest foreign customers for Rioja are Switzerland, Denmark, Britain, the Netherlands, the United States, Sweden, West Germany, Belgium, France and Canada. By far the biggest consumer, however, is Spain itself, for some two-thirds of all Rioja is still drunk there.

Key position

It will be clear that the *bodegas de crianza*, especially those with export licences, occupy a key position. They collect practically all the wine and then market it. The Rioja is dominated by these commercial firms, although of course they

often have close ties with the actual wine producers – or in part perform this function themselves. There are even a few bodegas that handle only their own wine. In France it is only in Champagne that a roughly comparable situation exists. As these bodegas have to store a legally prescribed minimum quantity there is a certain vastness of scale. The character of Rioja is not determined by numerous individual wine growers offering small quantities of mutually differing wines, but by a relatively limited number of producers who process large quantities into homogenous brand wines. In the nature of things this leads to a certain uniformity: the rich mosaic of wines offered by regions such as Bordeaux and Burgundy is missing from Rioja. Nor does it reach the optimum quality levels of some of the Bordeaux châteaux or Burgundy estates. But on the other hand Rioja excels in its production of a large volume of extremely reliable wines of good average quality, always at reasonable prices; and still with plenty of differences in style, taste and structure so that a journey of vinous exploration through the Rioja will be rewarded with many surprising finds.

Making the wine

Besides the usual way of making red wine Rioja has its own traditional method. An estimated one-third of all red Rioja is still produced in this way – and more than 70% in the Rioja Alavesa district. It is mainly the small growers doing their own vinification, the *cosecheros*, who keep it up. However, the method is also encountered on a bigger scale at some of the cooperatives and bodegas. After picking the ripe grapes are not crushed or destalked. They go straight into the fermentation tanks without further processing, skin, stalk, seeds and all. The tank used by the growers is a large, rectangular trough, usually of concrete, called a *lago*. It can hold from 23 up to 46 tons of grapes and as a rule it is filled up to 80% of its capacity. Small doses of sulphur dioxide are added during filling, about 6 to 9 g (0.2 to 0.3 oz) to every 100 kg (220 lb) of fruit. This universal practice is a protection against oxidation and eliminates unwanted types of yeast.

Intercellular fermentation

Partly as a result of being tipped into the collecting baskets and the fermentation tank, and partly through the grapes' own weight, a small amount of juice collects in the bottom of the *lago*. This begins to ferment and the carbon dioxide produced envelops the layers of fruit above, rendering it short of acid. As a result the enzymes present in the grapes are activated, causing what is termed intercellular fermentation inside their skins. Colour and flavour are extracted from the skin, while the primary aromas of the grape are trapped in the skin cells – resulting later in a fragrant, fruity wine. The *cosechero* does not simply look on in expectation during the fermentation process. From the second or third day he starts to tread the mass of grapes carefully by foot once daily and the lower layers of grapes are brought to the top (*remonta*) so that fermentation proceeds evenly. During fermentation the grapes gradually swell, finally bursting after ten or so days. This produces more fermenting must and thereby wine.

Treading the grapes

The first red wine drawn off the tank is the *vino de lagrima*. This has a lot of fruit and a good acid content, not much colour and limited alcohol (10 to 11%). Several men now work on the remaining mass. The grape pulp, still containing a lot of juice, is forked to one side of the *lago* and is then trodden vigorously by two or three men. This process is repeated several times. The wine thus obtained is called the *corazón*; this represents the best quality, with a robust constitution, a deep colour and a good deal of alcohol. Any remaining *marc* is pressed twice and a part of the resulting liquid (*vin de presse*) can be added to the wine. The quantities of the three types of wine per 10,000 litres – 2,200 (2,600 US) gallons – are roughly: 3,125 litres *lagrima*, 5,625 litres *corazón* (together making up about 85% of the total), and 1,250 litres of *vin de presse*. After being drawn off the wine continues to ferment, often in large wooden barrels, until all the sugar present has been converted into alcohol and carbon dioxide, and malolactic fermentation takes place. In this secondary fermentation the malic acid in the wine is turned into lactic acid, which is milder, and the wine itself becomes more stable.

Differences

The method of vinification just described has been employed for centuries in Rioja and has probably come down from Roman times. It is also used in France (and other countries), notably in the Beaujolais and Roussillon. The French call it *macération carbonique* and as this term is generally familiar, it will be used in the subsequent chapters whenever this traditional Riojan vinification method is being referred to. This is also done for the sake of clarity as the normal vinification process could equally well be labelled as 'traditional' in Rioja.

Macération carbonique and the ancient Riojan technique are not in fact quite identical. The most important differences are:

Making the wine

Making the wine

In France and elsewhere efforts are made to ensure that the grapes arrive as intact as possible. Therefore they are mostly transported in small stackable boxes. Most Riojans still use *comportas*, upright wooden tubs that can hold more than 200 lb and in which there is always some bruising of the fruit.

The Riojan vats are open; those used for *macération carbonique* always closed. That the Riojan wines are not characterized by volatile acid is due to the 'blanket' of carbon dioxide that covers the grapes. In addition the Tempranillo grape is highly resistant to oxidation.

Carbon dioxide is added during *macération carbonique*, but not in the Riojan method.

Sulphur is added to the grapes in the Riojan process, but not as a rule in *macération carbonique*.

Employed on an industrial scale

Despite the above differences the wines produced by these closely related fermentation methods are similar in character, allowing of course for the influence of soil, climate and grape variety. Colour, nose, aroma and suppleness are their most important positive characteristics. A lack of acid (including tannin with its keeping properties) may be looked on as a negative factor. As has been mentioned, it is not only the small *cosecheros* who vinify in the manner just described. Besides a number of cooperatives there are also various bodegas that employ the method on an industrial scale. The author has sampled splendid Riojas made in this way at Faustino Martínez, in Oyón, and Palacio, as well as Bodegas Alavesas in Laguardia. Bodegas Martínez Bujanda has gone one step further. This Oyón firm has put in tanks exactly on the Beaujolais model for *macération carbonique*.

The Bordeaux example

While fermentation through the action of carbon dioxide is the oldest technique used in the Rioja, the classic vinification method is actually the one most employed for making red wines. It was French winemakers who introduced the process here in the second half of the 19th century, sometimes in collaboration with Riojans who had studied it in Bordeaux, where it is the usual technique. In this method the grapes are crushed and destalked, then taken to the fermentation tanks (the *depositos*). These are mostly of concrete (sometimes lined with tiles or a neutral layer of synthetic material), steel, or stainless steel. More commonly than in Bordeaux the open wooden fermentation vats have disappeared; and where they are still in use it is generally just for storing wine. One of the rare bodegas working exclusively with wooden vats is Muga in Haro.

Lower fermentation temperatures

The increasing use of steel and stainless steel fermentation tanks is due to the fact that they are easy to empty and clean. One type is the 'self-emptying' tank from which the *marc* slips into containers by the force of gravity. The main reason for choosing steel, however, is that it gives the winemaker maximum control over the fermentation temperature. In contrast to concrete, steel is a good heat conductor. This temperature control – usually effected by passing cold water over the tanks – has become increasingly important in recent decades. Until the 1960s red Rioja generally fermented at 28–30° C, compared with 22 to 27° C today. This lower temperature indisputably gives better and more aromatic wines. In all types of tanks or vats the wine is regularly scooped up over the cap, or *sombrero*, of skins that floats on top. This is done to extract the greatest possible amount of colour and tannin from the skins and to prevent the temperature rising too high in the liquid, rich in bacteria as it is. After the first wine has been drawn off the remaining mass of skins is pressed once more. Some of the *vin de presse* so produced is nearly always mixed with the rest of the wine. Many *cosecheros* still use small horizontal presses

(in some cases hand-operated); most of the bodegas employ modern types. The last stage of vinification consists of the malolactic fermentation. For this the bodegas usually have concrete tanks on a floor directly beneath the fermentation room into which the wine drains by gravity.

New-style white wine

Many firms have reduced the fermentation temperature for red Riojas, as we have seen, and this is even more the case for whites. The result has been a remarkable improvement in quality. Before the 1960s most white Riojas lacked freshness and fruit, tasting flat and downright uninteresting while their colour was yellowish. With Bodegas Marqués de Cáceres and other pioneers in the van, however, a completely new vinification technique was introduced. The white grapes are picked the moment they are fully ripe, or just before. Overripe fruit is undesirable as it has a reduced acid content. After arrival the grapes are pressed as quickly as possible and the juice goes into the fermentation tanks. It is then left to ferment slowly at a low temperature (14 to 18° C) for four to six weeks. In this way the maximum fruit, and all the components of the grape, are transferred to the wine. With the Viura grape in particular this method achieves remarkable results: very pale-coloured wines with a lot of fruit, fine perfume and an unusually pure, fresh taste. And whereas the traditionally made white Riojas were nearly always aged in the barrel, the new style whites are kept well away from wood.

Cold stabilization

Not all the bodegas, however, have adopted this modern vinification method. Sometimes this has been through lack of the necessary capital to invest, but more often it is a matter of keeping on with old-style Rioja whites for the sake of faithful customers. This latter reason is justifiable in some cases, for there are certain firms

Making the wine

that make white wines of a good standard by the classic method and mature them in wood. Bodegas Marqués de Murrieta is one example. There are also bodegas that produce the new and old styles of white wines simultaneously – Federico Paternina, for instance. White Riojas hardly ever undergo a malolactic fermentation, for they more often have a shortage than a surplus of acidity.

Cold stabilization made its appearance in Rioja at much the same time as cool fermentation. White wine is particularly prone to the formation of tartaric acid crystals, which look like grains of sugar. They are absolutely harmless, completely neutral in taste and smell and do not affect the wine. They occur naturally, especially when there are temperature variations. Despite the fact that they are actually a proof that the wine has developed unhindered they often form a source of complaint from the public. To prevent these crystals forming in the bottle, tanks have been developed in which white wine can be cooled down for a few days to just above its freezing point. This causes precipitation of the crystals and the wine is then filtered.

The production of rosés

Cold stabilization, or cold treatment as it is also termed, is not only widely employed in Rioja for white wines but also for rosés (and occasionally for reds for drinking young). Today new bodegas are actually obliged to install the necessary equipment. In other aspects, too, the making of rosés shows similarities to the white wine process. Fermentation often takes place at low temperatures, vitality and fruit in the wine being the aim. Most rosé is produced by leaving the skins of black grapes (with sometimes a smaller quantity of white grapes) in contact with the must for a specified number of hours; in Rioja this period varies from 6 to 24 hours. The riper the grapes, the shorter the time. To achieve the same intensity of colour 6 hours of contact with the skins is sufficient in Ausejo in Rioja Baja; 12 hours in Cenicero, in central Rioja Alta; and 24 hours in Fonzaleche, in the western corner of Rioja Alta. A long period of contact is generally beneficial for the wine, for it is not only colour that is extracted from the skins but a number of other substances, too, including acids. Sometimes the skins and the must are separated immediately; in this case a light pressing transfers the colouring to the juice. The Garnacha Tinta is the grape most used for rosés in Rioja, followed by the Tempranillo and the Viura. A dark type of rosé – which could be regarded as a light kind of red – is called *clarete* in Rioja. It was once very fashionable but has now largely dropped out of use.

Sweet wines

Besides the types already mentioned Rioja also produces small quantities of semi-sweet and sweet wines (described on labels as *abocado* or *semi-dulce* and *dulce* respectively). Ideally these are made from overripe grapes which have so much sugar that not all of it ferments; the residue gives the wine its sweet taste. Usually, however, this type of wine is obtained by interrupting the fermentation of ordinary white must. The results achieved are not very interesting.

Pasteurization

Pasteurization is a sporadic phenomenon in which yeast cells and bacteria still present are killed by heating the wine, usually to 60° C for 30 minutes. The wine, however, loses character, backbone and vitality, so from the point of view of quality pasteurization is not a desirable practice and is suitable for only the very simplest of Riojas. Today in fact the same effect can be achieved by the less drastic method of filtering. One type that is often pasteurized is semi-sweet white.

Maturing the wine

Apart from the sometimes very successful *macération carbonique* wines, all red Riojas of any importance are matured in wood. The minimum period for each type is laid down by law. *Crianzas* and *reservas* have to spend a minimum of one year in the barrel, *gran reservas* a minimum of two. Even in small, non-exporting bodegas you therefore come across what to non-Spanish eyes seem rather large numbers of barrels. At the firm of SMS in Villabueana there are on average 650; 800 at Eguren in San Vicente de la Sonsierra; and 900 at La Real Divisa in Abalos. The numbers held by the big bodegas are truly impressive. Heading the list is Federico Paternina with 55,000, followed by Campo Viejo with 45,000, AGE with 35,000, Berberana with 32,000, and Franco-Españolas, Marqués de Riscal, Olarra and La Rioja Alta with 25,000 each. The other bodegas all have less than 20,000.

Bordeaux model

The form and capacity of the barrels is legally prescribed. They have to be identical with the Bordeaux type, the *barrique bordelaise* with its 225 litre or 50 (59 US) gallons capacity; and so in the Rioja they speak of *barricas bordelesas*, or just *barricas*. Anyone who knows the history of Rioja will realize that this type came in under French influence in the second half of the 19th century. The barrels have to be made of oak, but people are free to choose which kind. The great majority in the region are made from American oak, mostly originating in Oregon or Ohio. This is shipped to Rioja and made into barrels there. Murua in Logroño is by far the biggest cooperage, but you also come across smaller firms. Quite a few bodegas have their own coopers on permanent staff both to make and repair *barricas*. To a lesser extent some bodegas have stocks of barrels made from French oak (mainly from Limousin). These, too, are generally manufactured in Rioja, although a few enterprising bodegas have bought used barrels from Bordeaux châteaux. As a result of rising wood prices in America and France there are bodegas that are experimenting with Spanish and Portuguese oak, but so far the quantities involved are negligible.

American versus French oak

It is alleged that there is hardly any difference between American and French oak barrels. Nothing could be further from the truth. The American wood has a different cellular structure from the French, being denser and less porous. In addition American oak is generally used in 35 mm (1 4/10 in) thicknesses, compared with 22 mm (9/10 in) for the French. In the French barrels the wine therefore comes much more intensively into contact with oxygen and develops quicker. And then there are the aromatic aspects. The two kinds of oak influence the taste of the wine in somewhat different ways; the French wood imparts milder, and nobler, nuances.

Maturing the wine

The few bodegas that have a reasonable stock of French barrels obtained them quite deliberately. Campo Viego, for example, always keeps its *reservas* and *gran reservas* in French oak barrels for their first year of ageing. The biggest proportion of French barrels is held by Bodegas Marqués de Cáceres: half of its 10,800 *barricas* are of French wood. The fact that the owner was trained in France and was advised by a French oenologist may have something to do with it.

A vanilla aroma

Riojan barrels usually last a long time:

their average age is estimated at 15 to 18 years. During this long period of use a layer can be deposited on the inner walls of the barrel so that the wine no longer comes into direct contact with the wood, and only minimally with oxygen. Some bodegas, such as Marqués de Murrieta, use old barrels of this kind to keep white as well as red wines in the wood for very long periods – sometimes for decades. The wines keep perfectly in them and show amazing freshness and vitality in their old age. Wines aged in the barrel derive not only tannin with its preservative properties from the oak but also vanillin, which manifests itself in an aroma of vanilla. This is a characteristic of practically all barrel-aged Riojas. The wood itself also comes out in the wine with a suggestion of sawdust in taste and fragrance. New barrels naturally impart more tannin, vanillin and more of the scent of the wood to the wine than old ones do. It is therefore quite possible that Riojas from the younger bodegas, set up since 1970, will undergo a gradual change of structure. These firms started with new barrels, of course, which at first strongly marked the wines. But as the barrels become older – and so far as they are not replaced by new ones – the effect of the wood will diminish.

Treating the wine

Riojas are nearly always filtered before they go into the barrel. For this phase the majority of bodegas use an earth filter, but when they come to be bottled most wines are passed through a filter with cellulose plates or a membrane. At some firms the *reservas* and *gran reservas* are not filtered before bottling as all solid particles in the wine will have been deposited naturally during barrel ageing. Wines are regularly racked throughout this period, twice a year on average. This may be done with pumps or by hand; in the latter case the wine flows through a wide, open tank before passing into the clean barrels. In this way the wine receives an extra dose of oxygen: those thick, dense American staves make this necessary. Towards the end of their time in

the wood the wines are clarified. In this process the very lightest floating particles are removed by pouring a coagulating agent through the wine. This agent is albuminous – but actual egg whites are hardly ever used now. Only stringently conservative bodegas, like Muga, still clarify their wines wholly or partly with the beaten whites of eggs. In times past the blood of lambs or sheep was used: blood is also rich in albumen. Today, however, most firms use other forms of albumens.

Resting the wine

Ageing in the barrel is nearly always followed by maturing in the bottle. For this, too, there are legal minima according to type of wine. A striking feature here is that some bodegas attach great value to a long period in the wood while others place more emphasis on a long rest in the bottle for their wines. At firms in the latter category you find a large quantity of bottles in relation to the number of *barricas*. Marqués de Cáceres is one example with its average of 10,800 barrels in store and about 3 million bottles. This may be compared with Bodegas Berberana that produces a far greater volume with its 32,000 barrels but nevertheless keeps the same number of bottles in stock. The large AGE company also has a stock of on average 3 million bottles and has 35,000 barrels in its cellars. In bodegas with a shortage of space the bottles are placed in long deep ranks by hand. Other firms have replaced this time-consuming method by storage in wooden pallet boxes. The bottles are generally stored unlabelled and unwrapped. All this is done, and the bottles packed in boxes or crates, just before dispatch.

The categories of wine

The bodega system of Rioja is aimed at supplying the market with wines that the consumer can drink straight away. This in itself may be regarded as unique, certainly for a region that mainly produces red wines of quality. Legislators, however, realize that not all wines need to have the same maturity, and that there are various degrees of maturity. Riojas are therefore divided into various categories on the basis of maturity, all defined and protected by the wine laws. The consumer can read on every bottle which minimum ageing conditions it complies with. The author knows of no other wine region of repute in the world that offers its customers this service of immediately drinkable wines categorized according to their maturity.

The rise of the young Riojas

Details have been given in the 'Wine Legislation' chapter of how all bottles of Rioja have to be given a numbered back or neck label. These labels also state the category of the wine. Wine with no ageing in wood, or just a minimal such period, is called *vino sin crianza*. The three categories with barrel ageing are, as we have seen, *vino de crianza, reserva* and *gran reserva*. What is striking is that the first category, those with no time in wood, or virtually none, hardly existed before the 1960s. Until then the youngest Riojas produced had been mostly two or three years old. The picture that emerges today is quite different. Under the influence of a changed market and a new group of large, industrial-scale and very commercially-minded bodegas the *sin crianza* Riojas have become the most important category in volume terms. Sales for 1980 to 1985 present the following picture:

vino sin crianza	57%
vino de crianza	33%
reserva	6.5%
gran reserva	3.5%

In the long run, however, the proportion of *vino sin crianza* can be expected to decline, for with rising grape prices this category is becoming less competitive with comparable wines from other regions; and to justify higher retail prices the bodegas are being obliged to let more of their Riojas age in the wood. Intrinsically this is a good development. For if there is one factor that characterizes Riojas, especially the reds, it is this maturing of the wine in oak barrels.

Vino sin crianza

The category of *vino sin crianza* is not defined as such on the back labels: these give only the vintage year. They also differ somewhat in appearance from other back labels in having a yellow rather than a red background to the parchment map of Rioja. *Vino de cosechero*, the wine of the current year from small growers (and a few large bodegas) that is drunk so much in Rioja itself, is also sold as *vino sin crianza*. Bottles of this wine do not as a rule carry labels front or back, but just a neck label. In Spain in particular you also see *sin crianzas* with the letters *c.v.c.* on the back labels, standing for *conjunto de varias cosecha* (a blend of various vintages). In practice, however, this does not always mean that the wines in question come from various years. Many bodegas use these labels for convenience. Mostly they are applied to wines of the latest vintage, but if more than the legally permitted 15% of wine from another year is added then there is no need to change the labels.

Vino de crianza

The standards applied to red Riojas in the *crianza* category are a minimum one year in the barrel and one year's tank and/or bottle ageing. Therefore no Rioja in this category can be sold before it is two years old. There is some controversy concerning the obligatory twelve months in the wood. Some bodegas with a relatively large number of new barrels justifiably point out that a wine develops much faster in new oak than in old. It is also argued that account should be taken of the particular vintage. Not all years can tolerate the same length of barrel ageing and so a more

The categories of wine

flexible ruling is urged. For white and rosé Riojas in this category the obligatory time in the barrel is restricted to six months.

Reserva and gran reserva

The word *reserva* came into use at the end of the 19th century through French buyers who 'reserved' wines for their companies. Legally the term now applies to the category of red wines that have matured for at least three years, with a minimum one year in the wood. For whites and rosés the total ageing period has been reduced to two years, with a minimum of six months in the wood. To be entitled to the designation *gran reserva*, a red Rioja must have had at least two years in the barrel and three years' bottle ageing. The minimum statutory maturing in the wood for white and rosé *gran reservas* is six months, as for the *reservas*, but their total stay in the cellars has to be twice as long: four years.

The recurring vintage

A remarkable phenomenon has arisen in the Rioja because of these different categories. It is possible – and it does happen – for a bodega to bring out wines of the same year with long intervals in between. After all the *crianza* has been sold, the *reserva* from the same vintage may appear, and then the *gran reserva* a long time afterwards. Most bodegas select their wines by type: the longer a Rioja has to mature, the more Tempranillo there will be as a rule in its blend of grape varieties. However, it can also happen that the basic wines do not differ and that, for example, the *gran reserva* from a particular bodega is identical to its *reserva* in constitution, but simply matured for longer.

A varied supply

Every bodega cherishes its own ideas about the length and method of ageing and practically all of them have different kinds of red Rioja in their selection. As a result there is such a varied range of wines that it is really impossible to give an exact

Right:
At Bodegas Hacienda Palaciana,
a modest-sized winery in Elciego.

Below:
At the little bodega of Eguren in
San Vicente de la Sonsierra.

If a label describes a Rioja as, for example, '3° año' this usually means the wine is about two years old, for it has been bottled in its third year of life, the vintage date being counted as its first year. This is all rather confusing for the consumer. The now obligatory back or neck labels make the actual year of vintage quite clear, and it is these you should check if the front label does not state it.

The categories of wine

definition of the character of red Rioja. There are no very great similarities between, for example, Viña Faustino from Faustino Martínez, Castillo Ygay from Marqués de Murrieta, Banda Azul from Federico Paternina and Viña Pomal Reserva from Bilbaínas. Anyone wanting to characterize red Rioja will be obliged to confine himself to the most sweeping generalizations, to which there are always going to be a number of exceptions.

The essential characteristics

Yet the red wines of Rioja cannot be accused of a lack of identity. It is just as much there as it is in Bordeaux or Burgundy, California or Chianti. There are many aspects of the Rioja – and not just soil and climate – that are entirely its own and guarantee wines that are similarly its own. And nothing makes less sense than tastings in which Rioja is compared with Bordeaux. It is only in treatment and nurture that the two have points in common, and the contrasts are much more numerous: think of the grape varieties, the cultivation and the bodega system. Let us try to formulate the most essential characteristics of red Rioja:

Usually produced on a big scale.

Generally comes from different vineyards in more than one district.

Nearly always made from more than one grape variety, with Tempranillo the most important.

The older wines are held in tanks, casks and/or bottles according to legally prescribed regulations. Maturing in the wood lasts for at least one year.

Colour varies from a dark deep red to light brown, with the average shade lying in between.

Has a vanilla aroma to some degree if matured in the wood.

With the exception of the *macération carbonique* wines, not markedly fruity, although a mellow hint of ripe fruit is perceptible even in very old wines.

Seldom 'tired' despite a long period in the wood.

Accessible in character with almost a mildness of taste and nose and with gentle acids.

Of only moderate alcoholic strength, with the exception of the Garnacha wines from Rioja Baja.

Firm and yet elegant in structure, without any predominant taste elements and, in general, without any great depth or complexity.

Very vital, often to a considerable age.

Sold ready to drink.

A description like this, given its vagueness and its generalizations, reads almost like a political manifesto. Anyone who really wants to learn to know the wines of Rioja must let them speak for themselves. Every bottle tells its own story; every mouthful makes more things clear than a thousand lines of text.

Right:
*In October the leaves of the
Tempranillo vine start to show a
whole palette of colours.*

*As will be clear from the
assessment of vintages given
below, the Rioja by no means
corresponds year for year with
Bordeaux – contrary to what is
often believed outside Spain.*

Vintages

With the help of Manuel Ruiz Hernandez, the eminent director of the Estación de Viticultura y Enología at Haro, it has been possible to obtain assessments of the quality of the Rioja vintages from the beginning of this century. These are, of course, very broad and generalized and represent only a rough average – and that is how they should be used. It is quite possible that in a moderate year certain bodegas will nevertheless have produced some very good wines; and not all Riojas of a vintage described as excellent will themselves be excellent. Factors such as microclimate, selection of grape varieties and human skills also influence the ultimate quality of a wine.

For 1900 to 1970 only the 'very good' and 'excellent' vintages are listed; those from 1970 on are given brief descriptions.

1904 Very good	*1947* Excellent
1915 Very good	*1948* Excellent
1920 Excellent	*1952* Excellent
1922 Excellent	*1955* Excellent
1924 Excellent	*1959* Excellent
1925 Very good	*1962* Excellent
1931 Very good	*1964* Excellent
1934 Very good	*1968* Excellent
1942 Excellent	

1970 Very good. No night frosts in spring. Warm, moist summer, moderate autumn. Some hail in June. Mainly north winds.
Production: 24.8 (29 US) million gallons.

1971 Poor. Very wet spring, with some night frost in May. Attacks of oidium (mildew).
Production: 12 (14.3 US) million gallons.

1972 Poor. Cold rainy winter followed by bad spring and summer weather. A lot of oidium.
Production: 21.5 (25.5 US) million gallons.

1973 Good (and often very good). No night frosts, relatively dry spring, good rainfall during the growing cycle. Hot summer, warm autumn.
Production: 28.1 (33.28 US) million gallons.

1974 Good to moderate. After a damp, very cold winter, heavy rainfall in early spring. No night frosts. Warm summer, cool autumn.
Production: 28.6 (33.8 US) gallons.

1975 Very good. Moderate, dry winter. Late into bud. Wet spring. Warm summer and hot days during the harvest. Red wines for ageing of a deep red colour. White grapes much affected by rot.
Production: 18.5 (21.8 US) million gallons.

1976 Good. March very cold. Late into bud. Wet, hot summer. Ripening difficult and inconsistent quality. Wines soon ready for drinking.
Production: 20.5 (24.2 US) million gallons.

1977 Poor. Night frosts in spring followed by heavy rains, a cold summer and a moderate autumn.
Production: 14.5 (17.2 US) million gallons.

1978 Very good. Severe night frosts in April, warm dry summer, dry autumn. Successful wines, with fruit.
Production: 17.2 (20.3 US) million gallons.

1979 Moderate to poor. Very good weather conditions to August, then too much rain with rot prevalent as a result.
Production: 30.8 (36.4 US) million gallons.

1980 Good. Fresh, moist spring and then moderate temperatures. Elegant wines, mostly with only modest colour.
Production: 31 (36.6 US) million gallons.

1981 Very good to excellent. Frost in April and even snow. June part warm, part cold. Very warm harvest weather. Powerful, rounded wines.
Production: 29.7 (35.1 US) gallons.

1982 Excellent. Sunny, warm year (above 40° C in early July), but with sufficient rain. Powerful, rounded wines.
Production: 25.3 (30 US) million gallons.

1983 Good. Light spring frosts. Hail around Nájera, Cenicero and Lapuebla. August rainfall abnormally high. Reasonably warm harvest period. Wines with plenty of colour and acidity.
Production: 23.8 (28 US) million gallons.

1984 Good. Night frosts in May in Rioja Alta and parts of Alavesa. Hail in north-west in September and grapes lost through hurricane Hortensia. Stable, fruity wines with relatively little colour.
Production: 23.5 (27.8 US) million gallons.

1985 Good. Poor harvest expected originally but proved to be the biggest in recent history. Variable quality, but good on average.
Production: 37.4 (44.2 US) million gallons.

Gastronomy

'Eating a lot is unhealthy, but it is such an *agreeable* way of killing yourself', the manager of a bodega once remarked at table. This pronouncement was very typically Riojan. Eating well and at length is an extraordinarily popular activity here, pursued almost with passion. The many restaurants are full at midday and until late in the evening as well. In addition people here often eat *tapas* (snacks they can buy in any bar) or, in the early evening, the *merienda*, an 'in-between' meal. At home, too, the Riojans set about their food with verve. Their enthusiastic eating habits are stimulated by the region's plentiful supply of fresh produce. In the fertile, often irrigated river valleys a great range of vegetable and fruit is grown, the large numbers of sheep and other stock provide meat, and the nearby Atlantic offers abundant fish.

Specialities

Riojan cuisine is essentialy popular in character, full of flavour and nourishing. One regional speciality towers over all the rest: lamb chops – *chuletas de cordero al sarmiento* – clamped between large gridirons and grilled over the glowing embers of vine twigs. Red Rioja wines taste delightful with them. Besides the ordinary *chuletas* there are also the smaller *chuletitas*, often from very young lambs, *cordera lechal* or *lechazo*. Roast leg of lamb is often served and is a speciality of Haro's well-known Terete restaurant. Roast leg of young goat (*cabrito*) comes into the same category. There is a good deal of hunting and shooting in the Rioja Alavesa and in season partridge, quail, rabbit and various small game are on offer. Large quantities of *chorizos*, piquant pork sausages seasoned with paprika, are enjoyed by the Riojans, who eat them as a starter or as a main course. They also feature in other dishes: in the famous *Patatas a la Riojanas*, a kind of soup with potatoes, in *menestra de verdura*, a vegetable recipe, and in *pochas Riojanas*, which includes haricot beans.

Two meat dishes for stronger stomachs are *pimentos rellenos a la Riojana* (casseroled stuffed peppers) and *callos a la Riojana* (highly flavoured, with tripe and, again, *chorizos*).

Fish and vegetables

Merluza (hake) is frequently served in Rioja, prepared in a variety of ways. *Bacalao a la Riojana* is cod with tomatoes and red peppers. Sometimes you also see crayfish and trout (still present in the Río Oja, Río Iregua and Narjerilla rivers). Asparagus is tremendously popular in the Rioja. Despite its short season this noble vegetable can be eaten all year round thanks to the local canning industry. The asparagus, often thicker than your finger, is served simply with mayonnaise or a vinaigrette dressing. The 'tinned' taste that the asparagus acquires to some extent is no obstacle to the Riojans. Snails, cooked in olive oil with tomatoes and shallots, can also be ejoyed here. So can grilled mushrooms, fried peppers and *ajo arriero* (also called *sopa a la Riojana*) – a bouillon of cod with garlic, bread and eggs.

Meals are often ended with a sweet course. These include fruit, such as peaches in red wine; pastries, the very light *ruso* from Alfaro, for example; or other such desserts as flan, crème caramel, and *yema*, made from egg yolks, sugar and fruit with a layer of candy, nuts and dates. Besides the usual Spanish cheeses the Rioja has one of its own which is, however, difficult to find. This is called *Queso Camerano* and is a compact white goat's cheese of 8 to 28 oz, made to the south of Logroño in the hill villages of the Sierra de Cameros Nuevo.

Restaurants

Most eating places in Rioja are simple, informal and reasonably priced. Here is a selection of recommended restaurants, working through the region from west to east.
Briñas
El Portal de la Rioja
Labastida
Mesón los Claveles; Jatorena
Haro
Beethoven II; Terete; La Kika
Santo Domingo de la Calzada
El Rincón de Emilio; Parador Nacionál
Ezcaray
Hostal Echaurren
San Vicente de la Sonsierra
Hasta Toni
Cenicero
Conchita
Fuenmayor
El Valenciano; El Porrón
Laguardia
Hostal Marixa
Oyón
Mesón la Cueva
Logroño
Mesón la Merced (brilliant interior, excellent cuisine: see 'Logroño' chapter); San Remo, El Fogón, Avenida 21; Machado; El Cachetero; Asados Gonzalez; Asador Zubillaga
Lardero
Angelines
Viana
Mesón Borgia (one of the most creative small restaurants, just outside Rioja, in the province of Navarre)
Arnedo
Sopitas; Virrey (also a hotel and café)
Calahorra
Casa Mateo; Montserrat–2; Chef Nino; La Taberna de la Carta Esquina
Alfaro
Hotel Palacios

Above left:
Lunchtime in the small, and always crowded, Casa Mateo restaurant in Calahorra with feverish activity in the kitchen.

Left, centre:
Sopa de patates a la Riojana *is one of the region's best-known specialities.*

Below:
Serious trenchermen at Beethoven II in Haro. The names of local bodegas appear on the barrels in the mural relief.

Below left:
Roast leg of goat, cabrito asado, is another speciality often served in Rioja.

Rioja has its own mineral water. It comes from springs at Torrecilla and Cameros and bears the brandname Peñaclara.

José Luis Sanado Carinanos is the congenial chef and owner of Mesón Borgia in Viana (in the province of Navarre, just north of Logroño). Besides cooking at his restaurant he does meals for Bodegas Federico Paternina – evidence of that firm's good taste.

Left:
Rioja has its own official shape of bottle, but so far Campo Viejo is the only bodega to use it – as here for its rosés.

Below:
Quite a number of bodegas serve their wine in large brandy glasses, but the Bordeaux type is used at La Granja Remélluri.

Bottle sizes in Rioja are 0.7 and 0.75 litres.

Semi-sweet white Riojas should be served cooler than dry ones, at 5 to 6° C.

Enjoying Rioja

It will be clear from reading the description of the bodegas in the following pages that each firm produces its own style of Rioja and may excel in particular types. The reader will also learn of differences – sometimes very great – in the quality of the wines from the various bodegas. Anyone buying or ordering Riojas should therefore start by choosing the bodega. Is it a small concern specializing in long-matured wines? Or a firm operating on a massive commercial scale bringing out simple young wines at low prices? Should you expect lean, elegant Riojas from a particular house, or broad, meaty wines with a good deal of alcohol? Does a certain producer put the accent on fruity wines that have spent longer in the bottle than the cask, or does he choose to age his Riojas in the wood for the distinct oaky flavour this imparts? Anyone who knows his bodegas can, as it were, select to measure. Features of the vintages are given on page 53.

Choosing the quality

All the bodegas in the chapters that follow have their strong points delineated, as well as any weaker features. The most interesting wines from each firm are picked out and described, along with their labels. That the choice here is personal should need no emphasis. If you are buying Riojas for laying down it may make sense to choose ones with a high Tempranillo content. This grape produces wines that are resistant to oxidisation, in contrast to those from the Garnacha (the next most important black grape of the region). It is also important to look at the back or neck labels on a bottle of Rioja as these will indicate its legally defined category. The back label gives useful information, and it is here that the distinction is made between wines that have been matured in the wood and those that have not. It can sometimes happen that the main label says *reserva* while the rear label indicates that the wine is a *gran reserva*.

A convenient sort of wine

Red Rioja is an ideal wine for restaurants. Not only is it marketed ready for drinking, but even the oldest bottles hardly ever have any sediment and so they do not need to be decanted. In the region itself it has often been the writer's experience that bottles of 1968, 1964 or even earlier years were simply put straight on the table and the wine poured out without further ado. And the bottles once opened will often remain perfectly good for a day; this, too, is due to the Tempranillo grape, which gives a wine that is so consistent in its oxygen content. These advantages for restaurants obviously apply to drinking the wine at home as well. Rioja is one of the most convenient and 'consumer-friendly' quality wines in the world.

To enjoy a red Rioja at its best it should be served at 18 to 19° C – just below room temperature. The wine will often gain in richness as it comes into contact with the air. The glasses should therefore be not too narrow, nor should they be too full: then the wine can be swirled around, enabling it to absorb more oxygen. In passing it should be mentioned that the Rioja, remarkably enough, does not yet have a glass design of its own: another task for the Consejo Regulador here. Decanting the wine can help to air it; but the author has seldom seen this done in the Rioja.

The whites and rosés should not be served too cold, but at 8 to 12° C. A slightly higher temperature, 12 to 14° C, does the traditional, matured-in-the-wood white Riojas most justice.

The nearly 60 bodegas described on the following pages are arranged as far as possible in geographical order, from west to east.

Profiles of the Bodegas

Castillo de Cuzcurrita

The most westerly bodega described in this book stands in Cuzcurrita de Río Tirón, a village where wine has been produced for centuries. In 1650 it made 15,100 (US 17,900) gallons, 74,000 (US 87,000) gallons in 1750, and in 1850 a record 530,000 (US 625,000) gallons was achieved by the village. Today production hovers around 440,000 (US 520,000) gallons annually. Most of the wine is made by small *cosecheros*, but there is a larger bodega here, the Castillo de Cuzcurrita. This is based in and around a castle whose square tower rises high above the roofs of the village. The tower with its battlements and 5-foot-thick walls forms the core of a fortress built in 1367. For generations the castle was neglected and when in 1945 the Conde de Alacha (born Sainz de Incháustegui) became the new owner the structure was in a very bad state. In addition, as is clear from photographs in the family archives, considerable violence had been done to the original form of the stronghold. All manner of extensions had been built on, windows had been made in various places, and one turret had been replaced by a dovecot.

Perfectly restored

Helped by his two sons Fernando and Iñigo (who with their sister Maria Delfina are the present owners) the Conde de Alacha totally restored his castle. This took several years. The partly collapsed tower was restored to its original form, the battlements were rebuilt, floors renewed, rooms furnished, a park laid out and trees planted. The results are there to be seen. There are now tastefully furnished living rooms and bedrooms round the perfectly restored tower, and also a small chapel. The park is a feast for the eye. The Sainz de Incháustegui family only lives here in the summer, spending the rest of the year at Algorta on the coast near Bilbao. From there the family run the biggest bakery in the region: it was the income from this and from real estate that

Opposite page, above left:
Some of the bodega's stock of
90,000 bottles. Today it uses only
the Bordeaux bottle but in the
past the Burgundy model was
also in service.

Opposite page, above right:
There is a shortage of space in
this bodega's cellars, so the casks
are stacked directly one on top of
the other using supports. This
pattern fits in two more casks per
row.

Opposite page, below left:
Tractor and cart in front of the
imposing tower of the castle.

Opposite page, below centre:
The family coat of arms above a
drawing of the castle in its
present form.

Below:
A cellarman pours Fernandez
Sainz de Inchaustegui a glass of
wine in the castle grounds.

Conde de Alacha

RIOJA

CRIADO Y EMBOTELLADO EN EL CASTILLO

Bodegas Castillo de Cuzcurrita
Viñedos en la Rioja Alta

RESERVA 1973

The crianza and reserva I tasted were rather austere, even thin wines of little charm. The gran reserva had more class and its quite lively taste was more attractive; and it had vanilla, wood and some fruit. This Rioja, a 1973, had then had 8 years in cask (some of it was still ageing in the wood), with 1 year in tank and 2 years in bottle. Grapes: 85% Tempranillo, 15% Viura.

Some of the wine is bottled for restaurants etc. with their own labels.

Some white wine is produced here, although only for the bodega's own use.

The bodega's official foundation year was 1971. When the present owners took over the castle there were four families living there. One of its rooms was being used as a store place for wool.

The sitting rooms and sleeping apartments were built around the tower and so was the dining room with its hunting atmosphere. The castle can house – and sleep – 27 people, and it is full when the family arrive during the summer.

The castle has its own chapel with 16th-century priest's vestments. The collection of firearms forms a contrast.

Some of the castle's gateways are narrow but tall – designed for a horse and rider.

Castillo de Cuzcurrita

---

made the restoration of the castle financially possible.

Grapes from its own land

A document of 1774 describes the castle has having *tierras de pan y bino*: 'lands of bread and wine'. When taken over in 1945 Castillo de Cuzcurrita still had its own vineyard, but it was let out to 82 tenants. There came a time when the new owners brought this situation to an end and retrieved the land for their own use. In addition a piece of waste land next to the castle was planted with vines in 1971. This brought the total vineyard area up to 30 acres. It was decided that the grapes should be processed at the castle and so a bodega was set up, partly in the castle itself, partly in outbuildings; a move that was preceded by a course of study in France.

Frequent filtering

The bodega makes only red wine, from about 85% Tempranillo and 15% Viura grapes. The fruit is not destalked but just slightly bruised. The grapes ferment in white-painted concrete tanks. After fermentation is completed the wine remains in fibreglass tanks for 9 to 12 months and is then transferred to wooden casks. A proportion of these – all made of American oak – come from the sherry districts, for in 1969 when the bodega wanted to buy casks there were insufficient available in the Rioja. Depending on how the selection has been made, the wines stay in these *barricas* for two to five years. Racking takes place once a year. The wines are filtered relatively frequently. A six-year-old wine will usually have been through a filter four times – twice as often as at most bodegas. The total production of some 11,000 (US 13,000) gallons is bottled on the premises.

Introvert wines

For visitors a tasting cellar full of atmosphere has been fitted out in the castle, with thick beams and an earthen floor, and this is where I made the acquaintance of the bodega's wines. The first vintage it produced from its own vineyard was the 1971 – although it actually started to make wine two years earlier, using bought in grapes. Glasses of a *crianza*, a *reserva* and a *gran reserva* were served, in that order, of the 1978, 1975 and 1973 vintages respectively. The first wine had had one year in tank, two in barrel and two in bottle. I did not like it: I thought it a rather thin Rioja, lacking in body, fruit and depth. Charm, too, was not present, but acidity and harshness were. This mediocre quality could be due not only to the still rather young vineyard and the treatment of the wine (all that filtering), but also to the location and the microclimate. This western corner has the fewest hours of sunshine, the most rain and the lowest average temperatures of the Rioja Alta, if not the whole Rioja. It was the brothers Fernando and Iñigo who told me this. By way of illustration they said that on the Thursday before my visit it had been down to 3° C – in early October! Because of this special local climate the meteorological institute has set up measuring instruments in the vineyard at Castillo de Cuzcurrita.

The 1975 *reserva* was not very impressive either. It is true it offered a little more firmness, some fruit and considerably more wood (four years' barrel ageing) but it, too, had an acidic tinge, harshness and a personality that was not really attractive. The 1973 *gran reserva* proved to be by far the best wine, thanks to a quite lively and pleasant taste, with fruit, wood, vanilla and a mellow maturity. However, it was not an exuberant kind of Rioja: all the Castillo de Cuzcurrita wines could be described as introvert.

They are mostly sold under the brand name Conde de Alacha, but Castillo de Cuzcurrita and Señorio de Cuzcurrita are also registered brand names.

Bodegas Carlos Serres

As you drive into Haro from the south-west Carlos Serres is the first private bodega you come to after leaving the *autopista*. It is on the left, next to the local cooperative. This bodega was built in 1966, but the year of its foundation lies much further back. When the French wine merchant Alphonse Vigier returned to his homeland at the end of the 19th century he bequeathed his firm to his two colleagues Charles Serres (a fellow countryman from Orleans) and Cipriano Roig. They decided not only to continue dealing in wine, but also to make it, and so in 1896 they set up the Cipriano Roig bodega. The name Serres was added six years later. The location they chose was the famous Calle de las Cuevas in Haro, where they took over an existing bodega.

Increased capital

Up until 1932 the firm was called Roig y Serres. Then Carlos Serres Diaz, the son of Charles and the owner at that time, changed the name to Bodegas Carlos Serres Hijo. This last element (the Spanish for 'son') disappeared in due course. The third generation of owners, still the Serres family, elected to make the concern a limited company in 1975, with a capital of 25 million pesetas. This was increased to 42 million in 1980, with outsiders now acquiring shares (the Caja Provincial de Ahorros, for example). The capital was again increased in 1982 and 1983, to 86 and 103.5 million pesetas respectively. At present the shares are distributed as follows: Santos Montoro y Monthisa 50.75%; Caja Provincial de Ahorros 38%; and Tryp 11.25%. The bodega occupies a $3\frac{1}{2}$-acre site. Expansion is still possible for the present buildings take up only about one-third of this area.

BODEGAS

DESDE 1.896

Carlos Serres, S.A.

The Clarete label (formerly Fino Clarete) is used for wines that include the 3er Año crianza, which is given 6 months in tank, 15 in cask and 6 in bottle. It usually contains 80% Tempranillo (20% more than the flat, characterless wine of the year from this bodega) and the rest is Garnacha. Fruit, wood and vanilla are present in pleasurable doses. The wine tastes very good but does not have much depth or length to offer.

The Carlos Serres 5° Año approaches a reserva in quality but is still a crianza. It is matured for 12 months in tank, 30 in wood and 20 in bottle. This makes it a quite well-matured Rioja with distinct wood and vanilla. In addition it tastes fruity and is nicely rounded. Grape varieties: 80% Tempranillo, 10% Garnacha, 10% Mazuelo. Depending on the year I sometimes prefer the younger crianza, described in the previous column.

The Carlomagno, sold in a Burgundy bottle, enjoys a good reputation in Spain; and the 1975 won prizes in both Bordeaux and Zurich. Like the younger cask-aged wines from this bodega, this composition of 80% Tempranillo, 10% Garnacha and 10% Mazuelo has fruit combined with a rounded character, wood, vanilla and in the background a fresh tone. You should not, however, reckon on subtleties. This wine matures in the tank for 12 months, in cask for 55, and for at least 36 months in bottle.

The Bodegas Carlos Serres gran reserva usually has rather more colour and strength than the Carlomagno, as well as being older; it is matured for 12 months in tank, 48 to 60 months in cask and 36 to 80 in bottle. Distinguishing features are a dark-brown colour, a well-matured taste and nose and an almost too dominant aroma of wood. You also taste a good deal of tannin in it. Grape varieties are the same as in the Carlomagno.

Bodegas Carlos Serres

Rosé to red

It is not at all unusual to see a tanker drawn up in front of the bodega delivering wine. Carlos Serres has no vineyards of its own and buys in only wine. About 90% of this is selected in the Rioja Alta, the rest in Rioja Baja. The wine comes from both cooperatives and individual growers. The Riojas arriving here have already been fined and are immediately filtered. In addition red wines for selling young, the whites and the rosés then undergo cold treatment or stabilization. There was a time when this bodega specialized in rosés, particularly for the Swiss market, but interest in this type of wine has waned. Of the more than 220,000 (US 260,000) gallons now produced annually roughly 75 to 80% is red and the rest mainly white. Rosé is made in only very modest quantities.

Exports

For wines that are aged in the wood the firm has a stock of some 3,000 casks, all of American oak. They stay in circulation for eight to ten years. Some casks of Portuguese rather than Spanish manufacture were to be seen in the underground cellar. The bodega had ordered these – cheaper – *barricas* by way of experiment. When their ageing period is completed the wines are bottled in a spacious building, in the course of which they are pumped through a membrane filter. Two types out of the total range are pasteurized – the semi-sweet rosés and the white Riojas. The stock of bottles at Bodegas Carlos Serres fluctuates around 225,000. They are given various labels: the most important brand name is Carlos Serres, but Arméntia y Madrazo, Bodegas Vista Alegre, Castillo San Lorenzo and the ancient Roig y Serres are also used. About 60% of production is exported, with Germany, Switzerland, Britain, the Netherlands, Belgium, Mexico, the United States, Canada and Central America the most important markets.

Roundness and fruit

The range from this bodega shows a wide variation in quality. There are good wines, but also a number of only moderate ones. I would put the rather flat whites in this category, and the rosé, which lacks real freshness. Nor can I enthuse over the young red *sin crianza* – a completely characterless, dull product. Much of it is sold in 1- and 2-litre bottles. Quality only becomes perceptible at *crianza* level, a Rioja with a lot of fruit as well as ample wood and vanilla in the taste. This wine does not offer a great deal of depth or length, but sampling it is pleasurable nevertheless. Clarete 3er Año as it is designated is composed of 80% Tempranillo and 20% Garnacha. It is matured for 6 months in tank, 15 in cask and 6 in bottle. There is also a somewhat older *crianza*, the Carlos Serres 5° Año. The 1976 vintage of this wine won a gold medal at Vinexpo 1983 in Bordeaux. The percentage of Tempranillo was the same as for the other *crianza*, but half the Garnacha was replaced by Mazuelo. This wine has a distinctly mature tone to it, with a lot of fruit some roundness and a touch of freshness. Carlos Serres also makes a *reserva*, the Carlomagno, which is also characterized by fruit and roundness, supplemented by wood, vanilla and some freshness in the background. It is given a year in tank, 4½ years in cask and 3 to 3½ years bottle ageing. Its grapes are the same as for the older *crianza*. Finally, the *gran reserva* after a year in tank spends four to five years in wood and three to four in bottle. Wood and tannin are very much in evidence in this mature, dark-coloured Rioja.

Right:
The dining room.

Below:
Pallet crates full of bottles
stacked next to the casks. The
bodega hopes to extend the
premises and separate bottles
and casks.

Opposite page, above right:
There was a period when
shortage of metal compelled the
bodega to sell its Viña
Turzaballa without its wire
mesh. A label on the back
assured the customer that the
wine was the authentic article.

Opposite page, below:
View of the bodega, with general
director Juan de Lecande Busa,
who lives in Bilbao.

Like all the white and rosé Riojas
here, the red sin crianza is
stabilized at low temperature.

Total storage capacity of the
tanks is 660,000 (US 780,000)
gallons.

At Ramón Bilbao all the casks
are of American oak and stay in
use for 10 to 15 years.

The young red wine is called
Monte Llamo, the comparable
white is Monte Blanco.

Bodegas Ramón Bilbao

In the 1920s various bodegas were built in
Haro's celebrated Calle de las Cuevas. One
of them belonged to Ramón Bilbao Murga, a
Basque whose family had been involved
with wine since 1896. The building was
ready in 1924 and remained in use for more
than half a century. In 1975 new premises
were constructed for Bodegas Ramón
Bilbao on the western boundary of Haro, on
the road to Casalarreina, with the bodegas
of Federico Paternina, Carlos Serres and
the local cooperative as near neighbours.
By this time the Bilbao family were no
longer the owners. The founder had passed
the firm on to his son Enrique, and he in
turn had handed it on to his son Ramón,
who died in a car accident. His widow sold
the firm in 1972 to a stockbroker from
Bilbao, Florentino de Lecanda Arrarte, a
very active figure in the wine trade who
since 1946 had been joint owner and
manager of Paternina. Today it is
Florentino's son Juan who has the day-to-
day running of the bodega. He and his
father are the only proprietors of this

sociedad anónima. The cellars in the Calle
de las Cuevas are still appreciated and
remain in use for storage.

Wines bought in

Bodegas Ramón Bilbao has little vineyard
area of its own and what there is – 25 acres
– is planted exclusively with white grapes.
The firm derives little benefit from these as
about 90% of its annual sales of from
132,000 (US 156,000) to 154,000 (US
182,000) gallons consists of red wine. There
is hardly any interest here in white, or in
rosé. I was not given either types to sample,
which must be significant. Grapes are not
bought in by Ramón Bilbao, only made
wines. These are selected from private
bodegas; wines from cooperatives are
seldom if ever used. The biggest supplier is
an almacenista in Fuenmayor, which can
deliver wines from 185 to 200 acres of
vineyard. The Riojas purchased come in
between January and March for a short
stay in concrete tanks or closed wooden

vats. Wines that are to be aged in the wood
are transferred to the barricas at the latest
in the May after their vintage, passing
through a filter for the first and only time.

More ageing

The bodega plans to phase out the young
Riojas without wood ageing from its
collection. 'There is, after all, no prestige to
be earned with these', says Juan de
Lecanda. Besides this, there is murderous
price competition going on for this kind of
wine. As a result of this quality policy the
bodega has increased its stock of barrels
considerably, from 2,500 in 1981 to 3,000 in
1984. A new cellar was built in 1984,
appreciably enlarging the storage space for
casks and bottles. Once this was available
casks and bottles were separated, which
had not been possible before in the serious
space problem that the firm had had to
contend with. Ramón Bilbao does not plan
to extend total sales greatly, only to
concentrate on better quality. The stock of

The Monte Seco crianza is usually a very palatable wine with a vitality of taste, some wood and freshness. After staying in the tanks for several months it is given 16 to 18 months in cask, 10 to 16 in bottle. It has the same mix of grapes as the other cask-aged Ramón Bilbao wines: 65 to 70% Tempranillo, 20 to 25% Garnacha, the rest Mazuelo. Only the 1980 had more Garnacha than usual.

After 24 to 30 months in cask and at least 15 to 16 in bottle the Monte Rojo is entitled to the reserva classification. Brownish in colour, this wine is reasonably firm in constitution with a fresh core to it; wood and vanilla are not over-emphasized. This Rioja is sold in a burgundy bottle.

Despite being at least 6½ years old before going on sale (3 years' cask age and more than 3 in bottle) the Viña Turzaballa gran reserva shows absolutely no signs of decline. It is a well-matured but still vital wine, with fruit, suppleness, tannin, a hint of freshness and the familiar combination of wood and vanilla.

Only the very best qualities are selected for the Ramón Bilbao gran reserva. I am familiar only with the 1970, a wine with 3 years in cask and then 10 in bottle. It had a dark-brown colour, a nose that was well-matured with wood and vanilla, a mellowed taste, again with wood and vanilla, with tannin and even some fruit.

Bodegas Ramón Bilbao

---

bottled Riojas – about 800,000 bottles at the end of 1984 – will therefore be increased, probably to 1.5 million.

Cask-aged reds

The young red wines that are not aged in the wood undergo cold stabilization, just like the whites and the rosés, but not the other kinds. The Monte Seco *crianza* is generally a very nice wine, given 16 to 18 months in the wood and 10 to 16 in the bottle. The proportions of grape varieties are usually 65 to 70% Tempranillo, 20 to 25% Garnacha and the rest Mazuelo. These are in fact the percentages for all the better red wines from this bodega. As an experiment the Garnacha content was increased in the Monte Seco in 1980, which gave the wine more colour and strength. However, I prefer the 1981 with the normal proportions: this was livelier in taste. The Monte Seco goes into Bordeaux-shape bottles, but the burgundy type was chosen for the Monte Rojo *reserva*. Yet this wine does not really have a very different personality, with only slightly more structure and alcohol to it. Maturity, wood and vanilla are elements that are naturally present to a greater extent, thanks to 2 to 2½ years ageing in wood and 15 to 16 months in bottle.

A wine name from the past

The only label remaining from the time of the Bilbao family is that of the Viña Turzaballa, a *gran reserva*. The name was taken from two vineyards near Haro, the Turcos and the Zaballa. The wine in question is given 3 years in cask and 3 in bottle. It is a soundly structured Rioja in which the wood is not exaggerated, nor is the wine over-matured or tired. It, too, travels in a burgundy bottle, this time wrapped in a metal mesh. The bodega's showpiece is the Ramón Bilbao *gran reserva*, a wine that also receives 3 years in wood but spends much longer ageing in bottle. This Rioja is made only in exceptional years: after the 1970 vintage the next one did not come along until 1975 – and a decade after its birth it had still not appeared on the market. As it is given more bottle than cask ageing, this type of wine has to be protected against drying. Besides its very mature character there was still some fruit there, supplemented by wood, vanilla and tannin. Given the course that Ramón Bilbao has chosen it is clearly a bodega that will be increasingly worthy of interest and attention.

Federico Paternina

Federico de Paternina Josué was acting firmly in the family tradition when he founded his own bodega in 1898, the year in which he married. He was following the example of his father Eduardo who had started a wine business under his title of Marqués de Terán, encouraged by Baron de Rothschild. Federico started up at Ollauri, where he took over three underground cellars. The firm stayed in the family until 1919. It was then bought by Joaquín Herrero de la Riva, a Logroño banker. Federico de Paternina remained involved in the running of the bodega, however, until his death in the early 1930s. His son-in-law Luis de Rezusta stayed with the firm until 1939. The new owner developed a dynamic style of management. In 1922 he obtained the buildings of a cooperative just outside Haro, on the road to Casalarreina, and he opened a sales office in Madrid. In addition a French winemaker, Etienne Labatut, was brought in from the Bordeaux firm of Calvet. He worked for the firm until 1942.

A new group of owners, mainly Basques, came to power in 1940. They brought a lot of capital with them, enabling the bodega to grow more strongly than before. In addition it was now very energetically run by Maria Luisa Olano, from San Sebastián, who remained as managing director until 1949. During her regime shares were continually changing hands while the capital increased steadily.

On 18 July 1972 Federico Paternina was taken over by the Rumasa group. The nationalization of this group a decade later meant that the bodega passed into state control, but early in 1985 it was sold to Marcos Eguizabal (of Bodegas y Viñedos, Lan and Franco-Españolas).

A 'hangar' for wine

Huge amounts of money were invested in Federico Paternina in the Rumasa period. The complex at Haro grew into one of the most impressive in the Rioja, covering some 30 acres with half of this area roofed over.

The biggest building is the above-ground cellar for Banda Azul. This hall – hangar would be a better word – with its pinewood roof occupies at least 2½ acres. There are 35,000 casks stored here: nowhere else in Europe are so many to be found under one roof. Yet despite the dimensions of the bodega at Haro, Federico Paternina retains the character of a family firm. Many of the 150 or so employees here have followed their parents into this bodega. There is, for example, Alberto Oteo Garrido whose parents had worked for Paternina for a considerable time, and whose brother, son and two nephews are also employed there. Another example is provided by Doña Mercédes, who has worked at the bodega for around 70 years and who has two sons and four grandchildren in the firm. And the family of the almost legendary cellarman Federico López Davalillo has been associated with the company for five generations.

Authentic cellars

While the bodega at Haro has grown into a large, modern, wine factory, the cellars at Ollauri have changed scarcely at all. Electricity was put in, and a lift, and above ground a very comfortable reception suite, complete with salon, dining room, kitchen, and a small exhibition of wine objects, has been fitted out. Below ground, however, time has stood still. In the silent, dark galleries are the casks and bottles with the Paternina *reservas* and *gran reservas*. Here, too, is the *catédral del vino*, a vault closed off by wrought-iron railings with thousands of mildewed bottles from all the good years, the oldest dating from 1887. The temperature in these silent cellars remains at a constant 11° C, nor does the humidity vary from around 93%. The layout consists of four galleries each 500 feet long; the earliest parts date from the 17th century. They were dug out by Portuguese who worked on the land in the summer and in the cellars in winter. The passages run into the hillside; this is why their entrances lie 75 feet below the surface but their furthest points are 90 feet down.

No vineyards

Federico Paternina has no vineyards of its own. For the red Riojas ready-made wine is bought in, and must is normally bought for the whites and rosés. The quantities involved are by no means small: the firm produces some 2 (US 2.4) million gallons annually, of which about 70% is red, almost 20% white and 10% rosé. An exceptionally large amount was bought in the very good year of 1981: I was told at the firm that it had reserved 40% of the total Rioja Alta and Alavesa production for itself. The red wines go into around 100 tanks with capacities varying from 21 (US 25) gallons up to 110,000 (US 130,000) gallons. Thereafter the wines can be transferred to any point in the bodega by means of a system of pipes controlled from a central panel. The blending of the different kinds takes place in a separate hall where a further 22 tanks of 19,150 (US 22,600)

It is not only the Rinsol that has a different name and label for the American market: Banda Azul is called Blue Band; Banda Dorada becomes Gold Band; and Viña Vial carries the name Red Band.

Paternina wines are normally filtered twice. All the casks here are of American oak and remain in use for about 30 years.

This bodega has tanks with a total storage capacity of around 4.5 million (US 5.3 million) gallons.

The firm has two bottling installations, one with a capacity of 6,000 and the other 10,000 per hour.

The Banda Dorada is very successful as a not-too-expensive thirst quencher. Fermented at low temperature, this white Rioja has a mildly fresh, pure taste with some fruit in it. It is given absolutely no cask ageing, is bottled quickly and is meant for drinking within a year. Its grapes are 70% Malvasía, nearly 30% Viura and the tiny remainder is Garnacha; they are picked early.

Since the 1980 grape harvest the dry white Rinsol has been a new-style Rioja: fermented at low temperature, not brought into contact with wood and offering a good deal of freshness and fruit. For this light (11%), elegant creation only juice from the first pressing is used and it is made exclusively from Viura grapes. In quality Rinsol is one of the best wines in its category. Sold as Banda Blanca in America, it is sold in a very slender bottle.

Federico Paternina still makes a traditional white Rioja: Reserva Blanca, which is given 12 months in tank, at least 12 in cask and a minimum 24 months in bottle. New casks are never used for this wine – so that the wood scent does not become too strong. In its nose and taste this Rioja clearly offers a lot of character, vanilla and at the same time a remarkable freshness that remains for years. Viura is the grape variety used.

Federico Paternina

gallon capacity are installed. After filtering the red wines are then transferred to the barrel cellars. All the red Riojas are aged in the wood here and are at least three years old. For a few years Paternina made just one exception to this rule – for the Dutch market, shipping young, cheaper wines there. This was stopped in 1984.

Reserves for restaurateurs

There is an approximate total of 45,000 casks at Paternina, 35,000 of these for the Banda Azul brand alone. A further considerable number – 10,000 – is reserved for the Viña Vial brand. All the casks are of American wood, mainly from the state of Indiana. In principle they are kept in service for around 30 years and there are four coopers to maintain them.

Spanish restaurateurs can have their own reserve casks at Federico Paternina. A separate cellar has been fitted out for this purpose and it was officially opened in 1984. Riojas from these casks are bottled by hand. It was the American film actress Margaux Hemingway who opened this special restaurateurs' cellar in September 1984. The bodega dedicated the cellar to the Hemingways, and in particular to the memory of Ernest Hemingway, with whom the firm had close links.

Ernest Hemingway

Hemingway visited the firm of Paternina

BANDA AZUL

Annual sales of Banda Azul are around 600,000 cases. There are dozens of bodegas whose total production comes nowhere near this amount. Made from 70% Tempranillo, 20% Garnacha and 10% Mazuelo grapes, this is a supple, correct Rioja, reasonably robust in taste, but somewhat rustic, not really refined. A crianza, it has 12 months in tank, 12 in cask and at least 4 in bottle.

VIÑA VIAL

The Viña Vial has a higher percentage of Tempranillo than the Banda Azul (80 instead of 70%, with the rest Garnacha) and so has rather more class and elegance. In addition this crianza is matured for longer: 12 months in tank, 24 in cask and at least 12 in bottle. The bodega has given one of the storage areas at Haro modern insulation and this now serves as a cellar for Viña Vial; it contains more than 15,000 casks.

Paternina's Gran Reserva is aged in the cellars at Ollauri, 12 months in tank, for a minimum 24 months in cask and 36 in bottle. I have had the privilege of drinking several vintages of it, which all proved to be still vital some 30 years on. In the 1959, and other years, fruit, vanilla, wood and maturity combined in a balanced, mellow wine with charm, depth and length. I also recall more recent vintages, such as the 1964, 1967 and 1975, with pleasure.

A small quantity of the Conde de los Andes gran reserva is produced – only in exceptional years and never more than 12,000 bottles. This expensive Rioja is hardly ever on sale in Spain itself. As this wine stays in cask for 6 years there is a good deal of wood in its taste and nose as well as tannin (this lingers for a good time and is slightly dry). Substance, colour and strength are also fully present, so that this all Tempranillo wine can happily undergo a further 18 years' bottle age.

Federico Paternina

for 25 years in succession, the last occasion being in 1959 – when he signed the visitors' book for the first and only time. As always Hemingway was accompanied by a bullfighter, in this case Antonio Ordoñez, the inspiration, it is said, for *Death in the Afternoon.* Hemingway did in fact describe the 1959 bullfighting season in *The Dangerous Summer,* a book that did not appear until 1985, after being drastically cut and edited. Hemingway's visits benefited the bodega, but they did not always go smoothly from the hosts' point of view. The cellarman Federico López Davalillo has recalled how aggressive the writer could be in his later years. Sometimes he had his own collection of miniature bottles of whisky, vodka and other drinks with him to 'restore' himself after indulging in too much wine. Nevertheless the firm still admires Hemingway, and this is why his niece Margaux acts as its representative in America. The Hemingways were not, of course, the only celebrities to visit the

bodega. There have been many among its guests, including the Spanish Crown Prince, the film star David Niven and the Japanese ambassador.

Contrasts in white

Federico Paternina has its reasons for buying in must and not wine for its whites and rosés. The bodega is perfectly equipped for making the new-style Riojas, with a lot of fruit and freshness – in contrast to many cooperatives and individual growers. The dry white and rosé wines ferment at a temperature of 20 to 22° C. Lower temperatures would not be justified, according to the oenologists, because of the danger that fermentation would simply stop. During the slow fermentation process the maximum of fruit and other aromatic elements are retained in the wine. These Riojas are then stabilized through the cold treatment process. Most of them do not come into contact with wood. Only one white *reserva* in the traditional style is

aged in wood – for a year, with a further year in tank and at least 2 in the bottle. This white, which goes into a slender bottle with a metallic net over it, has a marked vanilla aroma, a taste full of character and a freshness at its core that it keeps for years. The Viura is the only grape used.

Excellent quality

Also made solely from the Viura grape is the Rinsol, a wine of which the new, fruity style was launched in 1981 (with the 1980 vintage). Only juice from the first pressing is used for this. It is a fragrant, elegant and pure product that must be counted among the best of all Rioja whites. The Banda Dorada tastes simpler and rather less fine, but this too is a nice Rioja white with freshness and fruit. In addition it costs less than the Rinsol, offering very good value. In this wine the Malvasía is the dominant grape (70%), with the Viura in a subordinate role at just below 30%, and a dash of Garnacha Blanca. Because of their

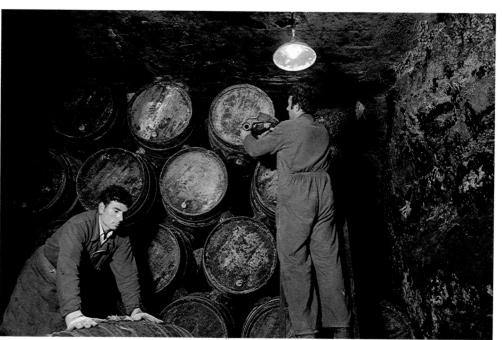

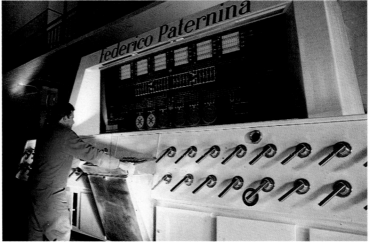

Federico Paternina

exemplary quality both the Rinsol and the Banda Dorada have been selected by the Consejo Regulador to represent the dry white Rioja category at all receptions, tastings and other such occasions. The two wines are also commercial successes, so much so that the bodega can no longer fully meet the demand. Production cannot be indefinitely expanded because high standards are asked of the basic product, the must. During harvesting and pressing the suppliers are subject to constant checks by half a dozen Paternina staff. In addition they are under instructions to pick the white grapes two weeks before the rest. This is not only so as to retain the fresh acids in the fruit, but also to harvest the white grapes quite separately from the black: in the Rioja the different kinds are often planted together in the vineyards.

In addition to its three dry white wines Paternina also makes a semi-sweet type, called Monte Haro. The rosé, Banda Rosa, undergoes a treatment comparable to that of the dry white wines. It is a pleasant Rioja, made from 75% Viura and 25% Tempranillo grapes. At Paternina the cold treatment method is used to stabilize both white and rosé wines.

Banda Azul

With 60% of all sales Banda Azul is Paternina's biggest brand by far. This *crianza* wine is given 12 months in tank, 12 months in cask and at least 4 months in bottle. New casks are never used for it, so that the wine does not take on too strong a flavour of the wood; new *barricas* are therefore "run in" on the must first. The proportions of the grapes varieties are usually 70% Tempranillo, 20% Garnacha and 10% Mazuelo (sometimes with a little Graciano). In the beginning of the Rumasa period the quality of the Banda Azul fell off considerably; the 1972 in particular was notoriously bad. Today, however, the level is steady again – though this is not a brilliant wine in any case. Even the 1981 wine, much extolled by the bodega itself, was no more than a technically correct product of average quality. I considered it a

supple, easy, reasonably firm wine but with nothing extraordinary about its nose and taste. Banda Azul is a not too expensive Rioja for people who are not too demanding, but want something reliable to drink.

Superior *gran reservas*

The Viña Vial is Paternina's other red *crianza*. This wine stays a year in tank, like the Banda Azul, but spends longer in the wood and the bottle – 2 years and a year respectively. Another difference is the higher percentage of Tempranillo – 80%. The rest is Garnacha. In terms of quality the Viña Vial has more to offer than the Banda Azul. It is a wine of some elegance and with nuances. Wood and tannin are more strongly present, together with rather more maturity and a touch of freshness. This wine was created by Federico López Davalillo's father, who was also a cellarman, together with the Frenchman Etienne Labatut. The name does not come from a vineyard, but from Ramón Vial, one of the members of the group who took over in 1940.

While the Viña Vial is of a higher quality than the Banda Azul it is in its turn overshadowed by the *gran reservas*. With these wines Federico Paternina demonstrates that even a large-scale producer can also turn out small quantities of excellent wine. I have been able to drink Gran Reserva of various vintages in Spain and elsewhere and all of them were delicious. In the 1959, for example, there were elements such as fruit, vanilla, wood and mellowness, harmoniously combined into a brilliant whole. A quarter of a century after its birth the wine seemed to have lost none of its vitality. More recent years, such as 1964, 1967 and 1975, also offer real class. Paternina's *gran reservas* spend a year in tank, followed by two years in wood and three years in bottle, and the cool, damp cellars at Ollauri have been set aside for this purpose. The blend of grapes is usually 90% Tempranillo, with a few per cent each of Mazuelo and Garnacha.

The rarest wine from this bodega is another *gran reserva*, Conde de los Andes.

Its bottles often come in a leather packing and a high price has to be paid for the wine. Only a very small quantity – never more than 12,000 bottles – from the very best vintages is ever considered for selection for this pure Tempranillo wine, which is stored for many years to mature. First it spends one year in tank, then 6 years in cask and finally more than 10 years (often 15 to 18 years) in bottle. And even then the wine still has sufficient backbone for further laying down. Among its characteristics are an often deep, dark-brown colour and a well-constructed, lingering (and sometimes slightly dry) taste with a lot of tannin and vanilla, and undertones of fruit and spice.

The Bordeaux bottle: a deliberate choice

Paternina holds an average 6 million bottles of all its Riojas in stock. This does not take up all its storage capacity: there is space for another 3 million. All the bottles are of the Bordeaux type. Federico López Davalillo once made a comparison of how various kinds of Rioja developed in Bordeaux and Burgundy bottles respectively: there appeared to be no difference. The bodega chose the Bordeaux form as it is easier to handle. Bottles of Paternina wine have received all kinds of rewards in their various categories, including international ones. Gold or silver medals have been won in London, Milan, and Ljubljana in Yugoslavia, and elsewhere. This will have contributed to the fact that of its annual production of around a million bottles almost a third goes abroad, with Switzerland, the United States, Germany, Britain, Denmark and France the most important customers. The once small firm in Ollauri has grown into a bodega with a worldwide reputation.

Bodegas Martínez Lacuesta

Haro

The statue that stands in the garden of Bodegas Martínez Lacuesta is a homage to a remarkable man. It was unveiled in September 1928 in memory of Félix Martínez Lacuesta, "son of the town of Haro", who had died six years earlier at the age of 49. Don Félix had meant a great deal to the town of his birth and the surrounding region. After studying law in Madrid he returned to the Rioja to start on a great political career there. He became president of the provincial assembly, civil governor of Teruel and Zaragoza, founder of the "Friends of Haro" circle, and was also involved in charitable work. He also earned his viticultural spurs. As chairman of the Sindicato de Vinos de la Rioja he set about the restoration of vineyards ravaged by the phylloxera, and at national level he led the Asociación Nacional de Vinicultores e Industrias del Vino. Finally, as an entrepreneur, he established his own bodega in February 1895.

Office in Cuba

The bodega was built just outside what was then the municipal boundary of Haro; one of the walls served as a *frontón* for the local pelota players. But Haro grew and today the bodega stands on a busy road that takes a lot of the traffic coming in from Logroño. Not long after he had set up the firm Félix Martínez brought in his brothers. There were five of them: José Crescencio, Emiliano, José Maria, Alfonso and Julio. A framed drawing of their six profiles hangs in the small reception room and office of the bodega. In 1902 the firm started exporting, mainly to South and Central America. There was even a branch office in Havana. In the firm's archives there is a colourful picture postcard that Emiliano sent his family from Cuba in 1908. Later European markets, too, were tackled. Bodegas Martínez Lacuesta has, for example, been supplying Riojas to the state monopolies in Finland, Norway and Sweden for more than 30 years. After the death of its founder the firm remained a family business. It still is today and the present management consists of Emiliano's son Luis Martínez-Lacuesta

Almarza and his nephew José Maria Martínez Allue.

Room for expansion

Although the bodega is now situated within Haro there is no shortage of space. A good-sized piece of the partly walled site is in fact still unused and could therefore be utilized for future extensions. The first building is still in service, although its wooden casks are no longer used for fermentation but for storage. Martínez Lacuesta owns no vineyards, nor does it make any wine. Everything is bought in the form of wine – a lot of it from the Rioja Alta, both from cooperatives and from individual growers. Annual sales are around 440,000 (US 520,000) gallons, of which 330,000 (US 390,000) gallons are red, 66,000 (US 78,000) gallons white and 44,000 (US 52,000) gallons rosé. Most of the wines are bottled in the bodega itself, but 20 to 25% is exported in bulk, going to Switzerland and Sweden, while Spain itself is a small customer for this. With the exception of the *reservas* and *gran reservas* the wines to be bottled go through a membrane filter. All the wines are passed through an earthen filter at an earlier stage, and white, rosé and young red Riojas (the *sin crianza* quality) are stabilized by cold treatment.

Ancient and modern

The filters and the cooling apparatus form a modern aspect of Martínez Lacuesta, and so too do the metal tanks that were installed up above in one of the halls in 1968. On the other hand this bodega still exudes the atmosphere of days gone by, not only because of the wooden vats and the old cellar directly behind them, but also because, for example, the wine is racked by hand. And memories of earlier times are also evoked by the atmospheric cooper's shop, still in full use by three *toneleros* for repairing ordinary-sized casks and making small ones. Many old tools of the trade hang on the walls; I also saw a unique item (the only one in the Rioja

The crianza *is the most attractive of the Martínez Lacuesta range. This wine is given 12 months in tank, 12 to 18 in cask and 6 to 12 in bottle. It is made from 80% Tempranillo grapes, 15% Mazuelo and 5% Graciano. Though not striking in character this is a pleasant wine with a certain fresh quality, elegance and some wood.*

Campeador, often a prize winner, is a reserva made up of 60% Garnacha, 30% Tempranillo and 10% Mazuelo grapes. The Garnacha gives it backbone without making it too full-bodied or alcoholic. This firm, reliable Rioja undergoes an ageing period of at least 1 to 2 years in tank, 3 to 4 years in cask and 1 to 2 in bottle – in this case the Burgundy shape.

The Reserva Especial appears at the Spanish royal court, but under a different label. It is a gran reserva, normally composed of 80% Tempranillo, 15% Mazuelo and 5% Graciano. A well-matured, but not tired Rioja, it naturally displays a good amount of wood in its perfume and taste, but without it predominating. Ageing: 1 to 2 years in tank, 5 to 7 in cask and then a minimum 3 years in bottle: of the Bordeaux pattern, fitted with a metal mesh. Open an hour before serving, or decant.

In 1903 the bodega opened a sales office in Madrid. It still exists but has moved to a new address.

The firm has a staff of about 30.

The wines here are usually racked twice a year to clean casks, sometimes three times.

In 1911 a wine from Martínez Lacuesta took the Gran Premio de Honor at an exhibition in Buenos Aires.

Wines in the cask at this bodega are sometimes not bottled until an order arrives. The biggest foreign customers include Sweden, Switzerland, Norway, Britain, Denmark, West Germany, the United States and Puerto Rico.

Bodegas Martínez Lacuesta

Rioja, according to the bodega), a device for cutting bungs for barrels.

American oak

In the various cellar areas the *barricas* are ranged in rows stacked four and five high.

There are some 7,400 of them, most made of American oak with just a few of French origin. They stay in service for quite a time here: usually 10 to 15 years. Then there is all the wine in bottles for the visitor to see: Martínez Lacuesta holds an average stock of 480,000. Besides these regular bottles

the bodega also uses special small ones, destined for a number of airline companies. (The Riojas the firm has supplied to Iberia for several decades now are not included here as these are in the normal-sized bottles.) Also in the cellars is the stock of vermouth, an aperitif that has been made since 1937 under the brand name Lacuesta.

Bodegas Martínez Lacuesta

Wood-aged reds the speciality

This bodega has more than a dozen different Riojas in its range, but they are not all of interest in quality terms. In my opinion this would apply to the red wines that are not matured in wood, the rosés (with or without cask ageing) and the whites (one that does not spend time in cask and four that do, including the semi-sweet Viña Delys and the Reserva Especial that stays there 3 years). It is the cask-aged red Riojas that constitute the speciality of this bodega. The *crianza* type goes on sale after two to three years, by which time the wine will have spent a year in tank, a year to 18 months in wood, and 6 to 12 months resting in bottle. It is not a Rioja with a great deal of personality, but it is pleasantly drinkable, with some wood and maturity and at the same time a fresh tone to the taste and a certain elegance. Its grapes are normally the Tempranillo (80%), Mazuelo (15%) and Graciano (5%). The Garnacha does not figure here, in contrast to what is probably the best-known and most-sold wine from this bodega, the Campeador.

The champion Campeador

The *reserva* Campeador is marketed in a Burgundy-type bottle and is made from 60% Garnacha grapes, 30% Tempranillo and 10% Mazuelo. Part of the Garnacha component comes from grapes grown on high south-facing slopes in the Rioja Alta (near Hormilla and Hormilleja for instance). They help to make the Campeador a firm, meaty Rioja, fully able to take a minimum of one to two years in tank, three to four years in wood, and one to two years in bottle. Its alcohol percentage is usually around 13, which cannot be regarded as excessive. Campeador is only produced in good years. That this is a quality wine is shown by the medals won in Czechoslovakia, Bulgaria and Switzerland and elsewhere.

Royal wine

Notwithstanding the very satisfactory turnover from Campeador, the bodega is even prouder of another of its wines: the red Reserva Especial that is bottled for the Spanish court – and therefore adorns the menus of many state banquets. The wine apparently accompanies the king on his journeys and is served on the royal aircraft. Naturally this wine is given a special label. The general public can buy the same wine but with a different label; the quality is identical, as is the Bordeaux bottle with its metallic mesh wrapping. This wine belongs to the *gran reserva* category, with one to two years in tank, five to seven years in cask, followed by at least three years' bottle age. The wood does not predominate in this Rioja either, probably because the bodega uses many old casks. A certain fresh quality and fruit are perceptible, and remain so for a good time. This is a Rioja that benefits from being decanted or opened ahead of serving: one hour's air does it a lot of good. Most of this and other Riojas from Bodegas Martínez Lacuesta remain in Spain, with around 40% exported to 40 other countries. The firm has various subsidiary brand names at its disposal – Bodegas Rocadria, Bodegas La Boveda, Bodegas Eurovin, Bodegas Atolon, Bodegas Peñarol – but only exceptionally has recourse to them.

Bodegas Rioja Santiago

As you come out from the centre of Haro the Rioja Santiago is the first bodega you see facing you across the Tirón, practically opposite the bridge. The oldest parts of this cellar complex date from 1904, when Angel Santiago Munilla built his new wine enterprise here. Almost a quarter of a century earlier, in 1870, he had started a small bodega in nearby Labastida. Increasing sales – to Brazil, Columbia and Cuba, among other places – compelled this entrepreneur to build anew. Angel Santiago was succeeded by his sons, Jésus and Angel. They expanded the firm in various ways; for example, Bodegas Vizconde de Ayala in Haro was taken over.

For a long time the cellars and the wines of the two companies remained separate, but today Vizconde de Ayala is just a subsidiary brand. The wines sold under this name are identical to those of the firm's other brands: Gran Condal, Castillo de Ezpeleta, Bilibio and Rioja Santiago.

The Pepsi Cola take-over

A still more important development was the creation of Spain's first bottled sangria. The Santiago brothers succeeded in getting this very typically Spanish product into bottles in a stable form, and with no danger of secondary fermentation. In the 1960s this bottled sangria was shown at a trade fair in New York. As a result an American importer – Monsieur Henri Wines, a subsidiary of Pepsi Cola – decided to take the new product. It was a tremendous success: so much so that in 1970 Pepsico decided to take over half the Santiago family's shares. Five years later it bought the rest. The sangria is now made in a vast factory just outside Labastida, where table and sparkling wines are also produced.

Disappearance of the square bottle

The sangria carries the brand name Yago Sant'gria and the sparkling wine is called Dom Yago. Consequently the name Yago has been dropped for the Riojas. Much the same has happened with the form of bottle the bodega had designed for its Rioja wines: tall and slender, with a square lower half. Once this type was being used for the sangria as well, the idea of Riojas being sold in it became progressively less acceptable to the market. The difference in image between the two drinks was simply too great. In addition there were some practical objections to this deviant model and so the square-bottomed bottle disappeared for all the Riojas, with the exception of the very old Gran Fino Enologica. This is perfectly reasonable, for this *gran reserva* spends a very long time resting in the bottle – 10 to 15 years. Vintages bottled before the square bottle was discontinued will therefore be around for a good while yet.

Although the influence of the Pepsi Cola dollars has clearly been felt, the day-to-day running of Bodegas Rioja Santiago is not determined by the Americans; on the contrary, the management of the firm has remained entirely Spanish. In the meantime the Santiago family itself has moved to Palma in Majorca.

Increasing turnover

The bodega does not have vineyards of its own, nor is vinification carried out here. Everything is bought in as wine, and the selection is made in Rioja Alta, Rioja Alavesa and Rioja Baja. At the time of my

visit around 275,000 (US 325,000) gallons was being produced annually, but this amount will be increased. Because of the increasing turnover the bodega was already then running out of space. This meant for example that the whole stock of 830,000 bottles had to be stacked rather than stored in the more practical pallets. The recent growth of this bodega has also been signalled by its increased stock of casks – more than doubled in the early 1980s to around 2,750. Most of these *barricas* are made of American oak, but some French casks – about one in five – are also in use. In principle the casks at Rioja Santiago remain in service for at most ten years.

Protective caps

The incoming red wines – 67% of the total production – are given their first ageing in very large wooden vats. There are concrete tanks for the red Riojas that are to be sold young, and for the white and rosé wines; in addition these three types are stabilized by the cold method. All wines are filtered at least once. At this bodega wines that undergo bottle ageing are given a special temporary cap over the whole neck. This is

Bodegas Rioja Santiago

intended to protect the corks – and therefore the wines – against possible insect larvae. I cannot judge how significant this pre-emptive measure is, but at all events it shows the care with which the better wines are surrounded.

Two types of white

A feature of any guided tour around Bodegas Rioja Santiago is a visit to the narrow, rectangular tasting and reception hall. You enter it, surprisingly, through a door in an empty vat. Besides a long dining table, a bar and the usual framed certificates, there is the inevitable open hearth arrangement for roasting lamb. During my visit, however, the fire was out for it was early in the morning and all attention had to be given to tasting. The technical manager José Luis Gímenez, with the firm for more than 30 years, had brought a number of representative Riojas from the cellar – various reds and a couple of whites. They did not let me taste the rosé (although amounting to 13% of production, and a combination of Tempranillo and Viura). Of the white on the other hand (20% of production) two types were served, the ordinary and the *semi seco*. The first kind was extremely pale in colour, with a touch of tannin in the taste and the nose, and it was also pure, fresh and not too acidic. The fruit and some fragrance were perceptible. The second variant was less sweet than I had feared, but in no way exciting. I was told that this wine was still being exported, to Germany, America and elsewhere, but that sales were declining steadily.

An easy taste

The youngest red Rioja, the *sin crianza*, does not come into contact with wood, but it is matured for 6 to 12 months in tank and 3 to 6 months in bottle. It is composed of 75% Tempranillo and 25% Garnacha. I thought it a not unpleasant wine, but a little too smooth, too easy of taste. The *crianza* came across rather more robustly and had some wood in nose and taste. However, it could have done with more fruit, more "bite",

density and depth. The blend of grapes was the same as for the *sin crianza*, but the ageing was different and longer: 12 months in tank, 12 in cask and 6 to 12 in bottle. As has already been mentioned, you may encounter these and practically all the other wines under various names – only the brands differ, not the quality. Gran Condal and Vizconde de Ayala are the most used of these brand names: remarkably enough, Rioja Santiago only comes in third or fourth place.

More Tempranillo

It was only at the *reserva* level that I thought the red wines really good. In this category I sampled balanced vintages, firm of taste, with maturity, wood and vanilla in them, although here too they lacked any real depth or intensity. Their nose was pleasant and they were correct in their aftertaste. Normally the *reservas* are made from 80% Tempranillo and 20% Garnacha. Before these wines are put on sale they

spend at least a year in tank, 2 in wood and 2 in bottle. With the really old wines, the *gran reservas*, it struck me that they all retained a certain freshness in their taste; and this was even the case with the Gran Fino Enologica 1964. Only a very few bottles of this wine are produced. Usually only enough for 300 cases is in vintages that are considered good enough. The normal *gran reserva* is available in more generous quantities. It is a robust Rioja in nose and taste, mature but not too much so, brownish-red in colour and pleasant in its dose of wood and vanilla. The *gran reservas* have the highest proportion of Tempranillo of all at 85%, and in these, too, the rest is Garnacha. The Gran Fino Enologica receives about five years' ageing in wooden casks, its younger equivalent two years.

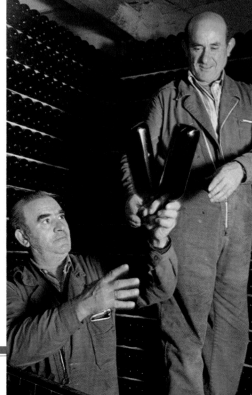

Haro

CVNE

In 1874 the Second Carlist War was raging in Spain. The city of Bilbao was under siege and many young volunteers had come forward to help defend it. Among them were the brothers Eusebio and Raimundo Real de Asúa. An old photograph from the early days of the siege shows Eusebio's company; he is in the foreground with a guitar in his hands and a bottle of Pauillac beside him. He had probably acquired a taste for this wine during his *lycée* days in Bordeaux. Some months later Eusebio, who suffered from asthma, was afflicted with severe difficulties in breathing; hunger and cold in the winter trenches were partly to

blame for this. After the war had ended his doctor advised him to move to a less damp climate – to the Rioja. One day in 1877 he set off south in a landau with just the coachman and the latter's wife, who was an excellent cook. Once in Haro, Eusebio Real de Asúa bought himself an apartment. His wife and children stayed on in Bilbao, only joining him in the summer holidays.

A collective enterprise

Haro at that period was completely taken up with wine. Agents from Bordeaux visited bodega after bodega to buy wines at favourable prices. Eusebio became friendly with both French and Spanish wine men, thereby getting to know the trade and forming the idea of starting his own bodega. This plan took on an increasingly definite form, particularly through conversations with his friend Isidro Corcuera from Logroño. The two men – both just turned 30 – had rather idealistic plans in mind: a collective trading firm devoted to the

nurture and export of wines. Isidro, who knew the vineyards and bodegas as well as anyone, would be responsible for the technical side of the business, Eusebio for the administrative. Louis Perré, Eusebio's French friend from the *lycée*, would be able to take on a considerable part of the commercial work. The Frenchman could also bring in a measure of security, thanks to his good relations with Champagne houses in Reims and the Cognac firm of Rémy-Martin. There were others, friend and relations (including his brother Raimundo) who were also allocated tasks and positions.

Compañía Vinícola del Norte de España

After looking at various locations it was decided to buy a site near the railway station at Haro; this would be convenient for dispatching the wine. On 24 March 1879 at Haro in the presence of a lawyer the *sociedad colectiva mercantil* Corcuera, Real

CVNE

Menu

ofrecido por la

Compañia Vinícola. del Norte de España

à su personal el 1.° de Enéro de 1901, para festejar el

GRAN PRÉMIO

obtenido en Paris, Exposición de 1900.

ENTREMESES VARIADOS

Consómmé
Paella à la valenciana
Ternera con alcachofás
Besugos à la inglesa
Capones asádos

POSTRES

Qhesos y frutas

VINOS

Compañia Vinícola
Champagne Compañia Vinícola
Café, cigarros y
Cognac Compañia Vinícola

Imp. de Portmar

MARCA REGISTRADA

Compañía Vinícola del Norte de España

BILBAO ✦ HARO

de Asúa y Compañía was duly established. The firm had an initial capital of 50,000 pesetas and its head office was in Bilbao. Eusebio became the managing director and remained as such until his death in 1895. His brother then took over the reins until 1914. The business had an exceptionally successful start and after about a year its capital had to be increased to 300,000 pesetas to cover the necessary expansion. There remained, however, a shortage of both wine and facilities and so in 1882 it was decided that a vinification centre should be built on the Haro site, and in addition a distillery in Alfaro. The investment required meant that the structure of the firm had to be altered into that of a *sociedad anónima* or limited company, a change that took place in June 1882. At the same time the name of the firm was changed to *Compañía Vinícolo del Norte de España*. The working capital was increased to 3 million pesetas. The statement of CVNE's aims told no more than the simple truth: "The purchase, making and selling of wines, which may also extend, directly or indirectly, to the cultivation of the vine, to the buying or renting and planting of vineyards, to the manufacture and acquisition of a large stock of casks and, in general, to all activities related to the trade in wines, distillates and liqueurs."

A champagne adventure

An energetic start was made to the work and within two years four buildings went up, for the making and storing of wine and to accommodate a cooper's workshop. A lot of equipment, including apparatus for the firm's own laboratory, came from France. The bodega began to produce various types and styles of wine. For a long time the red Riojas were imitations of well-known French wines. A Médoc and a Graves type were brought out together with a Rioja Spanish Burgundy, for the American market; and I have in fact seen the label of a white wine that was called Cepa Sauterne. There was little bottling done in those early years. Only a small élite got its

CVNE

wine in that way: perhaps that is why for a long time various CVNE labels carried the legend *"Para proveer al ó los Monarcas y Presidentes de las republicas de ambos continentes"*. Bottled wines were also sent to a number of international fairs, where they repeatedly won the highest possible prizes, as happened at Barcelona (1888), London (1889), Brussels (1897), Paris (1900) and elsewhere. One type of wine that had to be bottled from the start was, of course, the sparkling white. This was made by the *méthode champenoise*, and in fact cellar workers came every year from the Champagne district to treat the wine. There was indeed a period when CVNE had its own branch in Champagne. This was the house of Eugène Perré et Cie, set up in Reims in 1887 and named after Louis Perré's son. However, this firm closed after only four years. Later the *espumoso de Rioja* sparkling wine disappeared from CVNE's range altogether. Only old advertising material and preserved menus remain to recall this product of former years.

Early modernization

Through the years the firm continued to grow, not dramatically but steadily. In the process the name was corrupted to "Cune", simply because the capital V in the initials was wrongly taken to be U. Today everyone on the staff – from the caretaker to the chairman of the board – talks of Cune, and you even come across the name in this form on some of the labels. And so "Cune", not the initials, will be used for the rest of this chapter. As has been mentioned, expansion was always taking place, while a good deal of attention was also given to modernization. That this was a characteristic of the bodega at an early stage is clear from the machine now standing on display in the garden. This is a Malvoisin pasteurizer brought here with great difficulty from France at the turn of the century. It did service for some years sterilizing bottles as well as pasteurizing the wines. This curious contraption has long been out of use – nor is pasteurization carried out by any other means at Cune these days.

A contrast in entrances

The bodega is still near the railway station in Haro, where the complex now occupies 14 acres. Neighbouring businesses were bought up one by one. One fairly recent acquisition was a biscuit factory, whose manager had a swimming pool next to his house. The factory made way for cellars but the swimming pool is still there – at least for the present. Cune's old entrance was right opposite a railway embankment, with the first buildings behind the imposing iron railings grouped around a large yard. In those days they looked out over what was then a bleak, unsurfaced area with rails for transporting the barrels. Today, however, there is a charming garden with flowers, a lawn (where the pasteurizer is displayed) and shady trees, the first of which was planted in 1920. There are fine tall trees in other parts of the site as well. The new entrance, a few dozen yards in the direction of Haro, forms a considerable contrast. This is marked out by dazzlingly white walls and gives access to a vast asphalted area with room for articulated trucks to turn round in. Next to this square a fermentation hall exclusively for white wine has been built. Here there are steel, and also stainless steel, tanks, the latter type in use since 1984. Modern offices also adjoin the square, although the management is still based in Bilbao.

The biggest of the smaller bodegas

Although Cune is by no means shy of efficiency and innovation, it nevertheless respects the past. This is clear when you see the earliest part of the bodega. In the ground-level cellars, obviously inspired by Bordeaux, there are 42 splendid wooden vats still in use storing wine. Some of the cellars with their casks are full of atmosphere and take the visitor several generations back in time. As the bodega arrived at its present form through many successive stages, a maze of cellars, halls and passages has developed in places, both above and below ground. Everywhere there is wine, in tanks, casks and bottles. At Cune you are given the impression of a very large concern, but this is not so. Annual production amounts to around 770,000 (US 910,000) gallons; the firm itself refers to itself as "the biggest of the smaller bodegas". At rather more than 500,000 (US 595,000) gallons annually, the emphasis is clearly on red wine, although the 240,000 (US 285,000) gallons of white represents a goodly proportion. Rosé production, however, is only 22,000 (US 26,000) gallons a year.

Investment in vineyards

In the 1970s the Cune board of directors, on which the Real de Asúa family is still fully represented through their majority shareholding, decided on a big investment in vineyards. One of the factors in this was the fear that the emergence of so many new bodegas would put pressure on the supply of reasonably priced grapes, in particular of the Tempranillo. The result of this decision was a Cune estate of 1,160 acres that supplies around 65% of the grapes for red wine, 35% of those needed for white, and 50% of the rosé requirement. Not all of this land had to be bought in the 1970s. Existing property included a site in the Rioja Alavesa where since 1940 the elegant red Viña Royal had been made in a separate bodega. The vineyard of this name lies on the Camino Real ("Royal Road") near Elciego. Besides the 1,160 acres that Cune owns the firm has a further 370 acres under contract for the supply of grapes. Ready-made wine is bought in only small quantities.

Casks and bottles

Cune makes none of its red wine by the Riojan *maceration carbonique* system: all black grapes are destalked and crushed. Before they go into the casks all the red Riojas spend a year in the tanks (or in closed wooden vats). The time in the cask varies from one to three years. The firm

Left:
The old entrance, opposite the railway viaduct.

Below centre:
Drawing wine from a cask beside the big vats.

Below:
Some of the splendid wooden vats now used for storing wine.

Opposite page, below left:
White wines are fermented in this modern building. The tanks are of steel.

Opposite page, below right:
Bottles from the CVNE range.

With its tanks and large vats the firm has a storage capacity of at least 3.96 million (US 4.68 million) gallons.

An old wine press stands in the large dining and reception room, and photographs on the walls include one of the French maître de cuisine Paul Bocuse, who has visited the bodega.

The oldest bottle Cune possesses dates from 1883.

The bottles here are given an extra wash before being filled.

Cune's own vineyards are spread over the three Riojan districts.

The Cune Lanceros is a dry white Rioja with only 12% alcohol and made solely from the Viura. It is fermented at low temperatures in steel tanks and is stabilized cold. Besides a hint of gravel, a little fruit and the slightest suggestion of terroir can be perceived in its taste and perfume; for the rest, this wine is wonderfully fresh and pure in the mouth. It spends 2 to 3 months in wooden vats before bottling.

The white Monopole is a concept in its own right in Spain. The brand has existed since 1915. Sold in a slender green bottle, this wine has a very light colour tinged with green, and there is some wood and vanilla in both its taste and perfume. It stays for a year in cask (along with a year in tank and three months in bottle). Viura (80%) and Malvasía (20%) are its grapes. This is a delicious, balanced Rioja, with taste, fruit and a good aftertaste. Formerly a red Monopole was also sold.

CVNE

holds an average stock of 19,000 *barricas*. About 30% of them are of French oak, the rest of American. Most remain in service for quite a time – 15 to 20 years. There are no longer any coopers on the staff, as once there were. Cune has an abundance of bottles in stock: normally some three million. A good deal of space is kept for the Viña Real, of which *crianzas*, *reservas* and *gran reservas* from various vintages are always available. In September 1984, for example, the bodega had 600,000 bottles

of the 1973 Viña Real *gran reserva* in stock.

The reliable Clarete

The best-selling red wine in the range is the Cune Rioja Clarete 3er año. In Spain the demand for this wine is so great that the supply can never meet it. Nowadays this wine is made from 80% Tempranillo and 20% Garnacha, the Graciano and Mazuelo grapes having virtually disappeared from

the blend. A Rioja clarete was being sold by the bodega as far back as 1895 and the name Cune Rioja Clarete dates from 1929. It is a notably supple wine, with taste, some fruit, some wood, and a quality that is utterly reliable.

The first of the Viña Reals is the *crianza* 4° año, a wine that is matured for 18 months in the wood (6 months more than the Clarete). In principle all the Vina Real Riojas are based on the Alavesa-grown Tempranillo grape, usually nowadays with

Since Cune decided in 1982 to make an absolutely fresh rosé with no cask ageing its quality has greatly improved. This bodega's rosado is now among the best in the region, thanks to a fairly pale, orange-pink shade and a delicious taste with its slight suggestion of fruit. The Garnacha is the only grape used and the alcohol content is around 12.5%. This rosé, like all the white wines, is stabilized cold.

Experience teaches that you can order the Cune Rioja Clarete 3er año "blind", so reliable has it proved over the years. It has a rather soft colour and the noticeably supple taste offers an agreeable amount of wood, body and fruit. It is made from 80% Tempranillo, and 20% Garnacha. After 12 months in tank the Clarete has a further 12 months in cask and at least 3 in bottle.

The Viña Real plata (with silver lettering on the label) has a preponderance of Tempranillo in it, supplemented by some Garnacha. It is a quite rounded wine with firmness, a strong colour and an almost sultry bouquet; so the choice of a Burgundy-type bottle was probably deliberate. This Rioja is in the crianza category with 12 months' tank, 18 cask and 8 bottle.

The Cune 5° año spends 12 months in tank, 18 to 24 in cask and at least 6 to 12 months in bottle. Grape varieties are the Tempranillo (80%) and Garnacha (20%). Its features are a good deep colour with a brown tint to it, a mellow taste, body, wood and an aftertaste with tannin. This wine comes close in quality to a reserva but is officially a crianza.

The Viña Real oro exists both as a reserva and a gran reserva. Both are quite generous, firm wines that easily retain their vitality for 15 years. These compositions of Tempranillo (at least 80%) and Garnacha remain in the tank for 12 months, in the cask for 36. The subsequent period in the bottle can vary from 4 years to 8 or more. The wine is not filtered.

Excellent harvests were the occasion for Cune to create the Imperial trademark, to be used only for the best wines of the best years. These reservas and gran reservas are striking for their maturity, elegance and refinement. Their composition may vary according to the harvest, but the Tempranillo always accounts for at least 70% (often with a little Viura). Ageing consists of 12 months in tank, 36 in cask and at least 36 to 60 in its Bordeaux-type bottle. It is not filtered.

CVNE

Garnacha added. This explains why these wines have rather more colour, firmness and a more rounded quality than Riojas made only from the Alavesa Tempranillo. These same characteristics are found in a more mature form in the Viña Real *reservas* and *gran reservas*. A wine that could be placed between the *crianza* and *reserva* versions of Viña Real is the Cune 5° año. This is sold as a *crianza* but in reality it approaches the class of a *reserva*.

At the top of the range are the Imperial wines – a trademark that was registered in 1928. Only the best that can be selected from the best of years is considered worthy of the Imperial label: 1928, 1934, 1942, 1947, 1948, 1952, 1955, 1961, 1964, 1968, 1970, 1973, 1975 and 1976 are examples. The wines spend at least one year in tank, three in wood and three in bottle, and they are marketed exclusively as *reservas* or *gran reservas*. In general these wines are more elegant than those of the Viña Real range.

Spain's beloved Monopole

Since 1915 Cune has produced a dry white wine under the trademark Monopole. From the start it appears to have been a white Rioja with a lighter and fresher taste than the average. In Spain Monopole developed into an enormously popular product, with Cune selling about a million bottles a year. The grapes used are the Viura (80%) and Malvasia (20%). It is given a year in cask, which is just enough to impart an interesting suggestion of wood and vanilla, while the taste does not dry out or lose its freshness. Monopole is a balanced Rioja with 11.5 to 11.7% alcohol. It is an established fact that many bodegas have imitated this type of wine.

There is another dry white Rioja in the range in addition to the Monopole, the Cune Lanceros. This is made solely from the Viura grape and is only in contact with the wood for two to three months. It tastes very fresh and pure.

Another white Rioja is Cune's *semi dulce*, a semi-sweet wine that merits no attention. On the other hand I was pleasantly surprised by the Cune *rosado*, which has improved greatly in quality since the 1982 vintage. This rosé is made from the Grenache alone and of the dozen wines I tasted at Cune this was the only one that had had no ageing in the wood at all. It was lively in taste, fruity, light and delicious and, quite simply, belongs among the best of Rioja wines: a judgment that could also be applied to Cune as a whole.

Haro

Bodegas Bilbaínas

In order to ensure a sufficient supply of wine for his flourishing wine merchant business in Bilbao, Santiago de Ugarte y Aurrecoechea decided to buy a bodega of his own in the Rioja. That was in 1901. Santiago, then 38 years old, decided on H. Sauvignon y Cia, a bodega established by Frenchmen and situated near the railway station in Haro. Immediately after he had taken over, the name was changed to

Bodegas Bilbaínas. The business prospered greatly and in the second decade of this century two adjoining bodegas were bought so that production could be increased. Santiago de Ugarte, who was married to an Englishwoman, was already exporting a great deal, having set up friends as agents in various countries. To cultivate the British market, which was so important to him, he even established a branch in London in 1925. Bilbaínas London Ltd had its offices in Regent Street, together with

vaults under Charing Cross Station. One day the Spanish monarch paid this branch a visit, unannounced and accompanied by a friend of the then manager. As it happened some bottles had just that moment been broken and the manager was in rather a bad mood. When his friend asked him who he thought this visitor was he replied, irritably, "The King of Spain, no doubt" – and went on sweeping up the shards. He was considerably astonished to be told that indeed it was. The king found the incident highly amusing – and very Spanish. In 1966 the London office was closed and the building was sold to the Imperial Tobacco group.

Bodegas Bilbaínas

The third generation

Santiago de Ugarte retired in 1929 and handed the business over to his two sons. Responsibility now rests with the third generation. The chairman of the board is Gonzalo Diéz del Corral (who is married to an Ugarte), and the younger Santiago de Ugarte (grandson of the founder) is his deputy. They have further extended the bodega. The total floor surface of its buildings is more than 31,000 sq yds of which 3600 sq yds is underground. You reach the complex by taking the narrow street (where two lorries cannot pass one another) that runs between the railway embankment and the wall of the neighbouring Cune site and on to the station. The first row of bodega buildings faces on to the little station yard and they have a platform of their own. Opposite the entrance stands "the chalet", a house which the Ugarte family uses only in the holidays: they live in Bilbao and direct the business from there.

More white grapes planted

Just as the founder of Bodegas Bilbaínas wanted to ensure his supply of wine, so his successors have been anxious to create a continuity in the provision of grapes. The firm has therefore invested a good deal in vineyards. At present it has about 620 acres, of which 495 are fully productive. Most of this land is in the neighbourhood of Haro, along the banks of the Tirón, but the concern also has vines growing near Elciego, Laguardia and Leza. In Leza, in Rioja Alavesa, it has the El Pomal vineyard, from which Bilbaínas' best-known wine takes its name. The names of two other vineyards also appear on labels: Viña Páceta and Viña Zaco. What is striking is that of the 495 productive acres, nearly 300 are planted with white grapes (75% Viura, supplemented by Malvasia and a little Garnacha Blanca), and the rest with black (95% Tempranillo, 5% Garnacha, Graciano and Mazuelo): exactly the reverse of ratios at most other bodegas.

Sparkling wines

One of the reasons for the extensive planting of white grapes is the production of sparkling wines. These represent almost one third of the annual 220,000 (US 260,000) gallons of white. Bodegas Bilbaínas started making these *vinos espumosos* in 1912. They are not entitled to the Rioja *appellation*, even though grapes from the region are used for them – notably for the Royal Carlton, in which Viura grapes from the bodega's own vineyards as well as bought in wines made from the same variety, are utilized. The production process is like that used in Champagne, with the wines given not just the minimum nine months' rest after bottling, but at least two years. Royal Carlton is not topped up with a wine-and-sugar *dosage*: the words *brut nature* on the label are justified. The wine has small spiralling bubbles, a cool, pale cölour and a decent but not really fine or exciting taste, and there is a slight earthiness. A simpler quality is marketed under the name Lumen.

This bodega's range includes yet another unusual product, a mild brandy (37% alcohol) called Imperator. It used to be distilled on the premises, but nowadays this is done at a cooperative. In addition a small amount of bottled grape juice is marketed under the brand name Zuva. This comes from Rioja grapes only and is therefore expensive.

No more cask-aged whites

About 20% of the annual production of 220,000 (US 260,000) gallons of red Rioja comes from Bilbaínas' own land. The rest is bought elsewhere in the form of grapes or wine. After destalking and crushing the fruit ferments in self-emptying tanks; these red-painted metal *depositos* were installed in 1972. In principle the fermentation temperature is not allowed to rise above 26° C. The white wines are fermented in concrete. During my visit at the end of 1984 Santiago de Ugarte said that he was experimenting with low fermentation temperatures, between 16 and 22° C, in order to endow his wines with more fruit and freshness. With some regret in his voice he added that the market was compelling Bilbaínas to give up ageing its white Riojas in the wood, so this traditional type of wine was gradually disappearing. A cooling plant has been purchased for stabilizing the dry whites and rosés. The semi-sweet variants of both types are pasteurized; these wines go mainly to South America and the Caribbean. All wines are filtered twice.

Underground galleries

While part of the bodega is equipped with up-to-date plant, it also keeps a cellar from the previous century in use. It is linked via a tunnel with galleries dating from 1901. These wide passages, with casks stacked five high on either side, are a good 330 ft long. I saw mould on quite a few of the casks. Bodegas Bilbaínas has around 13,200 casks, all of American oak. The firm endeavours to replace them with new *barricas* after nine years; in the meantime they are maintained by three coopers. The wine here is still racked by hand; on average it goes into a clean cask every eight months. Once bottled all the Riojas stay for at least six months in the cellars. The stock of bottles normally amounts to 400,000.

Visitors welcome

Bodegas Bilbaínas exports 50 to 60% of its production, to Venezuela, the United States, Britain, Denmark, Puerto Rico, Switzerland and other countries, and also enjoys a good reputation in Spain. The firm is geared to the reception of visitors, especially small groups. A spacious reception-cum-dining room has been built, with a large open hearth, a tile picture of Haro, engravings of Spanish and German villages, two suits of armour and replicas of brandy casks which hold bottles of wine. At the entrance to this hall a small museum of wine tools and machinery has been fitted

VIÑA PÁCETA
BLANCO SECO
COSECHA 1980   HARO·RIOJA
Bodegas Bilbaínas, S.A.

Until 1984 at least the Viña Páceta dry white was given 12 months in tank, 6 months in cask and 6 in bottle. The intention, however, is to abandon wood ageing and to ferment the wine at a lower temperature. This will change its characteristics. What I tasted was a pale, fresh, rather austere Rioja: refreshing but without much fruit. Its grapes were 75 to 80% Viura, the rest Malvasía.

Imperator
Bodegas Bilbaínas, S.A.
HARO · RIOJA
VINO · TINTO
COSECHA 1981

At this bodega the Imperator trademark serves for a fairly simple white wine, a dry rosé, the firm's own brandy and a red crianza. This last wine consists of 60 to 70% Tempranillo and 30 to 40% Garnacha. It is a correct Rioja, with juice and robustness. It stays in the tank for 12 months, with 24 months in cask and a minimum 6 in bottle.

COSECHA 1981
POMAL JUNIOR
HARO·RIOJA
Bodegas Bilbaínas, S.A.

Like the Imperator red the Pomal Junior is a crianza. This is aged in the same way but has a different mixture of grapes – in fact the basis for all Pomal wines: about 60% Garnacha and 40% Tempranillo, plus just a little Graciano. A rounded quality, a certain freshness and a modest wood aroma characterize this wine. The Ederra Rioja is another crianza, with about 45% Garnacha and 55% Tempranillo.

Bodegas Bilbaínas

up. Here there are a number of hand-bottling machines, distilling equipment, an old, red-painted German filter and tools of the cooper's trade. If there was enough room the wooden fermentation vats would belong here: they are no longer used and stand idly in their dark underground cellar. Until 10 years ago they were still in service for the storing and blending of wine, but there came a time when the bodega's workers refused to go on crawling inside them to clean them out.

Low-temperature fermentation on the way

This bodega is characterized by its large range of Riojas. I have tasted at least 10 different kinds, and that does not include the semi-sweet wines. The pleasantest white Rioja, in my opinion, was the Viña Páceta, a blend of Viura (75 to 80%) and Malvasía grapes. It was a fresh, really dry, somewhat austere wine, clearly lacking fruit then. The alternative fermentation method – cool and slow – that is on the way will perhaps remedy this defect. Because of its acids this Rioja usually retains its freshness for a good four or five years. A simpler variant, which contains some Garnacha Blanca as well, is called Imperator. For the sake of completeness the brand names of the two best-known semi-sweet white wines should be mentioned: Cepa de Oro and the slightly sweeter Brillante. In the past all these wines, and the rosés, were given an ageing period of 12 months in tank, 6 months in wood and 6 months in bottle. But now, as has been seen, for white wines the time in the cask is on its way out.

Pomal in triplicate

The most familiar brand from Bodegas Bilbaínas is Viña Pomal. There are even importers who carry only this line. The Spanish court has ordered a good deal of it and, according to the bodega, Winston Churchill used to drink it regularly. The surrealist Salvador Dali was apparently another lover of this wine. Viña Pomal is a *crianza* by origin but it could also be sold as a *reserva*, for it is given one year in tank, three to five years in wood and at least one in bottle. It is composed of 60% Garnacha and 40% Tempranillo (with just a little Graciano). The Garnacha grape gives this Rioja a fairly broad taste and this is rounded off with a touch of wood and a certain maturity. You would look in vain, however, for character, concentration or finesse. Alongside this ordinary Viña Pomal there is the Viña Pomal Reserva – of which more is sold. The name again is rather imprecise for this is a *gran reserva*, which is usually sold only after 11 to 13 years. It has one year in tank, five in wood and five to seven years in bottle. It is very much the Rioja for people who like extremely mature wines with a lot of wood.

Since rising grape prices, inflation and other causes have made the older Viña Pomals rather costly, the bodega has been urged to create a younger, more favourably

The ordinary Viña Pomal is a more mature *crianza*, with 1 year in tank, 3 to 5 years in cask and a minimum 1 year in bottle. It is a mellow, supple Rioja with a fairly broad taste and the slightly "oxidized" tinge that all wines of this brand seem to have. This may be partly due to the large percentage of Garnacha.

The Viña Zaco *reserva* is named after a vineyard in Rioja Alta. It is an elegant rather than a concentrated wine, usually decently matured and still with some fruit. Its composition is 60 to 65% Tempranillo and the rest Garnacha. It matures for 1 year in tank, 3 to 5 in cask and 2 in bottle.

Although *reserva* appears on the label, this Viña Pomal is a *gran reserva* for it is given 1 year in tank, 5 years in cask and at least 5 to 7 years in bottle. This is the bestseller of the three Pomal wines. It is a Rioja for those who like a really well-matured wine. Like the other Pomals, however, it is somewhat lacking in depth and intensity.

Bodegas Bilbaínas carries several other *gran reservas* besides Viña Pomal. The lightest type is just given the firm's own name. The Vendimia Especial (see the label) is more robust and contains more tannin (60 to 65% Tempranillo, the rest Garnacha). Still more strength and class is in the Gran Zaco, the most substantial wine of the range, with a really deep colour, a good deal of wood and an excellent ageing potential of at least 20 to 30 years. Production is unfortunately extremely limited.

Bodegas Bilbaínas

priced version. And this is what has happened. In autumn 1984 the first consignment of Pomal Junior was bottled, with England its destination. The blend of grapes remained the same as for the existing types, but the ageing period was shortened to a year in tank, 2 years in wood and 6 months in bottle. It seemed to me a very acceptable and rounded product, with colour and some freshness – but my marginal note on all the Viña Pomals concerned their slightly "oxidized" style, a style that must be to an extent inherent in the preponderance of the Garnacha grape. I do not like this particularly myself, although others obviously find it no problem.

The rest of the reds

The remaining red wines have a preponderance of Tempranillo. The Imperator *crianza*, for example, contains 60 to 70% of this grape, with the Garnacha its second variety. It is not a really exciting Rioja, but by no means a bad one, for fruit and firmness are present. The same combination of grapes is found in the Viña Zaco, a *reserva* which I prefer to the comparable Viña Pomal. For me the best red wine in the whole collection is the Gran Zaco, a *gran reserva*. I cherish splendid memories of the 1962, which after some 20 years still had a full, vital, elegant taste to

offer. But the Vendimia Especial *gran reserva*, too, was a pleasure to taste. This seemed to be somewhat firmer of constitution, and with more tannin, than the same year's *gran reserva* sold with just the bodega name.

Bodegas Bilbaínas left me with the impression of an essentially conservative firm with all the potential of making good wine which, however, it does not exploit to the full.

Bodegas Muga

Although it was a period of crisis, Isaac Muga Martínez from Villalba, a village just north-west of Haro, started his own bodega in 1932. At the start the bodega was intended to process only grapes from the family vineyard. The location was the Calle Santo Tomás, a street in the heart of Haro. Isaac died in 1969 and the firm, which had grown in the meantime, passed immediately to his two sons, Isaac and Manuel Muga Caño. They moved the bodega out to the Barrio de la Estación on 4 May 1972, into a group of solid buildings that had served, among other things, as a wine bodega, a warehouse for colonial goods and a liqueur distillery. The family was not able to manage the necessary investment itself and so the Central de Inversión y Crédito (CIC), a centre for investment and credit, became a joint owner with 49% of the shares. This holding was later transferred to Mapfre, an insurance concern, but the majority interest remained in the hands of the Muga family. The chairman of the board is Manuel (born 1935) and Isaac (born 1940) manages the firm. Their whole life has been taken up with wine. A photograph from 1948, for example, shows a group of pickers posed in the Muga vineyard. Isaac senior stands on the right; Isaac junior sits in the centre, holding up a bunch of grapes.

It is said that Isaac Muga started making sparkling wine because his mother complained that it was so dear to buy. Isaac looked very thoroughly into the way in which his father was producing espumoso. More wine had to be made than could be consumed by the family so the bodega began selling it – with success.

The bodega exports about 20% of production, to Britain, France, the United States, Austria, the Netherlands and elsewhere.

Muga wines are filtered once, through cellulose plates.

A lead seal cap is sometimes used for the reservas.

The Muga crianza, marketed in a Bordeaux bottle, has as its basis 40% Tempranillo, 40% Garnacha, 10% Mazuelo and 10% Viura. It is a fragrant Rioja, light in all respects, with not much breeding or depth but with a silky, agreeable taste, some mellow fruit and a restrained aroma of vanilla. It is matured for 12 months in a large vat, for 12 in cask and a minimum 6 months in bottle.

The Prado Enea starts as a reserva, but after sufficient time bottle ageing it can be promoted to gran reserva. This wine is somewhat more powerful, more distinguished and with rather more nuances than the Muga – although here, too, the colour could be more intense. The proportion of Tempranillo is around 60%, complemented by 20% Garnacha, 10% Mazuelo and 10% Virua. Maturing consists of 12 months in a large vat, 48 in cask and a minimum 24 in the (Burgundy-style) bottle.

Bodegas Muga

Trusted suppliers

Bodega Muga is by no means large; it produces an average 74,000 (US 87,400) gallons of Rioja a year. This is mainly red wine, white and rosé together representing only 10% of the total. About 40% comes from the Muga vineyard, which lies on the right of the *autopista* as you drive north from Haro and covers about 54 acres. Isaac said that he was reducing the proportion of Tempranillo there to 60%, partly by replanting more Mazuelo vines and also some Graciano. What the bodega buys in consists mainly of grapes. The great majority of these have over the last 30 or so years been bought from the same growers, all with land in the Rioja Alta. The small amount that is taken in the form of wine comes from *cosecheros* who have been doing their own vinification for many years. Muga never buys from cooperatives.

Wooden vats only

In the solid-looking, well-insulated bodega the grapes are destalked and crushed. The whole vintage is then fermented in wooden vats holding around 4,000 (US 4,700) gallons each. Muga is a very traditional house – more so even than most bodegas of earlier foundation. After the first fermentation has run its course the red wine is racked to clean vats for its malolactic fermentation. As it is being drawn off a bunch of dried vine twigs is held under the tap, which serves to filter the wine. When the fermentation process has come to an end the red Riojas are left to rest for a year in wooden vats (or horizontal casks). Blending then takes place and the wines are racked to casks for ageing.

Fining with whites of egg

The bodega has 4,000 casks or *barricas*, all of American oak, which it normally keeps in rotation for around 12 years. Some of the new replacement casks – 80 to 100 a year – are made by a cooper on permanent staff. Once in the casks the wine is racked every four months, by hand. Visitors are always shown another "craft" aspect of this bodega: the fining of the wines with the fresh whites of egg. For this purpose the wine is pumped from the casks into one or more vats. Three eggs per hectolitre are used, which comes out at about six per cask. The egg whites are separated from the yolks and then whipped to a froth in a 22-gallon pail, usually with the addition of a little salt. Finally this is carefully measured into the vat. The eggs are supplied by a man who is also a pastrycook and confectioner, and

Bodegas Muga

therefore gets the yolks back for use in his wares.

Silky structure

Muga offers two kinds of red wine. The younger of the two is called simply Muga and spends a year in vat, 2 in cask and at least 6 months in bottle. It is a fragrant, rather refined and elegant *crianza*, made from 40% Tempranillo, 40% Garnacha, 10% Mazuelo and 10% Viura. This Rioja has no great intensity of colour, nor very much breeding, but on the other hand you encounter a silky structure, a soft, somewhat retiring fruitiness and a restrained aroma of vanilla. It is a most pleasant wine, but surpassed in quality by the Prado Enea, which is sometimes a *reserva*, sometimes a *gran reserva* (depending on how long it has rested in the bottle). This wine does not have a strong colour either, but it obviously possesses more distinction, more nuances and power. In May 1984 the Consejo Regulador underlined this wine's class by selecting the 1976 to represent the *gran reserva* category at all receptions, tastings and presentations. At 60% the Tempranillo is the dominant grape. The other varieties are Garnacha (20%), Mazuelo (10%) and Viura (10%). The wine is matured for a year in vat, or large cask, 4 years in cask and then at least 2 years in bottle. Prado Enea accounts for almost a quarter of the average stock of 450,000 bottles held by Bodegas Muga. *Reservas* are not set aside out of all vintages and it even happens that Muga considers no wines good enough for the *crianza* category. This was the case in 1972, 1977 and 1979, when all the red wine was sold in bulk.

White and rosé less interesting

In the reception area, done out in brown and red-brown colours, and with a tiled floor, brick alcoves and sturdy wooden furniture, there is a white wine and a rosé to taste as well as the reds. The white has the Viura grape as its basis and matures for 2 years in the vat only, not in cask, so it is

not a strictly traditional Rioja – but still less a modern one. Bodegas Muga does not ferment the wine at low temperature, nor stabilize it cold. I found the white less interesting than the two red Riojas. It was reasonably fresh in taste, but at the same time rather flat. More fruit and liveliness would have been welcome. This applied to an even greater degree to the rosé, the Almendora, a sometimes unpleasant-nosed composition of 80% Viura, 10% Tempranillo and 10% Garnacha. The rosé spends only four months in the vat.

Other products

Besides its Riojas, Bodegas Muga is making an increasing amount of sparkling wine: production is to grow from 35 to 40,000 bottles a year up to 100,000. This wine, made from the Viura, undergoes secondary fermentation *à la* champagne in the bottle. After this the bottles remain for at least two years in the cellar, for the longer the wine matures, the smaller and more

durable the carbon dioxide bubbles. And during this rest period the deposit produced by the secondary fermentation can impart subtle elements of taste and fragrance to the wine. Muga removes this deposit later in the traditional way, by means of concrete *pupitres* etc. The resulting wine – called Mugamart in Spain and Conde de Haro elsewhere – is always sold by the year of vintage, usually in two versions. The *brut* has 8g of sugar, the *brut nature* 1.3g. I prefer the drier variant, a fresh and pure-tasting wine without great depth or refinement, but a pleasant aperitif nonetheless. Muga may possibly bring out a *digestif* in the future, a *marc* from the Rioja. I have sampled this distillate at an early stage, when it had acquired just a tinge of colour, thanks to the oak casks where it reposed – and was destined to mature for many more years.

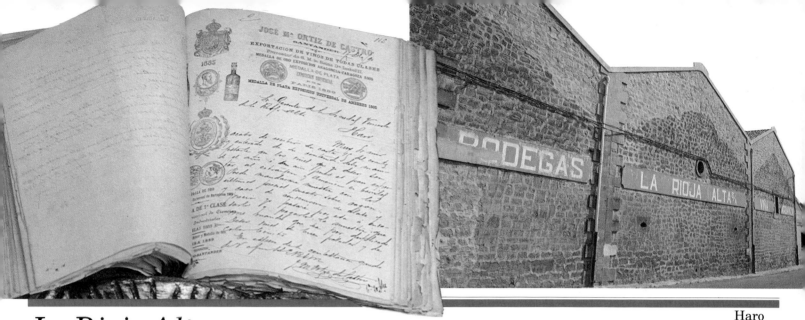

La Rioja Alta

At the end of the 1880s the French wine merchant Albert Viguier had cellars built opposite the López de Heredia bodega. Four prosperous Haro families, with Felipe de la Bellacasa, took them over in 1890. The founders were soon joined by Alfredo Ardanza Sánchez, who brought his vineyards with him; some of this land still belongs to the bodega, and Viña Ardanza is the best-selling wine. One of the founders, Mariano Lacort, subsequently started his own bodega in the same street; the building was later bought up by Bodegas Muga. The original *sociedad de cosecheros de vino* of La Rioja Alta was changed into a limited company in 1904 with its head office in San Sebastián. Almost 40 years later this was moved to Haro, where it has remained until today.

A number of the present owners are descendants of the families who founded the firm, but there are also industrialists (from steel, soft drinks etc.) among the shareholders and on the board of directors.

French cellarman

The firm prospered in the early years of its development and earned a good reputation. Its wines won a silver medal at the Bordeaux world exhibition in 1895, a silver medal at the Chicago World Fair in 1902 and the *grand prix* at Toulouse in 1911. At that time the bodega still had a French cellarman on the staff, Charles Gaillat, from the Médoc. His very precise notes have been preserved and give a good idea of how things were done in those days. And it was with the help of French experts that the young firm was enlarged. Later other expansions were to take place, as in 1970 and 1975. The present La Rioja Alta complex has a covered area of more than 3½ acres. The most recent acquisition is a battery of stainless-steel tanks. put in after the 1983 harvest. These are to be used for storing wine: their use for fermentation was still problematic in October 1984, for La Rioja Alta is a traditionally inclined concern.

Grapes and wine bought in

One feature here that shows how the past is revered is the fact that the original grey wooden fermentation vats are still in use – for both fermentation and storage. Even the concrete tanks here are not employed for fermenting the wines, just storage.

Average annual production consists of around 220,000 (US 260,000) gallons of red Rioja, 11,000 (US 13,000) gallons of white and 4,400 (US 5,200) gallons of rosé. About a third of the grapes for this output comes from the firm's own vineyards. These cover some 310 acres and are all in Rioja Alta, mainly near Rodezno (a hamlet south of Haro, just past Ollauri) and Cenicero. Another third is purchased in the form of grapes, the bodega stipulating that the fruit must contain enough sugar to produce at least 10% alcohol, and that it should include not more than 10% white grapes. The remaining third reaches the bodega in the form of wine.

Right:
The bodega has its own kitchen.

Below right:
Looking at the 'cap' of skins that has floated to the surface of wine fermenting in a wooden vat.

Bottom right:
To clean the wooden vats someone has to drop down through a narrow opening with a lamp.

TINTO FINO DE RIOJA

The youngest red wine from La Rioja Alta receives 8 to 10 months in tank, 18 months in cask and at least 12 months in bottle. This is the Viña Alberdi *crianza*, a pleasant, pure wine without a great deal of depth or length. But the taste has some wood, vanilla, fruit and a fresh quality. The grapes are 70% Tempranillo, with Garnacha, Graciano, Mazuelo and Viura.

SEXTO AÑO

The red Viña Arana (there are two unexciting white versions of it, dry and semi-sweet) has the same mixture of grapes as the Viña Alberdi – but is matured for longer in cask and bottle, 36 and 24 months respectively. It is a fairly light, reasonably mature *reserva*, but without a well-defined personality; but wood and tannin are clearly present.

With annual sales of 110,000 to 132,000 gallons (US 130,000 to 156,000), Viña Ardanza represents roughly half of La Rioja Alta's turnover. This *reserva* contains more Garnacha – 25% – than the other kinds; the Tempranillo is restricted here to 60% and the remaining 10% consists of Graciano, Mazuelo and Viura. It is a beautiful, complete, harmonious and quite generous Rioja with its alcohol at a good 13%.

La Rioja Alta

Around 25,000 casks

After the incoming grapes have been destalked and lightly crushed – at least those destined for red Rioja – the first and second fermentations take place. Then after filtering the wine is transferred to the cellars where the casks are: the bodega has a number of these cellars, both above and below ground. This is hardly surprising, for there are at least 25,000 casks; an exceptional quantity for a firm of this size, making it abundantly clear that it specializes in aged-in-the-wood wines. Of the annual 220,000 (US 260,000) gallons of red wine sold, 154,000 (US 182,000) gallons consists of *reservas* or *gran reservas*. All the casks are of American oak and are maintained by two coopers. The rotation of the casks proceeds slowly for in principle they are changed once in 20 years. Three teams of workers are kept almost continuously busy racking the large amount of wine ageing in the wood, each team dealing with about 50 casks a day.

Wine club

In a separate area of the bodega there are casks inscribed with people's names. These represent reservations for the Club de Cosecheros de la Rioja Alta SA, whose members can put their names to wines still at an early stage. This club was started in 1980 and has achieved a membership of around 2,000. One of the benefits of belonging is that members are regularly surprised with excellently produced, expertly written publications on the Rioja and its wines. The wines for the Club de Cosecheros are in fact no different from those in the ordinary range. The only difference is the label. The first vintages involved were the 1976, 1978 and 1980.

A great store of bottles

Although the casks, stacked five high, take up a lot of room in the various buildings and on the various floors of this bodega, a considerable quantity of bottles is also carried: around 2.5 million. The *reservas* and *gran reservas* are stacked on slats and the younger wines are in pallets. The Riojas are bottled with extraordinary care. They have to be – for otherwise La Rioja Alta would never have been allowed to supply its Viña Alberdi, for example, to the Sainsbury supermarket chain. This British firm imposes hygienic and other requirements of an almost legendary stringency on its suppliers. Sainsbury usually takes some 33,000 gallons annually: a formidable amount.

Early selection

The bodega makes its selections for its various brands at an early stage. The best wines are immediately separated from the rest. It is only in exceptional years that wine is picked out for the *gran reservas* 890 and 904. These Riojas derive their names from the year of foundation, 1890, and the excellent vintage of 1904 (which was also the year when La Rioja Alta became a limited company). After this the *reservas* are selected and the rest becomes *crianza*. Red wines are this firm's forte; the white and rosé it sells is not very inspiring. The white Viña Arana exists in dry and semi-sweet form; it is made from Viura and Malvasia grapes, is not aged in the wood but does spend 8 to 10 months resting in the tank and 12 in the bottle.

The Radiante brand also comes in these two versions. Other white wines which I have encountered in the past are the Leonora, with a little wood ageing, and the Metropol, which is matured in the cask in the traditional way. The only rosé that I know is the Vicuana, a combination of Tempranillo, Graciano, Mazuelo and Garnacha; it is given no wood ageing.

The younger red wines

The youngest red wine in the bodega's range is the Viña Alberdi, a *crianza* that has 8 to 10 months in tank, 18 months in cask and at least 12 months' bottle age. It is a most acceptable wine, not really deep, long or rounded, but pleasantly drinkable and very pure. Besides the wood and the vanilla, there is fruit and a certain freshness in its taste. The Tempranillo is the most important grape used, at 70%, supplemented by the Garnacha, Graciano, Mazuelo and Viura. The red Viña Arana, with same grape combination, comes into the *reserva* category because of its ageing period: 8 to 10 months in tank, 3 years in cask and at least 2 years in bottle. This is a pleasant-tasting rather light Rioja, sometimes tending almost to sweetness (the 1978, for example), and with more wood and tannin than the previous wine mentioned. It does not have a very pronounced personality, but it is a pleasure to drink.

Reserva 904, named after the excellent year 1904, is usually only put on sale after 10 to 11 years (8 to 10 months in tank, 6 years in the wood and at least $3\frac{1}{2}$ in bottle). Despite this its taste is not over-matured or tired; it can even be laid down for further development. Wood, vanilla and tannin are strongly present. This gran reserva is made from 80% Tempranillo, with the Graciano, Mazuelo and Virua varieties accounting for the rest.

Reserva 890 is a rare wine – small quantities are set aside for it only in outstanding years. It is given 8 to 10 months in tank, 8 years in cask and 6 years in bottle – so it is more than 15 years old before it leaves the cellars. Wood is strikingly present in perfume and taste – a very mature taste, but nevertheless vital and not dried out. The colour is deep, dark brown.

The firm has a small bodega in Labastida where reservas and gran reservas are aged in casks and bottles.

The bodega's basement dining room is often used by business firms and banks for meetings and dinners.

At the end of 1984 the bodega installed a whole new bottling plant. It gives the bottles an extra wash before filling.

A modest quantity of the better wines is sent out in wooden cases.

About 40% of production goes abroad, to markets including Britain, Denmark, West Germany and the United States.

Viña Ardanza

In quality and character the Viña Alberdi and the Viña Arana are both surpassed by the Viña Ardanza, a firm, generous and beautifully balanced Rioja. This is the most in demand of all the bodega's wines, representing more than half of sales. Viña Ardanza is treated as a *reserva*. Normally it stays 8 to 10 months in tank, $3\frac{1}{2}$ years in cask, and at least 2 years in bottle. That this Rioja has more strength than the two types mentioned above is partly due to a higher percentage of Garnacha – 25%. The Tempranillo amounts to 60% and the rest consists of Graciano, Mazuelo and Viura. A Burgundy-type bottle was chosen for the Viña Ardanza to symbolize its generous nature. The other red wines go into Bordeaux bottles.

Venerable duo

The highest percentage of Tempranillo – 80% – in a La Rioja Alta wine is found in its two *gran reservas*, the Reserva 904 and the Reserva 890. After 8 to 10 months in the tank these wines go into the casks for an extremely long time. The 904 usually spends six years in the wood, the 890 eight years. They are then left to age in bottle for a further long period: three and a half and six years respectively. The 890 is the rarer of the two types. In the first place it is made only very exceptionally, and the quantity of wine selected for it is also small. Only 38,000 bottles were laid down out of the 1968 vintage, for example, but it sometimes happens that the figure is as low as 7,000. Reserva 890 was produced from the 1964, 1968 and 1970 vintages, and 1973, 1976 and 1981 will probably follow.

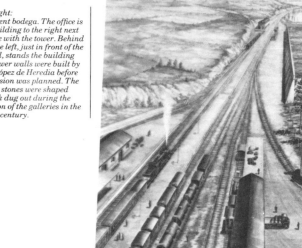

R. López de Heredia Viña Tondonia

The most striking bodega in the *barrio* around Haro's railway station is that of López de Heredia. It is distinguished by an Art Nouveau tower with pointed roofs and carved woodwork painted bright red, perched on top of a dwelling house. The firm was founded in 1877 by Rafael López de Heredia Landeta, who had been born 20 years earlier in the Chilean capital of Santiago. His parents – Spanish, and originating from the province of Alava, where the village of Heredia is situated – had returned to their homeland in 1869. After completing his business studies in the French town of Bayonne, Rafael saw great possibilities in selling Rioja wines to France. In the early years the French were in fact his biggest customers. The successful start made by the enterprise soon obliged it to extend its premises. In 1881 the cellars of the French firm of Armande Heff were acquired; and in 1892 a start was made on excavating galleries in the hill beside the bodega. The biggest of these, christened El Calado, ran for 235 yards through the hill, coming out by the Ebro.

An ingenious solution

This enormous project brought a problem: carting away the many tons of stone. Rafael López de Heredia hit on a brilliant solution. He brought in an architect and asked him to draw up plans for an ideal bodega in the future: if the firm maintained its prosperous development, what buildings would have to go up? After the designs were complete, 50 stonemasons arrived from Galicia to reduce the large pieces of rock to building stones. Low walls were constructed with these, outlining the shape of buildings to come, and the stone rubble was tipped into these enclosures – solving another problem. Rafael López de Heredia was convinced that within a few generations technology would be so far advanced that this rubble would no longer be a problem. In the mid-1970s Don Rafael's vision was realized. Mechanical grabs removed the rubble, the walls were completed and roofs were placed on them –

and a series of new buildings was ready for the bodega, in a short space of time and for little expenditure. The latter point was demonstrated when the firm had a small office built in roughly the same style near its weighbridge: it cost 2 million pesetas.

The Tondonia vineyard

Rafael López de Heredia was a striking personality (a photograph from April 1910 shows him grey-bearded, with bowler hat and cape, standing in the snow) and he directed his attention not only to the extension of the bodega, but also to the acquisition of vineyards. In 1913 he bought some 250 acres of land in one piece. It lay just east of Haro and was almost encircled by the right bank of the Ebro. It was given the name of Viña Tondonia. This slightly hilly land proved difficult to plant, but a year later the work was done. The label of the Viña Tondonia, the best-known wine from this bodega, was for many years printed with the years 1913 and 1914 on it, indicating when the vineyard of this name came into being. It was noticed, however, that the public sometimes took these to mean the years of vintage and so the figures were dropped. According to the bodega the Viña Tondonia lies in the wettest, coolest zone of the Rioja, so that it never produces heavy wines. At a later stage López de Heredia bought and planted three other vineyards, the Viña Bosconia, Viña Cubillo and Viña Zaconia. The firm now owns 420 acres of cultivated land.

Family concern

On 1 January 1924 Rafael brought his two sons into the business, Julio César and Rafael. At the same time the bodega became a limited company or *sociedad anónima*: Rafael López de Heredia Viña Tondonia. Julio César died in 1966 and Rafael in 1985. Until the last year of his life the very active Rafael was regularly in the cellars. As he had to go about in a wheelchair and lived in the tower, he had a special lift constructed that carried him straight down to the fermentation hall. The

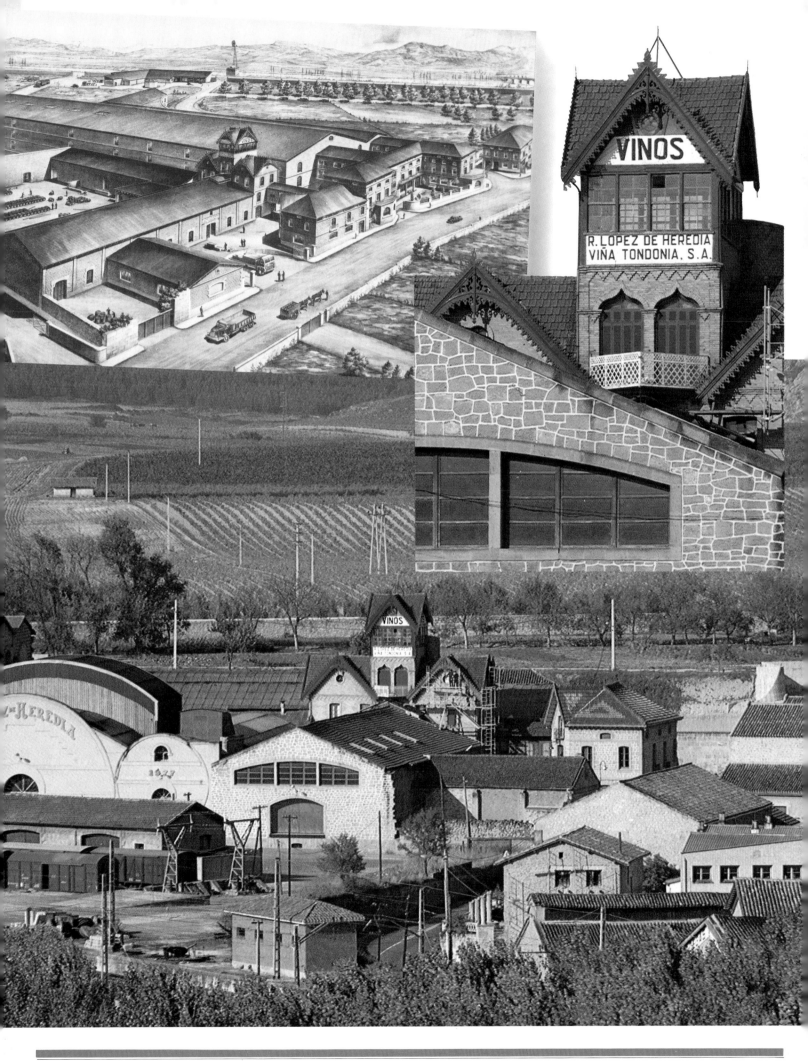

Like all the white wines from this bodega, the dry Viña Gravonia is composed of 50% Viura and 50% Malvasía, from its own vineyards. The wine undergoes a maturing process of 6 months in a large vat, 36 in cask and at least 6 in bottle. The colour is pale with a golden gleam; there is vanilla and a suggestion of gravel in the nose; and a refined, gently fresh taste with only a little wood.

The white Viña Tondonia comes from the vineyard of the same name. It is a striking, very fragrant wine, its perfume evoking associations with spices, herbs and vanilla. It is given 6 months in a large vat, 5 years in cask and a minimum 6 months in bottle. Despite this it retains a fresh core to its taste and an elegant structure. It makes sense to decant this Rioja so that the bouquet is fully released. Do not serve too cold.

The youngest red wine from López de Heredia, it nevertheless has 6 months in a large vat, 27 in the wood and at least 3 in bottle. Viña Cubillo often possesses a good deep colour with a tinge of brown, some maturity in the nose and a taste with fruit and elegance. It is not a great Rioja, or one with a long aftertaste, but it is agreeable and well balanced. Its grapes are 50% Tempranillo, 30% Garnacha, 10% Mazuelo, 10% Graciano: the recipe for all this bodega's red Riojas.

By putting its Viña Bosconia in a Burgundy bottle the bodega indicates that this is a red Rioja with rather more strength and generosity than the others. Usually this is true – but not always. The wine of the difficult year 1979, for example, was not at all full-bodied in taste. Viña Bosconia spends 6 months in a large vat, 4 years in cask and a minimum 6 months in bottle.

R. López de Heredia Viña Tondonia

lift shaft was tastefully provided with a pointed roof with matching red woodwork. The present chairman of the board of this wholly family concern is Rafael's son Pedro López de Heredia Ugalde. It was he who in June 1984 conducted King Juan Carlos and Queen Sofia round the premises, the only bodega the royal couple visited during their official stay in Haro.

The windmill

Down through the years López de Heredia has remained a strictly traditional concern, a bulwark of conservatism. There is abundant evidence of this, such as in the office building next to the entrance, the interior of which is the same as it was three generations ago. The panelling goes high up the walls, there are cream and yellow tiles on the floor, splendid old counters and pigeon holes, solid furniture and thick wooden doors with ground glass on which the words *dirección* or *probador* are engraved. Framed drawings, deeds and diplomas hang on the walls. And if you cross the site going towards the Ebro you come to the bodega's own windmill on the river bank, which is high at this point. This draws up ground water, supplying 80% of the firm's requirements.

Wooden fermentation vats

It hardly seems necessary to point out that López de Heredia still uses wooden fermentation vats. These are lined up in a large hall diagonally behind the office building. The larger ones, of 5,280 (US 6,240) gallons capacity, are used for red wine; the smaller type, holding 2,200 (US 2,600) gallons, for white. After fermentation all the wines stay in these and other vats for five or six months to rest, letting any sediment settle naturally. That this bodega believes in wood was demonstrated at the centenary celebrations in 1977. In an area behind the fermentation hall it was not a statue, plaque or anything of this nature that was unveiled, but five completely new closed oak vats of 15,800 (US 18,700) gallons capacity. These were intended for storing young wine. For the same purpose López de Heredia still uses the old *bocoys*, 132– (US 156) gallon barrels – in France they are called *demi-muids*. These were formerly employed mainly for transporting wine; five of them would be loaded on a cart, three below and two above.

Black mould everywhere

The extensive underground cellars also remain just as they always were. After descending a flight of 39 steps the visitor arrives in a silent complex of passages where all the walls and archways are covered with black mould. The temperature and humidity here are constant at 12° C and 80% respectively. A very special cellar is the *cementerio*, where the López de Heredia family has its private stock of wines, thousands of bottles from all the great years in their mould-covered recesses. In this totally silent room there stands a vast tasting table made out of the lower part of a fermentation vat. The cobwebs descend from the lamp above to a vine shoot standing on the table: you could think yourself in the dungeons of a haunted castle, or on the set for a tragic opera.

Coopers

All the *barricas* that López de Heredia uses are underground. There are about 14,000 of them, every barrel made in the cooper's workshop here from American oak. The bodega keeps at least five coopers on its staff. They maintain the barrels and carry out necessary repairs. The firm keeps its casks in service for a long time, for as long as they remain usable in fact. With very many of these casks the influence of the wood on the wine is therefore small. The result is that even the wood-aged white wines here can remain extremely fresh. Naturally enough, wine is still racked by hand here; nor is it to be wondered at that the wines are fined with fresh whites of egg.

A stock of 2.5 million bottles of wine is held here of which about 1 million are *reservas*. These wines are never filtered and are transferred straight from the barrels to

López de Heredia's bestseller is the red Viña Tondonia, sold in its sixth year after 6 months in a large vat, 5 years in cask and 6 months in bottle. It has refinement, style and a beautiful balance between fruit and wood. The wood is not predominant, nor is the vanilla aroma that goes with it.

In good years a quantity of Viña Tondonia is selected for gran reserva treatment: 6 months in vat, 6 years in cask and at least 3 years 8 months in bottle. The relationship with the younger Viña Tondonia is clear, but this Rioja usually has a firmer taste, more wood and vanilla, greater maturity and a stronger colour.

Opposite page, above left:
Some of the bodega's average stock of 2.5 million bottles.

Opposite page, centre left:
One of the last photographs of Rafael López de Heredia.

Opposite page, below left:
Exports manager Anastasio Gutiérrez.

Right:
Wooden fermentation vats in an old part of the bodega.

Below:
Signatures of the King and Queen of Spain from the guest book.

Bottom:
The private cellar of the López de Heredia family. Guests often come here for wine tasting.

The principle at this bodega is that all activities and processes are carried out by its own staff of about 50, which includes painters, mechanics etc.

The average annual production of 10,600 (US 12,500) gallons comes entirely from the firm's own vineyards.

The bodega uses no subsidiary brand names.

About 75% of production is sold in Spain. The rest goes to some 30 countries, including Switzerland, West Germany, Britain, the United States, the Netherlands, Denmark, France, Austria and Venezuela.

Except for reservas and gran reservas, all the wines are filtered once.

the bottles, patiently by hand. Care is taken that the bottles are filled as full as possible, with minimum space between cork and wine – which means a minimum of oxygen. This slows the development of the wine. Additionally all the bottles of *reserva* are given a temporary wax seal over the neck to protect the cork. This is replaced by the normal lead type years later when the bottles are labelled. A few other bodegas – Rioja Santiago, for example – have reintroduced this old system, although with the ordinary kind of temporary seal, not a wax one.

No crushing

R. López de Heredia Viña Tondonia produces an average of 265,000 (US 310,000) gallons a year. The larger part consists of red wine, although there is a fair amount – 25% – of white. Rosé represents less than half a per cent. The bodega's own vineyards supply about half of the grapes required and the rest is bought in in the form of grapes: the firm has 320 acres under contract with small growers for this purpose. All the grapes come from the Rioja Alta. When they arrive the grapes for red wine are destalked but not crushed, but during fermentation the stalks may be added to the must to increase the tannin content a little. Fermentation is followed by the six-month rest period mentioned earlier; after this the wines, now clear, flow into the barrels by gravity.

Refinement and style

All the red Riojas here have the same mixture of grapes: 50% Tempranillo, 30% Garnacha, 10% Mazuelo and 10% Graciano. The difference comes in the selections made and for how long they are matured. The youngest red wine is called Viña Cubillo. This is given the customary 6 months in vat, followed by 27 months in cask and at least 3 in bottle. It is an elegant, good *crianza* with maturity, a softly fresh taste, a measure of wood and a brownish gleam to the colour. The Viña Bosconia, the only red wine that López de Heredia markets in a Burgundy bottle, is more mature, mellower and usually broader in taste. It spends 4 years in the barrel and at least 6 months in bottle and is therefore entitled to the *reserva* classification. The Viña Tondonia 6° año also comes in this category. Wines bearing this name come solely from the Viña Tondonia vineyard. After 6 months in vat, 5 years in cask and a minimum of 6 months in bottle, Viña Tondonia has developed into a refined, stylish, splendid wine with a good balance between wood and fruit. Its nearest relation is the outstanding Viña Tondonia *gran reserva*, a Rioja that usually has more strength, wood and maturity; the 1973 first appeared on the market in 1984, by which time it had spent 6 months in vat, $6\frac{1}{2}$ years in barrel and $3\frac{3}{4}$ years in the bottle.

Exceptionally fragrant white

López de Heredia makes various types of

R. López de Heredia Viña Tondonia

white wine, including the semi-sweet Viña Romania and sweet Viña Zaconia. The accent, however, is on dry wines, all aged in the wood and made from 50% Viura and 50% Malvasia grapes. The Viña Gravonia, for example, is given three years in the barrel. In its nose this wine has some vanilla and a vague earthy hint. Its taste is agreeably fresh and elegant in structure. This wine comes from the firm's own vineyards, as does the white Viña Tondonia. The latter wine can be extraordinarily fragrant, with a perfume of spices, herbs and vanilla that almost drugs your senses, and lingers even in the emptied glass. It rests for around 5 years in wooden casks and then spends at least 6 months in bottle. Despite its age and its long contact with wood, the white Viña Tondonia retains sufficient freshness. The wood does not dominate the other taste elements or the elegant structure. After tasting this striking Rioja I asked the export manager Anastasio Guttiérrez what dishes he would serve it with. His answer was that the wine tasted excellent with the finer varieties of fish and with white meats; and he had recently enjoyed it with raw oysters – a successful combination that had brought him surprise and satisfaction.

The rare 1964

The most memorable white wine I was given to taste at López de Heredia was the

1964. This *reserva* has never been on sale, for the quantity – about 12,000 bottles – was too limited. It was purely and simply because of its exceptional quality that the bodega had kept this wine apart; and there was a special curiosity to see how a white wine from such a great year would develop. The first occasion on which this rare 1964 was presented was during the centenary in 1977. I was given a glass of it 20 years after its birth. Neither colour, nose or taste gave any indication of its great age. In fact the wine made an almost youthful impression and seemed suitable for laying down for a long period. I was told that it had been in the casks for seven years, but that very old ones had been used deliberately so that the influence of the wood could be minimal and the oxidation very limited. The refined character and the freshness of this Rioja therefore remained entirely intact.

A deviant rear label

The story of R. López de Heredia is not complete without a mention of its own rear

label. This does not contain the customary, official, even legally prescribed terms such as *crianza, reserva* etc., but a formula from the Consejo Regulador guaranteeing that the wine in question is entitled to give Rioja as its place of origin. The bodeja has always sold its wines as *vino de Rioja* without any further details other than its year of bottling. An exception was made for the firm and it was given permission to continue labelling in this way. It was allowed to go on using its own style of rear label – as it had done for an estimated 25 years.

Although bottles of López de Heredia are shipped out to about 30 different countries, three-quarters of production remains in Spain itself. The reason for this is simple: demand always exceeds supply. Given the quality of the wines, this is hardly surprising.

The youngest bottled red wine from Bodegas y Viñedos is the Lar de Sotomayor crianza. This composition of 70% Tempranillo and 30% Garnacha spends 24 months in tank, 12 in cask and 12 in bottle. It is a somewhat rustic, traditional Rioja with a robust taste, good wood and vanilla and a slight note of freshness. It can develop further in bottle.

The name Marcos covers both a crianza and a reserva. The latter offers the better quality, especially since 1975. Earlier vintages used to taste somewhat dry. Tempranillo (80%) and Garnacha (20%) are the grapes. The reserva stays for at least 3 years in tank, 3 in cask and 2 in bottle. For still older wines the bodega uses the gran reserva brand name Don Marcos.

Below:
Ollauri, with vineyards in the background.

Opposite page, above left:
Cleaned comportas stand drying in the sun; picking can begin.

Opposite page, above right:
Five coopers work at López de Heredia.

Opposite page, below left:
The grapes arrive.

Opposite page, below centre:
The grapes in their comportas are wheelbarrowed into the fermentation hall.

Opposite page, below right:
One of the underground galleries where casks are stacked five high.

The bodega has been in existence since the 14th century, but it was completely revitalized in 1970.

A fine old wine press stands to the left of the entrance.

The above-ground part of the building in Ollauri dates from 1830.

The vinification section Tudelilla has a storage capacity of 550,000 (US 650,000) gallons.

The new "emperor" of the Rioja, who owns (in order of take-over) Bodegas y Viñedos, Franco-Españolas, Lan and Federico Paternina, is Marcos Eguizábal Ramires. There is a picture of him on page 96. Born in Villar de Arnedo his father was a wine merchant and Marcos had 13 brothers. At first the family sold wine in bulk (still in skins then), but later in bottles as well. The quality was high: Eguizábal

senior entered some 30 competitions in the region, winning 28 of them. His Rioja Tio Julio even achieved an "excellent" rating at Bordeaux. So Marcos Eguizábal became familiar with wine at an early date. After setting up successful enterprises in various areas of business (including a dessert grape concern in Almería), this Riojan returned to his native district. He has many plans, including experiments with new grape varieties.

Bodegas y Viñedos

Many old bodegas in the Rioja have the characteristics of an iceberg: the part showing above the surface forms only a fraction of the actual whole. Bodegas y Viñedos in the heart of Ollauri is a good example. From outside it looks like a small concern, but it stands above a large complex of cellars that goes down nearly 50 ft. The oldest part of this system dates from the 14th century and has Moorish style arches. That the cellars have been intensively used is apparent from the very worn steps. At all events they have been in almost continuous use for storing wine since the beginning of the 19th century. In 1813 this was the Paternina family's first cellar. The Bodegas Federico Paternina's present cellars – also very ancient – are in Ollauri as well. Bodegas y Viñedos uses this underground system mainly for storing bottles of wine. There are usually some half million bottles of Rioja ageing here: 10,000 bottles in one alcove, 65,000 in an area further in, and so on. The temperature

remains at a virtually constant 11.5° C and the humidity at 80%. Mould is everywhere on the walls, as well as on the casks of *reservas* placed here. Technical manager Lorenzo García told me that the mould can give the wine a slight aroma of mushrooms.

Vinification centre

However, even with all its cellars, the bodega in Ollauri does not represent the whole picture. Wine is not made here; this is done in Tudelilla, a little town deep in the Rioja Baja. Behind the big weighbridge there is the Bodegas y Viñedos vinification centre. Given the name of this firm – *viñedos* means vineyards – you would expect it to have a considerable area of vine-growing land of its own; but in fact it has hardly any and nearly all its grapes have to be bought in. Wine ready made is only exceptionally purchased: it can happen that not a drop is needed for years on end. The bodega selects its grapes in all three

districts, so that they come in from Rioja Alta and Alavesa as well as Baja. The grapes intended for red wine are left as intact as possible: they are simply destalked and seeded. This means that the fruit undergoes a sort of semi-*macération carbonique*. In the concrete fermentation tanks the temperature is kept below a maximum 27 to 28° C. Rosé and white are fermented four to five degrees below this. The annual production from Bodegas y Viñedos is around 660,000 (US 780,000) gallons. The firm bottles only 20 to 25% of this itself; the rest is sold in bulk to other bodegas. All the bulk wines are stabilized by the cold method, and the rosé and white Riojas bottled on the premises also undergo this treatment.

Ageing in two bodegas

The red wines for bottling spend at least two years in the tank in Tudelilla, or are moved earlier on to Ollauri where there are

Left:
Casks in one of the underground passages at Bodegas y Viñedos.

Below:
Marcos Eguizábal. After buying Bodegas y Viñedos he took over Franco-Españolas, Lan and Federico Paternina a few years later, in early 1985; this gave him control of about a quarter of Rioja production.

Bodegas y Viñedos

large closed wooden vats plus a very big cask, in which wines can also be stored. After fining and filtering the red wines go into casks. There are about 1,600 of these, distributed between the two bodegas. They are made of American oak and remain in service for about 20 years. The wines are racked every six months. The last treatment consists of a second filtering, through cellulose plates this time.

In Ollauri there is not only the bodega's office, but also a pleasant reception and dining room. At the bar here, opposite a stained-glass window, I have tasted the whole range of the bottled wines. The youngest red that is featured is a *crianza*,

the Lar de Sotomayor. It is made from 70% Tempranillo and 30% Garnacha grapes. The wine seemed to have a full-bodied taste, a fresh tone and the familiar wood-vanilla aroma. I thought this Rioja rather traditional and rustic in character. In contrast with the readily and quickly drinkable wines from other bodegas, it seemed to me that this was a *crianza* that could develop further in the bottle.

The older wines

For me the best wine at this tasting was the Marcos *reserva* of 1975. After 3 years in tank, 3 in cask and 3 in bottle this proved to

have become an excellent Rioja: with nuances in its perfume, a taste you could chew on, and still with the potential for further ageing in the bottle. The proportion of Tempranillo here is 80%. The 1973 was at a somewhat lower level, although it was far from unpleasant; it was just that it was a little drier, lighter and, naturally, more aged. This wine, too, was sold as a *reserva*. The designation *gran reserva* is allocated only to really mature wines – only to the 1970 among the samples I tasted. This brownish coloured wine, called the Don Marcos, also seemed slightly too dry to my taste.

Improvements possible

About 80% of Bodegas y Viñedos' production is of red Rioja; a little more than half of the rest consists of rosé. The bodega was not able to give me really young vintages of either rosé or white – only four-year-old wines. The rosé had the Garnacha as its basis and tasted round and fat rather than fruity and vital; on the positive side it should be reported that the alcoholic strength was limited to 11.5%. The pale-coloured white wine was pure, fresh and light (10%), but did not have much else to offer. It was made from 70% Malvasia and 30% Viura. Both wines carried the brand name Lar de Sotomayor, but I have also seen them labelled La Emperatriz. While Bodegas y Viñedos should be complimented on some of its red wines, the rest of the Riojas it bottles could do with improvement: and it is by no means impossible that this will come. For after the firm had experienced various changes of owner, in 1982 a majority shareholding was acquired by Marcos Eguizábal Ramirez, a dynamic entrepreneur who at the beginning of 1985 also took over Franco-Españolas, Lan and Federico Paternina. This energetic man lives in Madrid, but feels himself very much involved in his businesses and visits them frequently.

Bodegas Beronia

Ollauri

Between 900 and 800 BC many nomadic tribes migrated into the valleys of the Ebro and its tributaries. One of these tribes was the Berones, tall, strong people with fair hair. They found a sheltered, well-wooded area with a mild climate, situated along the Ebro, and there they settled. At full moon they worshipped their gods and they had a deep respect for the stars and other natural phenomena. Later the Berones were to mingle with the neighbouring Basque people, particularly in the Tirón, Glera and Najerilla basins, and they also founded the first villages here. Their land was called Beronia and it largely covered the present Rioja. Bodegas Beronia was named in honour of these early inhabitants. The firm was founded by a group of friends from San Sebastián, who built their own bodega just outside Ollauri in 1973; and their first wines were made in that same year.

Taken over and expanded

A little less than a decade later, in early 1982, the firm changed hands. Gonzales Byass, the sherry and brandy house, bought 86% of the shares. This company, based in Jerez de la Frontera, had been looking around the Rioja for more than four years in search of a suitable acquisition. The arrival of Byass had immediate consequences. Within two years the tank capacity for fermentation and storage was almost quadrupled, to 506,000 (US 600,000) gallons. At the same time the number of casks was doubled, to more than 5,000, and the cellarage for bottles was increased tenfold. Naturally, production rose as well. At the take-over Beronia was making around 55,000 (US 65,000) gallons a year; two years later it was 143,000 (US 170,000) gallons.

Specialist in reds

The bodega is surrounded in almost idyllic fashion by vineyards on all sides. From the

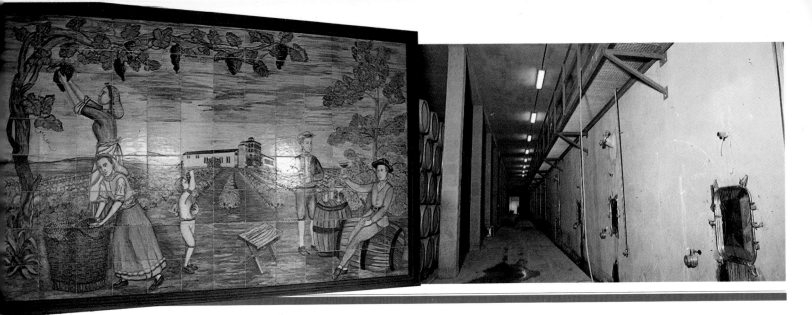

reception area on the top floor of the office building you have a splendid view of these surroundings. The adjacent 17 acres are the only vineyards that the company itself owns. They are planted exclusively with black grapes (mainly Tempranillo) and in 1984 were still supplying 10% of the grapes required by the bodega. Obviously, with the increase of production this percentage will drop steadily. Beronia is equipped to process around 500 tons of grapes during the harvest; the rest is bought in as wine. The bodega specializes in red Rioja. White represents only one tenth of the volume and there are no plans to increase the quantity. Rosé is not made at all.

Cold treatment

The red wine the company makes itself or buys in comes from grapes that are destalked and crushed in the normal way. In this bodega the temperature is not kept especially low during fermentation: for red wine the ceiling is 32° C; this was in fact the case before Gonzalez Byass took over. Vinification has not been drastically altered. Partly to stabilize the wines for export (risen from nothing to about half of sales since 1982) they are all given cold treatment. In addition they are filtered twice, once through earth and once through sterilized plates.

Continuing control

Although there may be a question mark concerning the number of treatments the bodega subjects its red wines to, extreme care is taken over ageing in the wood. It therefore sees to it that new casks are used only for new wine, believing that it is young red wine that is most improved by intensive, very direct contact with oak. Wine in new, or nearly new, *barricas* is racked three times in the year. This, too, is done deliberately to further the maturing of the young wine. After the racking the empty casks are thoroughly cleaned out: with hot water the first time, then with cold on the two subsequent occasions. Not all the casks are made in the Rioja; around

60% of them come from Jerez de la Frontera. Gonzalez Byass, after all, uses oak casks on a large scale for its sherry. In all cases the wood comes from the American state of Ohio. Beronia's serious approach to the storing of its wines is also apparent from the stringent quality control. Every wine from every cask is tasted each month. The bottled wines (it keeps an average of around one million in store) are also followed through. Every three months one sample bottle from the *reservas* is opened; this is done every two months for the other wines.

The effect of wood ageing

To demonstrate the importance of ageing in the wood, professional visitors are often offered an unusual tasting. They are served three glasses, each filled with a Rioja at a different stage of its development. The first wine I tasted had had about one year in the tank and also its first filtering, but had not yet come into contact with wood. The second wine, from an earlier vintage, had six months in cask behind it. The third, from the same year as number two, was almost ready for bottling after 18 months in wood. The differences between these three wines were striking. The second one was already considerably more exciting in taste and nose than the first; the wood has clearly added a dimension. The last wine offered more wood, and at the same time greater maturity, better balance and more refinement. Wood, patience and care are essential for almost all red Riojas – as the Beronia tasting unmistakably showed.

Two main brands

The firm sells its younger types of wine, both red and white, under the brand name Berón. The older kinds carry the name Beronia (with Beridia sometimes also used for identical wines). In the first instance only the Beronia line was marketed in Spain, but both this and the Berón went abroad from the start. The Berón red receives a maturing period of a minimum 12 months in tank and at least the same in

cask. It is a supple Rioja, with sufficient wood and a pleasant taste. It is made from 60% Tempranillo, 30% Garnacha and 10% other grape varieties. The white Berón is given just 12 months in the tank. It has a very refreshing taste which seemed to me better than its nose. At 90% the Viura is by far its most important component, supplemented by other unspecified varieties.

Impressions of the older wines

As a *crianza* the Beronia red is given 12

Bodegas Beronia produces about
13,000 to 15,500 (US 15,500 to
18,000) gallons of dry white
Rioja annually, and there are no
plans as yet for more. The wine
ferments at 18 to 20° C and, like
all the red wines here, it is
stabilized cold. Viura (90%) is
the most important grape. There
is a slight green tinge in the
colour; and a lot of freshness in
the taste as well as fruit. The
perfume can sometimes be
somewhat dull.

The red Berón mostly goes on
sale after a minimum 12 months
in tank and 12 months in cask. It
is made up from 60%
Tempranillo, 30% Garnacha and
10% various grapes. Some wood
and vanilla is clearly perceptible
in nose and taste; it is a Rioja
that is easy and supple in the
drinking.

The bodega produces its
crianzas, reservas and gran
reservas under the brand name
Beronia. Wines in the top
category are the most robust,
although this is never a firm for
heavily powerful wines.
Characteristics are purity,
suppleness, the presence of
vanilla, slight nuances and a
refined maturity. In all cases the
Tempranillo is the most
important grape (70%), followed
by the Garnacha (20%).

Bodegas Beronia buys most of its
grapes and wines in Rioja Alta;
only about 20% comes from Rioja
Baja.

The most important foreign
customers are Britain, West
Germany and Netherlands.

In order to compare its products
at consumer level with those from
other bodegas, Beronia regularly
buys considerable quantities of
bottles of wine in ships and these
are then tasted at Ollauri.

Bodegas Beronia

months in tank, 18 in wood and 18 in bottle. These are minimum times, often exceeded in practice. In comparison with the Berón this wine contains rather more Tempranillo (70%) and less Garnacha (20%), with the proportion of other varieties remaining the same. The same mixture is found in the *reservas* and the *gran reservas*. The 1978 I tasted was a wine that after six years in wood had some brown in its colour, vanilla in its scent, a softly mature, but not especially full-bodied taste, some unobtrusive nuances, a slightly fresh tinge and a reasonable aftertaste. I thought it a little short of concentration and "meat". But it should be pointed out here that I have only tasted older wines from the period before the Gonzalez Byass take-over. It is possible that wines from this bodega from 1982 onwards will gain in strength and structure. A 1982 sampled young gave some indication of this. Whereas the *reservas*, after 12 months in tank, have at least 18 months ageing in wood and the same time in bottle, for the *gran reservas* this maturation period is extended to 2 years in cask and 3 to 6 in bottle. The 1975 *gran reserva* naturally tasted fuller and more mature than the 1978 *reserva* mentioned above. I also made the acquaintance of Beronia's first wine, the still very vital 1973. There was an abundance of noble wood present here, for all the casks were new then.

Although not all its wines are really impressive, Beronia may well be a bodega worth following. For Gonzalez Byass not only possesses a great deal of capital and the necessary expertise, but with its sherry and other products it has shown that the concept of quality is high on its list of priorities – a watchword in fact. And its serious approach to the business in hand at Bodegas Beronia is irrefutably shown by the investments it has made there.

The Montebuena brand name is used on labels for the younger types of wine, such as the dry white (100% Viura) and the red sin crianza (75% Tempranillo, supplemented by Viura and Garnacha). The juice and modest fruit of the white Rioja gives it a good deal of charm (but not breeding); the red has a nice, supple taste in which a touch of ripe fruit can be discerned.

This is the label of the wine that is sold as a crianza, after 12 months in tank and 12 in cask. Its quite strong colour usually has a dark tint – as with all the red wines from this cooperative – and wood and vanilla are clearly manifested in nose and taste. This wine is reasonably full in the mouth; in addition the 1980 had a touch of caramel. Grapes are the same as for the Montebuena.

The Castillo Labastida reserva is matured first in the tank and then 24 months in cask, followed by 12 to 24 in bottle. In its supple, not really deep taste, there is a good deal of vanilla and it has a strong, dark-red colour. In some vintages an aroma of ripe raspberries can be picked up. Although Labastida is included in the brand name of this Rioja, on most of its labels the cooperative uses simply "Bodega S. Coop." as its business name.

Only a very limited number of cooperatives have casks, let alone a gran reserva in their collection; Labastida forms an exception to both rules. It sells a gran reserva that has spent about 1 year in the tank, 3 in cask and at least 3 years in bottle. The wine is dark coloured, soundly structured and vinous, with a mellow well-matured taste. There is a mesh over the bottle.

The Labastida Cooperative

The Labastida cooperative is one of the most recent to be founded in Rioja Alavesa and dates from 1965. Its white buildings stand on the edge of Labastida, on the Brinas side. Most of its 160 or so members live in Labastida itself, but there are also some in Briñas and Salinillas de Buradón. Every year the cooperative processes between 2,000 and 2,500 tons of grapes, which amounts to an annual production of about 350,000 (US 415,000) gallons. Nearly 90% of this is red. In contrast to the traditional Rioja Alavesa method, the black grapes are destalked and crushed: *macération carbonique* is not employed here. Fermentation takes place in rectangular, white-painted concrete tanks, which are also used for storage. A few years after being set up the cooperative bought wooden casks. In the beginning not only some of its own red Riojas were aged in

these, but also wines from other bodegas in the district. This no longer happens and the 1,000 casks it possesses (500 of them bought in 1983) are now used solely for the benefit of the cooperative. They are all of American oak.

One of the better cooperatives

The proportion of wine that the Labastida cooperative handles in the bottle is still limited – about 20%. It is, however, increasing gradually and part of it is even exported. Among regular customers for its bulk wine are La Rioja Alta, Domecq and Bilbaínas. The concern employs various brand names for its bottled red wines. The youngest of these is sold as Montebuena or Cavas Oro Vales. This is a Rioja with a reasonably deep colour and a pleasant, supple taste, well provided with mature fruit. The *crianza* has been given the name Viña Solagüen. This in fact receives one year in cask. Wood and vanilla are

definitely present; in addition the 1980 had a hint of caramel. Even more vanilla was discernible in the Castillo Labastida *reserva*, a dark-coloured, supple wine that is marketed after at least one to two years in cask plus two years in bottle. The cooperative also produces a *gran reserva*, a sound, vinous Rioja with considerable wood in its perfume and full-bodied taste. The Tempranillo is predominant in all these red wines, with 75% or more, the rest comprising Viura and Garnacha grapes. Although I did not sample the rosé I did make the acquaintance of the dry white wine. Although the cooperative does not yet have cooling plant available it nevertheless managed to retain some fruit in this dry Rioja. This makes it a charming, softly fresh, pure wine. The must for the bottled variant – of the Montebuena brand – is pressed out by the weight of the Viura grapes themselves.

This bodega's bottled wines show that it must be reckoned among the best of the Riojan cooperatives.

In all probability red wines from this small bodega contain 40 to 45% Tempranillo plus an undetermined mix of other varieties. The wine that carries the above cream-coloured label usually has 3 to 3½ years in cask. It is clear-coloured Rioja, with an elegant, fresh slightly juicy taste, a little terroir and a correct aftertaste. "This is how all Riojas should be," is what Francisco Martinez de Ayala said of his 1980.

The Viña Mendiate label is generally used only for older wines, along with that of Viña Mendiguria. Among those I have tasted was the 1970, a Rioja that after nearly 15 years was still vital, with freshness and even fruit. Wood and vanilla were not really strongly in evidence. The wine had an elegant taste, yet offered rather more "backbone" and length than the type described left. The 1970 had been in cask for more than 10 years.

Right:
Besides bottles the tasting room also has cooper's tools, mementoes of bullfights and many other, often dusty, items.

Below:
Martinez de Ayala, father and son, in the tasting and sales room of their bodega. Behind this room the wine matures in casks and bottles. Vinification takes place elsewhere in the village.

Below right:
The family coat of arms.

Bodega Martinez de Ayala

The cellars of Bodegas Martinez de Ayala lie behind the weathered facade of a large town house in Labastida. Its atmosphere is unique. In the two large chambers that serve as hall, storage place, sales and tasting areas, dusty tools hang on the dark-grey, thick stone walls along with signed photographs of long-forgotten bullfighters and many other reminders of the past. And in this property, which is at least three hundred years old, the cellar where the casks are stored has an earthen floor, mould-covered walls and a cobwebbed wooden ceiling. It simply could not be more traditional. Its owner, Francisco Martinez de Ayala, the grandson of the man who founded this small firm in 1880, talks of the "only craftsman's bodega left in the Rioja". It used to operate under the name of Bodega Bordelesa, which is still painted over the entrance to the cellar with the casks. Francisco's grandfather started out with a cooper's business and for that reason had many contacts with Bordeaux.

Traditional methods

It is not only the appearance here that is traditional: the methods are too. Thus the grapes go into the open wooden fermentation vats stalks and all; and you would look in vain for filters at Martinez de Ayala. The wines are simply fined. As in the past, the grapes are not picked or vinified separately – they are all lumped together. Francisco himself owns some 15 acres, planted with an uncertain mix of grapes. Probably there is 40 to 45% Tempranillo while the proportions of Graciano and Mazuelo must be very small. Besides its own grapes the bodega also processes fruit from a few other properties. Some made wine is also purchased. Total annual production is 13,200 to 15,400 (US 15,600 to 18,200) gallons. All but half a per cent of this is red wine. It is sold in small casks as well as bottles (about 30,000 in a year).

Characteristically Alavesan

The 400 casks the firm has at its disposal are mostly old. The wines often stay in them for an undetermined time, for frequently they are only bottled as the need arises. The same rather casual approach applies to labelling. I had the impression that the customer could, in a manner of speaking, decide what label he got. Martinez de Ayala's red wines are very typically Alavesan: somewhat light in colour, fresh and elegant. On the one hand I thought they lacked fruit and concentration, but on the other I enjoyed their elegant structure and great vitality. The better vintages from this house remain perfectly drinkable for 30 to 40 years.

Francisco himself tipped the 1981 as a very great wine, one he probably would not be there to experience at its best.

Left:
Labastida's main street with its two churches in the background. The one with the tall tower is centrally situated; the one to the left is built further out on a hill.

Below centre:
A private house was built above the new bodega, completed in 1983.

Below right:
Javier de Santiago, joint owner of the bodega.

The black grapes are crushed and destalked here – the traditional Rioja Alavesan wine-making method is not followed.

The wording on the label illustrated is to be altered; the name Señorio de Arana is to be used.

The bodega is not yet equipped for cold stabilization of wines.

Tank capacity is about 176,000 (US 208,000) gallons.

In addition to stainless-steel tanks there are fibreglass ones for storage.

This firm does not export much.

This bodega buys most of its grapes and wines directly from growers, in San Asensio, San Vicente de la Sonsierra, the Logroño area and elsewhere.

Bodegas Señorio de Arana

The wine merchant Gonzalo Rojas, who lived in Bilbao, bought his own bodega in Laguardia in 1905. The little firm – Rojas y Cia – acquired an excellent reputation and it is said that even French importers came here specially to buy wines. After the death of its founder the bodega passed into other hands. The present owners are José de Santiago and his son Javier. As they were cramped for space in Laguardia they moved the business to another site, just to the west of Labastida. There in 1983 work on a completely new bodega was finished, including a house for Santiago senior to live in. The name of the firm was also changed. Señorio del Oja was used at first (it can still be seen on older labels and boxes), but later the Consejo Regulador forbade this and so the firm is now called Bodegas Señorio de Arana.

Stainless-steel tanks

The advantage of building a new bodega is that you can derive the maximum benefit from the latest technological developments. Wood and concrete are no longer used for vinification at Labastida. Fermentation here takes place in stainless-steel tanks. In other aspects, too, the firm makes a modern, functional impression. Atmosphere is a forgotten concept here. The bodega owns just over 6 acres of vineyard, not enough to meet its requirements, and so some 200 tons of grapes have to be bought annually, together with some made wine. Production fluctuates between 33,000 and 55,000 (US 39,000 and 65,000) gallons a year, with the emphasis on red. The cellar for the casks is underground, where 600 of them are stacked four high. The red wines are filtered before going into the casks, a process that is repeated before bottling.

Three brand names

The bodega operates with three names for its Riojas: Viña del Oja, Sommelier and Viñaldea. According to the cellarman the quality is the same. The sin crianza is a nice, but not very memorable wine. The crianza was rather more captivating, thanks to a concentrated taste, a vanilla aroma, a pleasant maturity and a solid colour. As with the other red wines the Tempranillo dominates, with around 90%. I tasted only one reserva from this house, the 1973. It seemed rather light in taste to me and I thought it somewhat lacking in intensity. These and other wood-aged Riojas I tasted here were made in the old cellars at Laguardia; it is possible that their standards will improve with vintages from the new premises.

La Granja Remélluri

The most idyllically situated bodega in the Rioja is La Granja Remélluri. To reach it you take the narrow, winding road out of Labastida in the direction of Ribas and the Sierra de Cantabria. At the entrance to the estate there are still no buildings in sight. You come to them only after driving for a few hundred yards over an unsurfaced road, again a winding one. The bodega lies more or less at the foot of the mountains, at a height of nearly 1,000 ft. The view over the Ebro valley is marvellous and the silence complete. Wine has been made in this out-of-the-way spot for a very long time: parts of old stone presses, for grapes and olives, have been found on the land here, as well as stone troughs in which the grapes used to be trodden by foot. Other reminders of the past are the medieval stone coffins you come across. The name *granja* (Spanish for "farm") arose because Cistercian monks practised farming and horticulture hereabouts for the monastery of Nuestra Señora de Toloño. In fine weather you can see its ruins up on a neighbouring hilltop; 300 monks once lived there.

Total renovation

Around 1960 the estate – in full La Granja Nuestra Señora de Reméllur – was in a sorry condition. The vineyard had not been replanted for decades and the house served as a rudimentary hunting lodge for a group of men from Bilbao. There was neither electricity nor running water. Water had to be drawn from a well. Then the property was acquired by Jaime Rodríguez Salís, an entrepreneur from Irún, near the French frontier about halfway between San Sebastián and Biarritz. Together with his family he set about renovating the estate. It cost a great deal of time and money; all the more so since Rodríguez (born 1926), a great wine lover, quadrupled the vineyard area through purchases of additional land. When these transactions had been completed a start was made on replanting

La Granja Remélluri

the existing vineyard, and planting the land lying waste. This took place in the mid-1960s and not long afterwards the building of cellars was begun, for wine could not as yet be made at Granja Remélluri; at that time the grapes were sold to other bodegas.

From wood to stainless steel

In the Rioja there are unfortunately a good many examples of relatively recent bodegas built with little taste and scant regard for their surroundings. The Rodríguez family resolved to do things differently. A handsome building for vinification and maturing was designed, and fitted out and furnished with great attention to detail. For the walls of the first hall with its vats, for example, large pieces of local stone were cut to size by masons from Galicia, and so the building looks about two centuries old. To start with, used wooden vats were bought for fermenting the wine; later new ones were also ordered. With an eye to better temperature control, however, Jaime Rodríguez decided to abandon wood for stainless steel: in 1984 he therefore built a new vinification hall alongside the earlier one and it was ready just in time for that year's harvest.

Painters and paintings

The living quarters were refurbished with great care, making this one of the most tasteful houses I have seen in the Rioja. Meals are eaten in the special atmosphere of the large kitchen, where vegetables from the garden are also bottled. Many paintings hang in the living room with its panoramic outlook. Some bear the signature of the well-known Basque painter Montes Iturrioz; others are the work of Jaime's wife Amaya. Jaime's grandfather also painted and a number of his impressionistic works hang here. During the grape harvest in particular there is a lot of painting done at Granja Remélluri, when it is customary for artist friends to stay here. The Rodríguez family lives on the estate for the whole summer and visits it weekly during the rest

of the year. The drive out from Irún takes about two hours.

Fashionable restaurants

Granja Remélluri processes only grapes from its own land. The whole property totals 124 acres, 79 of them growing fruit-bearing vines. A mixture of 80% Tempranillo and 20% Viura, Mazuelo and Garnacha was decided on. In addition Jaime Rodríguez is experimenting with some old, well-nigh forgotten Riojan grape varieties. The average harvest amounts to some 23,100 (US 27,300) gallons. Although exports are on a rising curve, the wines are

still sold mostly in Spain itself. The bodega has a good relationship with a number of fashionable, influential restaurants who sell its wine under a special label (*Seleccionado por*). And so you find Granja's Rioja at Ama Lur in Barcelona, Zalacaín and Principe de Viana in Madrid, and Arzak and Akelarre in San Sebastián.

Spotlessly maintained

At many estates in Rioja Alavesa the grapes still go into the fermentation vats stalk and all. Here, however, the grapes are destalked and then lightly crushed. The

Only the free-run wine (vin de goutte) is used for this Rioja; the vin de presse is sold. After maturing for 6 to 12 months in the tank, 24 to 26 in cask and at least 12 in bottle, a sound, pure wine emerges, with a firm elegance, a beautiful element of vanilla and a harmonious composition. In quality this Rioja is among the best of the region – even though parts of the vineyard (80% Tempranillo, 20% Viura, Mazuelo and Garnacha) are relatively young.

Opposite page, above left: The wooden fermentation vats used in the early years – still here although since the 1984 harvest stainless-steel tanks have been employed.

Opposite page, above right: In the small cask cellar. There is a larger one twice the length.

Opposite page, below: Jaime Rodríguez with his daughter Amaya in their living room at the estate.

Right: The wine in context.

Below: In the large kitchen.

La Granja Remélluri

wine then stays in the tank until March, when it is transferred to the casks. There is no filtering at this point, in contrast to the general practice in Rioja. Some of the 1,500 casks at the bodega's disposal are of French, some of American oak. In the early days Jaime Rodríguez bought 300 *barriques* from Château La Lagune in the Médoc district of Bordeaux. The rest of the casks were all made in Logroño from American oak. The wine is racked twice a year and the only time it is filtered is just before bottling. During these activities the greatest possible care is taken with general tidiness and cleanliness. This bodega always looks immaculately kept, whether in the three cellars with the casks (two of 165 ft in length, one of 330 ft), the vinification areas, the bottling hall or other rooms.

Exemplary quality

Only one kind of wine is made at Granja Remélluri, a *reserva* (it is hoped eventually to produce a *gran reserva* as well). This Rioja spends 6 to 12 months in tank, 2 to 3 years in wood and at least a year in bottle. The wines I tasted were of an exemplary quality, the more recent vintages being the most impressive. The increasingly better control of vinification, the maturing of the young vines and the arrival of new casks will all have contributed to this. Particularly from 1980 onwards the Riojas produced here have been of an excellent standard, and the wine from the difficult year of 1979 also seems to have been successful. Among the characteristics of the Granja Remélluri wines are a reasonably deep colour (more so than is customary in Rioja Alavesa), a pleasant perfume with some vanilla, and a sound, pure taste with style and a firm elegance. In addition they are possessed of a sound balance. I would reckon them to be already among the best of the district, and their quality will undoubtedly improve still further.

Bodegas Eguren's own land is planted with 75% Tempranillo vines, 10% Garnacha and 15% Viura and Malvasía. The grapes come in in small blue plastic boxes – as intact as possible.

Bodegas Eguren uses the brand name Sierra de Cantabria. The oldest and best type of wine here is the crianza, made mainly from Tempranillo plus some Viura. It receives 1 to 2 years in the tank, followed by the same lengths of time in cask and bottle. These Riojas are of decent quality, albeit somewhat rustic (with a good deal of tannin and an element of old wood). They possess more colour and strength than the average Alavesa wines.

Bodegas Eguren

It sometimes happens during the annual fiesta at San Vicente de la Sonsierra that you cannot get into Bodegas Eguren's original building through the front door. It stands in the main street where there is an *encierro* held daily, with young bulls charging to and fro. The Eguren family has been making wine in this village for four or five generations. One of its ancestors, a Basque, came here one day to buy Rioja – and married the daughter of the house. It was not until 1958, however, that Eguren became a commercially operating bodega of any significance. The brothers Guillermo and Vitorino put their vineyards and capital together, in conjunction with their brother-in-law Martín Cendaya. In the early years the whole of their production went to other bodegas, but in 1974 they decided to supply wine in bottle to individuals and restaurateurs. This meant that space had to be found to store wine in tanks, casks and bottles, as well as for a bottling plant, filters and other equipment. The old bodega with its wooden fermentation vats and large horizontal casks could not be extended, and so the firm moved into garage-like premises below some apartments.

Growing vineyard acreage

Bodegas Eguren produces about 110,000 (US 130,000) gallons a year, of Red Rioja only (white and rosé are purchased outside and merit no further mention). This amount will increase considerably, for the acreage of vineyard owned is being doubled, from 185 to 370. The plots are near San Vicente de la Sonsierra, near Labastida and near Páganos, so all are in the Rioja Alavesa. So far the bodega's vineyards have delivered around 70% of the grapes required, but this percentage will perhaps decline. The rest is bought in in the form of grapes and wine. Eguren vinifies in the traditional manner. The grapes go into the fermentation vats (mostly concrete) with their skins and stalks without being crushed first. To give the wine sufficient colour and tannin the fermentation is allowed to proceed fairly slowly, often lasting 11 or 12 days.

More wine in the bottle

A good deal of the production is sold as "wine of the year" – *vino de cosechero*. It has a respectable quality and a little judicious fruit. A *crianza*, however, is also produced. The manager, Guillermo Eguren, gave me three vintages of this type to taste. These were not the characteristically light, fresh Alavesan wines but Riojas with colour, tannin, a reasonable strength and a suggestion of (old) wood. In one of them, the 1976, I also tasted a vague hint of ripe fruit. The *crianzas* are aged for one to two years in casks of American oak; the bodega has 800 of them. Before the wines go into the casks they are passed through an earthen filter, and through a plate one when they are bottled. Bodegas Eguren bottles about half of its production, but this proportion is increasing gradually. The brand name Sierra de Cantabria is used for all the bottled wines.

Left:
Between two horizontal vats director Antonio Martínez Balmaseda tastes his wine. The firm belongs to Francisco Fernández de Navarrete, Marqués de Legarda, who lives in Madrid.

Below:
Vineyards near Abalos. Bodegas de La Real Divisa processes only grapes from its own vineyards plus fruit from its employees' plots.

Wines that stay more than four years in the wood are not filtered. The rest are filtered just before being bottled.

The casks of American oak that this bodega buys remains in use for 20 to 25 years.

The average stock of bottles varies around 75,000.

Bodegas de La Real Divisa

In the little hill village of Abalos, just beside the square, stands one of Europe's oldest wine cellars. It belongs to La Real Divisa and dates back at least to 1367. Over the gateway are carved a vase and three lilies, the old royal arms of Navarre. Despite this great antiquity, serious wine making has only been practised here since the second half of the 19th century. The then owner, the Marqués de Legarda, was one of the first to make a better-quality Rioja with the help of French experts, but it was not until 1965 that the bodega started bottling on its own account. Today no more wine is sold in bulk. This little firm – producing about 24,750 (US 29,250) gallons a year – is still the property of a Marqués de Legarda, together with his family and a score of small shareholders. Since 1972 it has functioned as a limited company.

Wooden beams

All the grapes for Bodegas de La Real Divisa come from its own 69 acres in Abalos, which are planted with 80% Tempranillo, 15% Viura and 5% Garnacha. Only red wines are made. In the brown-tiled area set aside for the purpose the grapes are destalked and crushed. They then ferment in concrete tanks. For maturing the wine there are large horizontal wooden casks (where it spends 10 months) and roughly 900 barrels. Fifty of these are renewed per year. Some of the barrels are in a very old ground-level cellar with a rough, worn stone floor and a pattern of beams supporting the ceiling. Most of the some 75,000 bottles are underground in the magnificent cellar on various levels that dates from the 14th century or earlier.

A dark-toned taste

For me the nicest wine from La Real Divisa is its *crianza*. After its period in the horizontal casks it spends one to two years in barrel and 2 to 8 months in bottle. Generally there is a refined quality to the dark-toned taste, which tends towards bay and liquorice. The wood is only perceptible in the background. The *reserva* seemed to have lost somewhat in colour and strength in comparison with the *crianza*, and the *gran reserva* was too much dominated by less-than-noble wood for my taste. It is given four years' barrel ageing, which is one to two years more than the *reserva*. The bodega also produces a young Rioja, the Gran Maestre, but I was not given this to sample. It stays in the barrel for 6 to 12 months.

That the owners of the La Real Divisa are looking forward to the future with optimism is clear from the fact that in 1984 a start was made on building an office and a reception hall in living quarters over the working area.

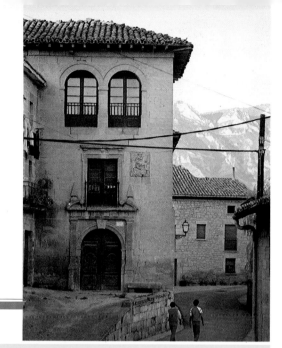

Bodegas SMS

Villabuena is a small village in the middle of the Rioja Alavesa. It is surrounded on all sides by green vineyards and most of the villagers make their livings from wine. This is hardly to be wondered at, for the grapes here are of good quality. For as long as anyone can remember they have always sold for just that little bit more than those from the surrounding area. After the local cooperative, the biggest bodega is the SMS, a concern that produces 33,000 (US 39,000) gallons a year. The name is derived from three families: Samaniego, Milans del Bosch and Solano. It was used for the first time around 1942. Before then the bodega had been called the Marqués de la Solana; honours earned under that name included a gold medal at the 1929 International Exhibition in Barcelona. The exact year of foundation is not known, but it is presumed to lie between 1860 and 1870. At all events, the name of the bodega appears in a deed of 1890. The present owners are six brothers of the Simón Milans del Bosch family, with Juan Pablo as managing director. The bodega stands at the southern entrance to the village, but Juan Pablo himself lives in the 13th-century tower house that Villabuena is built around.

Increasing area planted

Bodegas SMS processes only grapes from its own estate. At the time of my visit about 75 acres were productive, with a further 25 recently planted. In addition another 50 acres was available for expansion. Since 1979 it has been possible to destalk and lightly crush the grapes; before then the traditional Alavesa system had been applied throughout. Most of the fruit is fermented in wooden 4,400- (US 5,200-) gallon vats. There is no temperature control and with no intervention fermentation takes 8 to 15 days. After the *fermentación de primavera* (the spring, or malolactic, fermentation) has run its course the wine is transferred to the casks. Some of these are underground in an authentic, cool damp cellar dating from the 17th century. With increasing production the number of casks is to rise from 650 to around 1,000.

Some casks are destined for the Club de Degustadores Bodegas SMS, a "circle of friends" established in 1981 for whom *reserva* wines are laid down.

Reservas rich in tannin

The Simón family specializes in red wine, of which it produces three variants: a *crianza*, a *reserva* and a *gran reserva*. The grapes for the two latter types are not destalked, the principle being to maintain the classical method for these. I found the 1970 *gran reserva* still had a lot of tannin 14 years or so after its birth, and was dry in taste and aftertaste. The *reserva* Pagos de Torcuato

was fresher, with more vitality, but again with a good deal of tannin and a vague suggestion of bitterness. Its aroma seemed rather "stalky" and it lacked a fully-rounded quality. Wines of this sort need not one but two decades of patience. The *crianza* seemed somewhat more accessible and was firmly rounded, with a little earthiness and even fruit. I did not think it a truly fine, well-nuanced wine, but its quality was broadly speaking worth a "satisfactory". All the wines were made from roughly 88% Tempranillo and 12% Viura. SMS keeps an average 60,000 bottles in store.

Hors d'oeuvres.

Below left (inset):
Fernando Salamero, who has the day-to-day running of the bodega.

Below:
One of the courtyards at the bodega.

In 1872 and 1878 Marqués de Riscal won a silver and a gold medal respectively at Paris exhibitions. In other years and other places medals and diplomas were also carried off. Since 1950, however, the bodega has not taken part in such events.

In 1925 a bottle of Marqués de Riscal went for 100,000 pesetas at a charity auction in Barcelona.

The bodega produces a tiny amount of sweet white wine for local churches: four bottles a week.

Elciego

Herederos Del Marqués De Riscal

After a period of exile in Bordeaux, Camilo Hurtado de Amézaga, bearer of the title of Marqués de Riscal de Alegria, was one of the first to realize the Rioja's potential as a wine region. In the middle of the 19th century he started on the building of a large bodega just outside Elciego, on the Cenicero road. Underground galleries were to form an important component of the business and in 1850 some 200 quarrymen arrived from Galicia to excavate them. Ten years later the bodega was ready at last. A bell dating from 1860 – made in Bordeaux – still hangs on the front of one of the buildings. As the marquis was a great lover of Médoc, that was the kind of wine he tried to make.

This was why in 1860 he planted some of his 494 acres of vineyard with French grape varieties. Figures from that year reveal that Tempranillo, Graciano and Viura accounted for 75% of the vines; 25% was made up from Merlot, Cabernet Sauvignon, Cabernet Franc, Malbec (all from Bordeaux) and Pinot Noir (from Burgundy).

Bodega on the French model

The French element in this bodega was later reinforced when, in 1868, the marquis took Jean Pineau into service as his estate manager. Eight years earlier the province of Alava had brought this Frenchman over from Bordeaux to advise its wine growers. Pineau not only carried out further experiments with French grape varieties, but was also in at the birth of a big expansion programme, intended to produce a bodega to equal the most progressive in the Médoc. The architect undertook detailed studies in France to this end. The new bodega was completed in two stages. It was to be nearly seven decades before it was enlarged again. French influence long remained evident; Frenchmen worked here right up to 1940.

Herederos del Marqués de Riscal

Slow pressing

For its operations from 1883 onward, the bodega introduced the Bordeaux system of vinification in its entirety into the Rioja. The grapes were no longer left to ferment whole but were first destalked and crushed. Fermentation took place in wooden vats, and wooden tanks were used for blending. For maturing the wine the bodega naturally had *barricas bordelesas*, the 50 (US 59) gallon casks used everywhere in Bordeaux. In the casks the wine was fined and racked exactly as in France. The bodega's methods have not been substantially altered since that time, although the wooden fermentation vats were replaced by concrete tanks in 1940. Those fine, red-painted casks are still in service, however, for storing young wine. The 20 round horizontal presses also date from the early days. In these around four tons of *marc* (the mass of skins left after the first pressing) can be pressed. They used to be worked by hand, but motors were attached in 1920. They operate very slowly, which can only be to the benefit of the wine.

International recognition

The innovative, dynamic way in which the marquis (who had also founded the newspaper *El Día* in Madrid) went to work was not restricted simply to the making of wine. Commercial and promotional aspects, too, received his full attention. Not long after the original opening of the bodega, in 1862, he started bottling his own Riojas. He was the first to put metal meshes on his bottles, around the beginning of this century. It has been ascertained that empty Riscal bottles were being filled with wine from other firms, usually not even from the Rioja, and it was to counter this practice that the bodega began putting an *alambrado*, a net, over its bottles. This was secured under the bottle and, in those days, sealed with wax as a guarantee of authenticity. The only period when it became impossible to make and fit these meshes was during the First World War. The bottles were then given a special label certifying that they did indeed contain genuine Rioja from Marqués de Riscal.

The bodega entered its wines for international competitions at an early stage. And with some success, for in 1865 a first prize was won at Bordeaux. There was astonishment on all sides and the jury did not at first believe that this was a Spanish wine; although the bottles entered, it should be noted, contained exclusively Rioja made from the Tempranillo grape. In 1872 there was another competition in Bordeaux. Again the jury was most complimentary, praising the wine for its very Spanish character. But this one had been made purely from French grapes! The two medals and the *diplome d'honneur* depicted on the labels for generations now are a continuing reminder of the prizes won at Bordeaux.

For kings and dictators

The bodega's achievements at international fairs meant that its reputation grew steadily; but success at Brussels in 1910 had a very special consequence. The Spanish king, Alfonso XII, was present at the prize giving and must have uttered an "Olé!" when it was announced that Marqués de Riscal had come first. The monarch decided forthwith to serve only this particular Rioja, and even invited the marquis to his subsequent wedding. Since that time the firm has maintained a good relationship with the Spanish court. Wine was supplied to the king every year (including in the Franco period); and during my visit I saw three 1982 casks in one of the cellars marked *Cosecha Real para su majestad el Rey Juan Carlos I*. His father, too, had had three casks of "royal vintage" reserved for him. But it is not only crowned heads who have been lovers of Marqués de Riscal wines. Mussolini and Hitler, for example, sent aircraft to Logroño to fetch cases of Rioja from this bodega, which transported them from Elciego to the airfield in a Bedford truck. Brezhnev apparently served Marqués de Riscal at a family wedding, and Fidel Castro orders an annual average of 400 cases.

Four families

After the death of Camilo Hurtado de Amézaga the firm passed into the hands of his heirs. Its official name was changed to Vinos de los Herederos del Marqués de Riscal, SA, and this has remained unaltered since. The present owners are distributed among four families; the Salamero family holds the biggest share and runs the business. In one of the other three families there is still a Marquesa de Riscal. She was born towards the end of the Second World War and holds a few shares.

After extensions in 1950 and 1970 the bodega site now occupies 645,600 ft², of which 451,920 are roofed over. The buildings stand on both sides of the road. One of them is the solid former residence of the founder. Although a fire here in 1959

destroyed many photographs and documents, the portrait of the founding Marqués de Riscal was spared. It hangs in one of the rooms and shows an intelligent-looking man with a sensitive mouth and long, spreading side whiskers.

French grape varieties still

In 1860 the bodega possessed 494 acres of vineyard, and that is still the case: but the scattered plots of those days are now more concentrated. Black grapes are grown on 469 acres; nearly 75% of the vines are Tempranillo and the rest Cabernet Sauvignon with a little Merlot. The last two types, not authorized in this region, are permitted here because the bodega has used them right from its foundation year. There were also plantings of Cabernet Sauvignon in 1910 and again in the post-Second World War years. As the Cabernet Sauvignon and the Merlot require different cultivation from the Tempranillo, the 123 acres growing them are provided with poles and wires along which the branches are trained. The French grapes are not used for all the bodega's red wines, only for the *reservas*. Here the proportion has varied from 10 to 50% and above, decided on at each vintage; nowadays it is generally around 15%. This has been the position for nearly all the *reservas* since 1970; earlier in this century higher proportions of French grapes often occurred: 50% in 1952, 45% in 1935, 60% in 1925.

The Cathedral of Wine

The bodega produces about 440,000 (US 520,000) gallons of red Rioja a year. Its own vineyards account for 40% of this; the best is bought elsewhere in the form of grapes. Of the home-grown grapes that are processed, 95% consists of Tempranillo (from Rioja Alavesa) and the rest Viura. After fermentation is completed the red wine goes into casks, of which the firm has at least 30,000 (all these *barricas* are made of American oak; no French wood is used). They are distributed over various cellars, but principally in the underground

galleries. There are 49 of these – 2½ miles long altogether. The casks are nowhere stacked more than four high, because of the arched ceiling. Also underground is Riscal's famous Catedral del Vino, with bottles from all its good years. In many cases they are covered with a grey-white mould and the oldest date back to 1860, the founding year. When the Second World War broke out this cellar was chosen as a possible safe storage place for all the region's art treasures, but in the event it was never used for this purpose. Besides the bottles I saw a very special corkscrew here. Apparently it was designed at the bodega specifically for drawing the corks from horizontal bottles. The corks of the bottles in the 'cathedral' are in fact replaced about every 15 years.

Ageing in the wood: the Riscal practice

Wines resting in the casks are racked relatively frequently: every three months in the first, second and third year. This is done because the firm does not wish to filter the wines at the bottling stage. Fining here is still done with fresh white of egg. The average is six egg whites to a cask. The *crianzas* go on an ordinary bottle line, but the *reservas* are still drawn off the casks by hand. Other types of red Riojas are not known here: the term *gran reserva*, for example, is never used. After bottling the *crianza* remains for at least six months in the cellar, the *reserva* four to five years. Normally the bodega has 2.5 million bottles in stock. All the wines are bottled after three to three and a half years.

Characteristic Alavesa wines

Many laudatory words have been written about the older Marqués de Riscal vintages by Jan Read, Hugh Johnson and others whose expertise I rate highly. There can be no doubt that the *reservas* from this bodega are long-living, more elegant than concentrated, and with the fresh tone that characterizes many Alavesa wines. It would seem obvious to compare them with Bordeaux, but the wines themselves give

Herederos del Marqués de Riscal

little occasion for this. The only actual French factor here now – the grapes – are too much part of the Riojan whole to be of real significance. In fact it may be questioned whether the Cabernet Sauvignon can really thrive in the Rioja Alavesa with its mainly limestone soil. In the Bordeaux region itself this variety gives glorious results in the gravelly vineyards of the Médoc, but is reduced to an entirely subsidiary role on the limestone plateau of Saint-Emilion.

Wherever the truth may lie, the older *reservas* from Herederos del Marqués de Riscal are often very good wines. I remember the elegant 1962, which was only fully ready for drinking after 20 years or so, and combined charm with grace. Some other successes from this house were the *reservas* from 1975, 1970, 1968, 1964, 1958, 1954, 1952, 1950, 1947, 1941, 1938 and 1934 – and this is by no means all of them. However, it has also happened that the bodega has selected very light wines as *reservas*, the 1973 being a relatively recent example.

Variable quality

Although a lack of colour and intensity may be defended, in the *crianzas* included – for this is, after all, the style of this bodega – there can be no excuse for a quality that varies within the vintage. I have for example, tasted two clearly different versions of the 1980. One was extremely acceptable (fairly light colour, pleasant perfume, supple taste with an element of ripe fruit tending towards strawberry); but the other seemed to be on each occasion blessed with quite the wrong aroma (for me it summoned up memories of the American grape juice called Grapette). And I know, too, of at least one importer discovering similarly unacceptable variations of quality in another vintage. In my opinion it is especially important with light Riojas to strive for as high and as completely consistent a quality as possible. It is only under these conditions that this type of Rioja can remain acceptable. Other bodegas can perhaps build up a market for wines

with a lot of colour, strength and generosity; but Herederos del Marqués de Riscal, with its lighter wines, must seek its reputation for total purity of composition. Any dissonance is immediately perceptible in delicate wines. The not-too-distant past shows that this bodega is able to do this. It

Both white wines – from what is officially called Vinos Blancos de Castilla, SA – have metal nets on their bottles. The ordinary kind is in a slender bottle, the Reserva Limousin in a Burgundy-type.

The Marqués de Riscal rosé is bottled about two years after the harvest.

You eat in style in the bodega's dining room, at an oval table with a white cloth and napkins embroidered with the monogram M.R. A white-gloved waiter serves you. The vegetables mostly come from the firm's own garden.

The Marqués de Riscal crianza is made principally from the Tempranillo with at most a very little Viura. The grapes come from the Rioja Alavesa. At its best this is a graceful, supple wine, with a light vanilla aroma, a pleasant perfume and a touch of ripe fruits, particularly strawberries and blackcurrants. After a time in the tank, the wine is matured for 3 to 3½ years in cask and then for at least 6 months in bottle. Unfortunately the quality has fluctuated with different bottlings, which has done the bodega's reputation no good.

The reservas from this bodega spend the same time in cask (3 to 3½ years) as the crianzas, but then have a longer bottle rest. They generally leave the bottle cellar after 4 to 5 years. For these wines French grapes from the firm's own vineyards are used, as well as Tempranillo (with sometimes a little Viura). The percentage of French grapes (mainly Cabernet Sauvignon, plus a little Merlot) lies mostly around 15, but can rise to 50%. The best reservas are elegant but long-lasting Riojas, which can be graceful and charming, and in which neither vanilla nor wood predominates.

Herederos del Marqués de Riscal

is to be hoped, therefore, that there will be a return to a consistent quality, regaining the confidence of all those who have criticized the firm in Spain and beyond.

White wines from Rueda

The bodega produces around 33,000 (US 39,000) gallons of rosé a year but I was not given any to taste; 'It is a compromise', said managing director Francisco Salamero. White wines did appear at the tasting although they were not Riojas. In 1970 Herederos del Marqués de Riscal set up a firm for white wines in the Rueda region,

about 125 miles west of the Rioja. This was done under the leadership of Francisco Hurtado de Amézaga, great-grandson of the founder. This modern installation, equipped with stainless-steel fermentation tanks, supplies three kinds of white wines. The ordinary dry type is made from 80% Viura and 20% local Verdejo grapes and undergoes no cask ageing. It possesses a lively taste with fruit and a cool freshness. The Reserva Limousin has just the Verdejo as its basis and is given three months in casks of French oak (it used to be six months). I thought it a pleasant, supple wine, again with a cool note to its taste (the Rueda plateau has a lot of limestone). A

third type of white is too simple to be sold as a Riscal wine. The bodega owns some 125 acres in the Rueda, supplying nearly one third of the grapes required.

Riscal exports about 60% of its production to more than 80 countries.

Left:
"Domecq oblige" is the motto on the family coat of arms.

Far left:
Stalks are carried away by a conveyor belt.

Below:
Pickers near Elciego with the white Domecq buildings in the background.

Below right:
Ripe Tempranillo grapes.

Elciego

Bodegas Domecq

Elciego is an old village – ancient in fact; it dates back at least to 1072, for it appears from documents of that year that a certain Arnaz Diaz of "El Cieko" bequeathed a great house and lands to the monastery of San Millán de Cogolla. The village, like many others in the Rioja, is built on a hill. It can be recognized from afar for its church has two tall, dissimilar towers. According to legend the village acquired its name, which means "the blind man", from one such inhabitant who in times past ran a market stall for travellers and mule drivers. Visitors who walk round Elciego find themselves taken back several centuries in time. Along the narrow streets

and around the shaded Plaza Mayor they will discover many fine large houses with family coats of arms carved on their façades or corners. The undoubted prosperity of the village in the past is shown, for example, by the enormous sum it paid to obtain its independence from Laguardia in 1583.

Most of the bodegas in Elciego are also old; so if you drive out on the Leza road, negotiating a sharp bend after a few hundred yards and being confronted by the cool, modern buildings of Bodegas Domecq amounts almost to a culture shock.

The biggest wine estate

After its brief association with Seagram (*see* the Bodegas Palacio chapter) Pedro Domecq decided to build a bodega of its own in the Rioja. As is well known, Domecq has for more than 250 years been one of the most important sherry producers. And in 1874 it was the first sherry house to start making Spanish brandy. The firm now prides itself on being the world's biggest brandy producer. Increasingly Pedro Domecq is turning its attention to table wine. Evidence for this lies not only in its vineyards in Mexico, but also in its tremendous investment in the Rioja. A

The white Rioja labelled Domecq Domain is made solely from Viura grapes and is pale in colour and fresh, pure, fairly light and refreshing in taste. The taste tends more to tannin than to fruit. The wine stays for about 5 months in the tank and at least 8 in bottle. Only juice from the first pressing is used. Viña Eguia – also white – is of lesser quality.

Identical wines, both crianzas and reservas, are marketed under the names Domecq Domain or Privilegio del Rey Sancho. The crianza has 12 months in tank, 14 in cask and 12 in bottle. An almost elegant Rioja somewhat lacking in concentration, but with vanilla, a degree of maturity, a touch of freshness and an agreeable purity. This wine is sold mostly outside Spain.

Domecq gives this reserva 12 months in tank, 30 in cask and at least 20 in bottle. In most respects – colour, strength, alcohol, maturity, aftertaste – this type is better than the crianza, but not overwhelmingly so, nor is it really deep-coloured, full-bodied or possessed of many nuances. As with all Domecq reds, Tempranillo from Rioja Alavesa is the only grape.

I have seen this bodega's gran reserva labelled as Domecq Domain and as Marqués de Arienzo, and in various bottles. The wines are the same and are matured for 12 months in tank, 24 in cask and a minimum 48 in bottle. Of all the Domecqs, this shows the most strength, maturity and depth without, however, being really full-bodied or rich in nuances.

Below:
Group of young pickers.

Bodegas Domecq's subsidiary brands are Bodegas Iton (called Txoko in the Basque country) and Sociedad General de Viñas (with the trademark Conde de Montiga). In addition the firm produces kosher Rioja which is sold under the Soreika (Spain) and Abarbanel (export) names.

About one-third of production goes abroad, to the United States, Britain, the Netherlands, Denmark, West Germany and elsewhere.

Domecq's vineyard is still relatively young, which may be one reason for the wines still rather lacking depth and concentration.

The first vintage at the new premises was the 1975.

Carbon dioxide is introduced into the fermentation tanks. The grapes are half crushed. The bodega has 54 metal tanks with a combined capacity of nearly 1.25 million (US 1.48 million) gallons. In addition a further 946,000 (US 1.12 million) gallons can be stored in other types of tanks.

Bodegas Domecq

total of 1,360 acres of vineyards has been purchased in the Rioja Alavesa, which amounts to roughly 8% of all the land in the district suitable for growing grapes. No other Riojan bodega has so much land of its own.

A different mode of planting

About 320 acres of Domecq's estate consists of traditionally planted vineyards with an average area of between 1¼ and 2½ acres each. These were bought in 1972 from a large number of small growers and they normally yield 284 gallons per acre annually. In addition Domecq created 667 acres of new vineyards with an average plot size of 20 acres. These plots, planted in 1973 and 1974, have a significantly higher yeild: 378 gallons per acre of red wine and 567 per acre of white (both figures represent the legal maximum). A remarkable fact about these recent vineyards is that they are entirely planted in the Bordeaux manner, which is officially prohibited in Rioja. The vines grow vertically, their branches trained along stretched wires, and the method of pruning has been adapted accordingly. Results are favourable, and quality good, and so the people at Domecq are convinced that in the long run not only will this method of planting be legally recognized, but that it will be widely imitated. On one plot, not far from Laguardia, the bodega is experimenting with sprinkler irrigation – with the permission of the authorities.

Some 495 acres have not been planted yet. They are lying fallow and are intended for future expansion. Planting on the land already in use consists of 88% Tempranillo grapes and 12% Viura.

Colour extraction

The same drive and efficiency that have characterized the planting of the vineyards is apparent in the design of the bodega.

Bodegas Domecq

With an eye on the projected growth a generous site – some 15 acres – has been bought. Almost half of this has been built on now. On arrival the black grapes are immediately destalked and lightly crushed. Fermentation – they talk of a *semi-macération carbonique* here – takes place in vertical metal tanks. They contain a system that automatically brings the fermenting juice to the top, over the floating mass of skins. This promotes colour extraction which, for the mostly rather light red wines of the Rioja Alavesa, is a useful feature. Fermentation usually lasts for 8 to 12 days; the temperature in the tanks does not rise above 30° C. In addition to its 770,000 (US 910,000) gallons the bodega also produces 110,000 (US 130,000) gallons of white and 88,000 (US 104,000) of rosé annually. The white grapes are not destalked but go into the presses skin and all.

Modern equipment

It hardly needs pointing out that this modern concern is equipped with modern apparatus. Heating the halls to start malolactic fermentation in the red wines is no problem at all. Bodegas Domecq also possesses an installation that enables wines to be stabilized by the cold method. White and rosé wines are always given this treatment, but not red (although this is being experimented with, as I saw on one visit). After the secondary fermentation has run its course the red wines are divided into three qualities. The better types are aged in the wood; Domecq keeps an average 15,000 casks in store, all of American oak. The cellars in fact have room for twice as many. There are two coopers on the staff to repair damaged casks. After bottling (when the wines are filtered for the second time; the first is just before cask ageing begins) the wines are given a further period of rest. This varies from a minimum 3 months up to 20 or more. For storing its bottles of wine Domecq uses large wooden boxes that can be moved by forklift trucks. The firm has the space for over 2.1 million bottles but the present stock does not exceed 600,000 to 1 million.

Buying in grapes and wines

Despite owning so much land, Domecq is nevertheless obliged to buy grapes and wines from elsewhere. It makes its white Riojas exclusively from grapes it has processed on the premises, but 70% of the requirement for red is purchased in the form of wine, one supplier being the cooperative at Labastida. Both wines and grapes are carefully selected; everything for the red wines comes from Rioja Alavesa. Purchases for the rosé are made in the Rioja Baja. I know nothing else about this latter wine: I was not given it to sample on either of my visits to the bodega, so clearly it is of no very interesting quality. The Domecq Domain is the best of the white wines on an obviously higher level than the Viña Eguia. It is made from the juice of the first pressing only. It is a pale, pure, fairly light wine; not very fruity, but certainly refreshing. Its basis is the Viura grape. It is the firm's custom not to market the Domain Domecq until late in the summer after the vintage, in contrast to other bodegas which launch white wines of this kind in the spring.

Variations in red

Viña Eguia – a brand that is mainly sold in Spain – is also the simplest kind among the red wines, with an easy, supple taste in which fruit can vaguely be determined, but little depth or concentration. On a higher level is the Domecq Domain, a *crianza* that has had 12 months in tank, 14 in cask and 12 in bottle. Vanilla is unmistakably present in the aroma, while the wine tastes pleasant, with a certain ripeness, a slightly fresh tone and an agreeable purity – all this without being really rich in colour, full-bodied or strong. Exactly the same product is called Privilegio del Rey Sancho in some countries. The bodega also let me sample the Domecq Domain *reserva*, a wine with rather more colour, alcohol and maturity. It is matured for 12 months in tank, $2\frac{1}{2}$ years in cask and at least $1\frac{1}{2}$ years in bottle. Quality rises again with the *gran reserva*. Both the examples I tasted – the 1975 and 1976 – had a fairly deep, brownish-red colour, a matured nose with wood and vanilla, together with a decently mouth-filling taste, but again not intense or strong, with some nuances, tannin and also vanilla. They are somewhat lacking in harmony.

Domecq is not a bodega that you would choose for concentrated, meaty wines full of character, nor for very fine ones possessed of many subtleties. But in the great area between these two poles the firm offers a series of very reliable, carefully made Riojas that nearly always offer good value for the money.

Elciogo

Hacienda Palaciana

It was in the second half of the last century
that the Marqués of Legarda created a
number of vineyards on his land near
Elciego and Abalos. This was in the period
when the French were showing great
interest in the Rioja as their own vineyards
were being attacked by the phylloxera. The
marquis also built a small bodega in
Elciego, over cellars dug out of the rock in
the 17th century. After just a few years he
closed down the firm and it was not brought
to life again until 1965. A descendant of the
marquis, Blanca Fernandez de Navarrete y
Sáinz de Tejada, together with her brother
and her husband, Manuel Iglesias Sarría y
Puga (an uncle of the famous singer Julio
Iglesias) decided to reopen the bodega. They
called it Hacienda Palaciana, after the
family estate La Palaciana in Elciego. An
adjoining plot of 37 acres supplies all the
grapes; neither grapes nor wines from
elsewhere are used. The land is planted
with 77% Tempranillo vines, 3% Graciano,
19% Viura and 1% white Garnacha.

Traditional methods

The grapes are handled in the traditional
way, that is to say they are tipped whole
into open concrete fermentation vats
(lagos). The young wine that is not suitable
for ageing is sold in bulk. The rest – about
60% – is matured in the wood and in bottle.
The firm has around 150 casks, all of
American oak, which remain in use for 10
years on average. There is no filtering of
the wine, which is simply fined with white
of egg. The youngest wine, the 3° año,
spends 6 to 12 months in tank, 2 years in
cask and the same period in bottle, after
which it is sold. In addition the firm carries
wines that are given five or more years to
age in the wood. Official terms such as
crianza, reserva and so on are not used by
Hacienda Palaciana, which is not yet a
member of the Consejo Regulador.

Rustic character

According to the cellarman all the cask-
matured wines had approximately the
same composition: 80% Tempranillo

grapes, 10% Graciano and 10% Viura. The
older wines appealed to me more than the
3° años (although these were by no means
bad Riojas). I became acquainted with the
1975, for example, which had spent five
years in the cask. It had a respectably dark
colour, a pleasant, unobtrusive perfume
and a taste in which vanilla, tannin and
maturity were present. Its character
seemed somewhat rustic rather than
refined, but nevertheless I thought it a pure
and good-tasting wine. This bodega sells on

the home market, mainly in Bilbao,
Vittoria, Madrid, Barcelona and Cadiz; it
does not export.

Bodegas Alavesas

The village of Laguardia occupies a commanding position in the landscape of Rioja Alavesa. It is built on a hill that rises to 2,083 ft above sea level giving sweeping views on all sides. The rectangular, still partly walled nucleus of the village is rich in atmosphere and very ancient. At the foot of the hill, however, stand buildings that are clearly of more recent date, among them some apartments and the wine firm of Bodegas Alavesas. The latter stands on the narrow road leading from the bottom end of the village to Elciego. There can be no doubt that, given the appearance of this bodega, purely functional requirements have had precedence here over more aesthetic considerations. For this angular, sand-coloured building could hardly be termed handsome and it strikes a visually discordant note in the setting of this unique village and its surroundings.

Only local grapes

Bodegas Alavesas was founded in 1972. In that year the prosperous industrialist Miguel Ángel Alonso Samaniego (of the Laboratorios Alther pharmaceutical factory, well-known in Spain) brought together wine growers, mainly from Laguardia, with the aim of starting a bodega. Alonso was to provide the capital, the group of growers, the land and the grapes. Agreement was reached, a limited company was set up and in 1973 a totally new bodega was built. Miguel Ángel Alonso has since died, but his family still have the majority shareholding. At present Bodegas Alavesas owns 222 acres of vineyard, scattered over a good number of plots around Laguardia. These vineyards no longer supply anything like enough wine for the bodega's requirements – only about a quarter in fact. To cover the rest of its production Bodegas Alavesas buys in exclusively grapes – no wines – and only from the Alavesa district. These bought-in grapes come from about 100 small growers.

Before being sold the Solar de Iriarte crianza normally has spent 12 months in tank, 12 in cask and at least 3 in bottle. There is some mellowness in the deep-red colour, some vanilla in the aroma, some suppleness in the taste. It is a little lacking in depth and length, but is certainly pure. A Tempranillo wine, like the Solar de Samaniego crianza, which receives an extra 12 months or more bottle rest.

Solar de Samaniego reservas are kept for 30 months in tank and then for 18 in cask and a minimum 30 in bottle. During its cask ageing the wine is racked 3 to 4 times a year, like the other wood-matured reds. Dark, brownish colour, medium depth, mature in nose and taste, but not tired. Lacks depth, length and concentration. Pleasant, with a slight fresh touch to it.

For the gran reservas the strongest wines most likely to benefit from a long ageing period are of course selected. They are usually rather more full-bodied than the reservas, but otherwise not strikingly different – just further developed and with more wood (3 years in tank, 2 in cask, followed by at least 4 in bottle). Like the reservas they are not fined, but filtered lightly before bottling.

Bodegas Alavesas

Vinification

It is a Rioja Alavesan tradition to ferment black grapes with their stalks and seeds. However, this does not happen at this bodega: stalks and seeds are removed from all the fruit. The grapes are not subsequently crushed, so they go into the concrete fermentation tanks fairly intact. Here what the bodega describes as a *semi-macération carbonique* takes place, in which the fermentation develops partly within the fruit. It usually lasts for 12 to 15 days and immediately after this malolactic fermentation is started up. This is stimulated by the use of heating apparatus. After this secondary fermentation the red wine goes straight into tanks to cool and shortly afterwards it is separated out into its various qualities.

Underground storage

The better kinds of red wine are aged in wood in the underground cellar, where the casks are stacked five high in rows. Normally Bodegas Alavesas has about 9,000 casks at its disposal, all of American oak. They are used for an average 12 years. Storage for bottles is also underground. Alcoves in the large – and little used – dining and reception areas next to the cask cellar form one of the store places for the bottles of *gran reservas*, usually around 30,000 bottles. During my visit I happened to see how these alcoves were filled: it took no fewer than six men, on a two-level staging – a very time-consuming and expensive business. Elsewhere in the bodega rather more sensible means of storing filled bottles are employed. The average stock of bottled Rioja stands at around 2 million.

Success with young red wine

The Tempranillo grape is the sole basis of all the red wines from Bodegas Alavesas. The youngest of these wines is the Cosechero, which is sold as wine of the year (*vino del año*). It is blended from the wines with most fruit, from tanks where *macération carbonique* has been most closely approached. It was first marketed in 1981 and had considerable success. The 1982 had an even better reception, winning at least six prizes in various countries. Production now runs at over 44,000 (US 52,000) gallons a year – and is rising. In 1982 Bodegas obtained equipment for stabilizing whites and rosés by the cold treatment method; whether this has benefited the quality of these wines may be doubted. The white Solar Joven is a wine with body and freshness and a quality that is correct – but no more. Real fruit and breeding are lacking, and this applies to an even greater degree to the rosé. Of the wines from this bodega meant for drinking young the red Cosechero is clearly the best, with generally a deep colour, a supple, fairly "meaty" taste, a sound structure and a little fruit. Perhaps in the course of time this wine will become more aromatic and have more fruit, for experiments with a longer fermentation at a lower temperature are being conducted.

Poets on the labels

The youngest of the wood-aged red wines carries the brand name Solar de Iriarte; the rest are called Solar de Samaniego. Tomás de Iriarte and Félix Maria de Samaniego wcrc 18th-century Spanish poets, and rivals, and famous for their fables. Of the two Samaniego enjoyed the greater reputation. He was born in Laguardia and lived and worked there. His bust is in a graceful, open pavilion in a little park on the north side of the village, with the eternal Sierra de Cantabria serving as a mighty backdrop. These brands represent the bodega's quality line. It also uses the brand name Bodala for cheaper wines of a lesser quality. Simpler wines are also marketed under the Bodegas Cantabria name. About 80% of the bodega's production is sold in the bottle; exports in bulk go only to Switzerland.

Pure and elegant

On tasting the *crianzas*, *reservas* and *gran reservas* it struck me that all the wines were in fact elegant, but somewhat lacking in concentration and depth. They were thus true to their origin – Rioja Alavesa, where the lightest, finest type of red Rioja is made. None of the cask-aged wines had a really deep colour, and a slightly fresh tone was present in all of them. Each of them seemed very pure. Naturally they all to a greater or lesser extent had elements of wood and vanilla in nose and taste – but even in the older wines the wood aroma did not predominate. I would never describe the more mature red wines as truly exciting or subtly nuanced, but their elegance and purity make them very pleasant table companions – when veal is served, for example. And even the *gran reservas* keep their vitality for a long time.

Laguardia

Bodegas Palacio

Bodegas Palacio's reputation in Spain comes not only from its wine, but also from the grape juice it produces. For generations Mosto Palacio has been known as one of the best grape juices in the country; it is an altogether wholesome drink that contains no preservatives. Three to 4 million bottles are sold annually, principally in northern Spain. According to a spokesman from the bodega the quality and purity of this juice have had an undoubtedly positive effect on the image of the wine. For those who drink the grape juice the name of Palacio has in fact become synonymous with quality.

The juice and the wine are produced totally separately. No Riojan grapes are used for the juice – they are much too expensive. Grape concentrate is brought from the south of Spain.

Via Domecq to Seagram

The official year of foundation of Bodegas Palacio is 1894. Its founder, Ángel Palacio, had in fact been involved with wine 31 years earlier. He came from Bilbao and around 1890 he bought a number of vineyards in the Rioja Alavesa. Not long afterwards he started building a bodega to process his own grapes. Laguardia, the 'wine capital' of Rioja Alavesa, was the chosen location. Palacio found a site on the road to Elciego, below Laguardia itself. Cosme and Manuel, Ángel Palacio's sons, further expanded the business and started producing the grape juice at the beginning of this century. Despite their busy existence the brothers found time to be very active in the cause of their Catholic faith and they also gave a good deal of attention to the religious monuments of Laguardia.

In 1972 the Palacio family disappeared from the picture when all the shares in the concern were purchased by Pedro Domecq. Subsequently this sherry, brandy and wine giant made over half of the shares to the Canadian firm of Seagram, but this association was not a success. The partners separated at the end of 1973: Domecq set up its own bodega and Seagram became sole owner of Palacio. The original buildings had long since been given up: Bodegas

Palacio is now a modern-looking structure that stands almost opposite, and downhill from, Bodegas Alavesas.

Tempranillo from Alavesa

The firm's own land covers only 25 acres – much too small to meet its needs – situated around the bodega. For its annual 462,000 (US 546,000) gallons of red Rioja the firm buys in black grapes exclusively from the Rioja Alavesa, practically all of them Tempranillo. The grapes are obtained from growers up to a maximum of 9 miles away, so that oxidation during transport is kept to a minimum. In contrast to Rioja Alavesan tradition, all the fruit is destalked. Fermentation takes place in tall metal tanks. Temperature control is normally no problem, for the weather quickly turns cooler during the grape harvest in this part of the Rioja. In 1982, for example, picking began in a temperature of 27° C, but two weeks later snow fell. In any case, temperature is kept below 30° C during the first fermentation, being checked every hour while this is proceeding. For the second, or malolactic, fermentation of the red wine Bodegas Palacio has a hall where the temperature can be raised; this facilitates the process and there are never any difficulties. Young red wines (up to and including the *crianza*) undergo the same cold treatment as all the whites and rosés.

Nouveau

Since 1981 this firm has been enhusiastically making a Rioja "of the year" – a *nouveau*. It has been found that the Tempranillo gives a wine that is "sensational for drinking young". Introducing this type of Rioja brought many problems in Spain at first. Because of its lack of the traditional vanilla and wood aroma the wine was not regarded as a Rioja; in addition it was apparent that in the public mind maturity and quality were but two aspects of the same thing. This young wine was simply mistrusted. However, those who did try this new creation found it good – and came back for more; so much so that Palacio's wine of the year already represents a third of the turnover. I have enjoyed it intensely. It is generally characterized by a deep colour, a perfume with elements of berries and soft fruit, and a substantial, juicy taste with just a little tannin in it. Deservedly this Rioja has already carried off various prizes.

A preference for bottle ageing

With its more mature red wines the firm works on the principle that Alavesas benefit more from bottle ageing than from time in wood. Rioja Alavesan wines are

Bodegas Palacio

rather liable to oxidation and contact with oxygen is naturally greater and more intense in casks than in bottles. And at Bodegas Palacio they are not very keen on having too pronounced a taste of wood in their wine. This is another reason for the preference for maturing in bottle, and the fact that old wooden casks are used as far as possible. In practice what it means is that the Glorioso *reserva* is given one year in tank followed by one year in cask, then two years in bottle. For the *gran reserva* the two latter figures are two and three years respectively. An average of around 12,000 casks are held in stock and the number of bottles was due to rise to 4 million in 1986.

Improved quality

When tasting the wines, in the well-equipped laboratory next to the computer room, I was struck by the fact that the quality seemed to have improved

Since 1981 this bodega has made a delightful young red Rioja, meant for drinking in the year after its vintage. This Rioja Palacio is basically a Tempranillo wine, but may sometimes contain a small proportion of Viura. Flavours of berries and soft fruits may be present in its aroma and taste. The wine has a lot of colour, a substantial, juicy taste and a dash of tannin.

Palacio's crianza is sold as Castillo Rioja and Pórtico Rioja. The two are the same, from 90% Tempranillo and 10% Garnacha grapes. It is given 12 months in tank, 12 in cask and 6 to 12 months in bottle. Quality has improved clearly from the 1981 vintage. A sound structure, some fruit and a modest wood flavour.

The Glorioso reserva – very successful for 30 years now on the Swiss market – usually spends 1 year in tank, 1 in cask and 2 in bottle. It generally has a respectably deep colour, a very correct, not too light taste, vinous in character. Wood and a measure of maturity are unmistakably present. Quality will probably improve still further from the 1981 vintage on.

Like the crianza and the reserva, the gran reserva is made from about 90% Tempranillo and 10% Garnacha. The wine stays for 1 year in tank, 2 in cask and a minimum 3 years in bottle. Colour and taste can sometimes be rather lighter, more elegant than with the reserva. Mature bouquet, with some vanilla. Still very lively in taste after 10 years.

Below left:
Wines from the Palacio range.

Below right:
The Bodega's own laboratory, directed by Jesús Tobía.

Bodegas Palacio

significantly since 1980. At least as far as the red wines were concerned: the whites – about 440,000 (US 520,000) gallons annually – bought from the cooperative at Cenicero and the rosés – some 22,000 (US 26,000) gallons – did not prove very interesting, including the recent ones. The successful red wine of the year provides a clear example of the improved standard of quality; and this is also true of the *crianza* Castillo Rioja (also called *Pórtico Rioja*). The 1981 appeared to surpass the 1980 in all respects. I later heard the explanation: from 1981 the bodega bought in grapes to vinify on the premises, whereas before that year (at least from 1974 on) it chiefly bought wines. Where vinification had hitherto been left to others, the whole process of making the wine was now controlled by the bodega. The amount of investment has been phenomenal – fermentation and maturing tanks with a total capacity of 2.42 million (US 2.86 million) gallons had to be bought, apart

from anything else – but the quality has indisputably improved.

Growth limited

At the time of my visit it was still too early to sample a *reserva* made from grapes vinified by the bodega itself, but the Glorioso 1978 I tasted came over as extremely correct, with sufficient firmness, fruit and colour, and wood was apparent in both nose and taste. I am curious to know whether the quality of the post-1980 *reservas* will also improve; I certainly expect it to, and the same would then apply to the *gran reservas*. As far as

its red wines are concerned Bodegas Palacio would seem well worth following. The statement that this firm is not going to expand in an irresponsible way showed, I felt, a positive attitude. Palacio wants to sell 500,000 cases a year at most. More would not be regarded as desirable, for above this ceiling problems could be expected keeping up quality.

Right:
Harvest time at Viña Salceda, with tractors towing loads of grapes. In theory the bodega can process 8,000 tons per vintage, but the largest quantity so far has been 6,000 tons.

Below:
The bodega stands by a bridge over the Ebro. The sign, in Castilian and Basque, marks the start of the province of Alava.

Exports of Viña Salceda are gradually rising: 10% of volume in 1983, 20% in 1984.

Casks are stacked five high here, as at many bodegas. They are all made from American oak and replacement every 10 years is the rule.

VIÑA SALCEDA, S.A.

Viña Salceda

Elciego

The drive from Cenicero to Elciego takes you across the Ebro. On the right, immediately after the bridge, is the Viña Salceda bodega, with a main building that looks rather like a chalet. Building on this triangular site, between the road, the Ebro and a tributary, started in 1973. The bodega was then called the Larrea y Rabanera, after being known for a time as Cepas de Elciego. It started as a joint venture among various Elciego wine growers but was transformed into a limited company when the success of its wines obliged it to expand and thus to acquire new capital. The name Viña Salceda has been used since January 1976 and comes from one of the members of the board of directors, Count de la Salceda. At present there are about 200 shareholders, none with a majority holding. There is a special cellar in the bodega with black metal racks where shareholders can store their bottles of Rioja.

Red wine only

The bodega itself owns 50 acres of vineyard, providing wine for about one-eighth of production. One plot lies next to the bodega and here, by way of an experiment, the vines are trained along metal wires: a method of planting that is not yet officially permitted in the Rioja. Only the Tempranillo is grown on the bodega's own land. What is bought in is also mainly Tempranillo, for this bodega makes only

123

The *Viña Salceda* crianza is a successful wine, made from 95% Tempranillo and 5% Viura grapes (as are the other red wines from this bodega). Subtleties or concentration in perfume and taste should not be expected; nor is this a really firm, striking Rioja. But it has some maturity and tastes pleasant. Before being sold it rests for 12 months in the tank, 16 to 18 in cask and at least 6 in bottle.

This bodega offers its reserva and gran reserva under the Conde de Salceda name. The former type may disappear: its 2½ years in the wood (after a year in tank) and 3 years in bottle entitle it to gran reserva classification; which has been the case from the 1978 onwards. Colour reasonably deep, wood and vanilla in aroma and taste, but not dominant. More robust than the crianza, without being really powerful. Supple, somewhat smooth taste.

Viña Salceda

red wine. Apart from the Tempranillo there is just 5% of Viura used. Purchases comprise both grapes and wine, roughly in the ratio of 70 to 30. The great majority of both come from the Rioja Alavesa, the remainder from Rioja Alta.

No expansion forecast

In the neat, clean cellars the fruit is destalked and pressed immediately on arrival. Fermentation then takes place in concrete tanks. Viña Salceda has a storage capacity of 330,000 (US 390,000) gallons, not including the average stock of 5,000 oak casks, nor the 350,000 bottles. The last expansion of the bodega was in 1978; further enlargement is not anticipated for the moment. The present average annual production fluctuates around 132,000 (US 156,000) gallons; here there could be an increase, of some 10%. The wines are still sold mainly in Spain, although exports to the United States, Denmark and Britain are gradually increasing.

Pleasant and reliable

I tasted the Viña Salceda wines in the bodega's reception hall, situated behind a spacious dining room with a bar, and giving a view out over the Ebro valley. I have also frequently come across bottles of wine from this firm in Spanish restaurants. Only three kinds of wine are carried: a *crianza* (Viña Salceda), a *reserva* and a *gran reserva* (both called Conde de la Salceda). The first type has *4° año* on the label and spends 16 to 18 months in cask after 12 months in tank; it then has at least 6 months in bottle. Its colour is not really deep, but soft and mellow-looking. There is maturity and mellowness in nose and taste, too, with some wood. I did not find this a remarkable wine for it tasted rather flat and lacked depth and subtleties; the bodega markets what is clearly a commercial *crianza*: a reliable wine that is pleasant to drink, but with few exciting facets to discover. These aspects improve with the *reserva*, which has more wood and vanilla to offer and comes

across as firmer. But the depth, length or personality of this wine are not impressive either. This does not alter the fact, however, that Viña Salceda wines have repeatedly won prizes in Spain and elsewhere, as the many certificates in the bodega bear witness.

The *reserva* is kept for a year in tank, 2½ years in cask and at least 3 in bottle. This means that it could actually be a *gran reserva*, and this term will be used for the 1978 onward. The reason for the bodega not bringing out a *gran reserva* before was simply that the labels for the 1973, 1975 and 1976 wines had already been printed.

Cenicero

Bodegas Riojanas

The wine town of Cenicero lies about halfway between Haro and Logroño, sandwiched between the busy N232 and the railway line. The name Cenicero means literally "ashpan" and is derived from the Latin Cinisariam. It is presumed that the name arose because the Romans cremated their dead here, but in the place itself I heard another version. There is said to have been a cattle market on this site in times past. The traders usually arrived with their cattle the day before the market and kept themselves warm overnight by burning cow dung – resulting in a lot of ash the next morning.

On 7 August 1636 Philip IV granted municipal privileges to Cenicero. Another important year in its history was 1904 when, in recognition of the efforts made by its people after a great train disaster, King Alfons XII bestowed on it the title *Muy Humanitaria Ciudad* (Most Humane Town).

Statue of Liberty

The Cenicero of today has the usual big church and, in addition to many old houses, a number of modern apartment blocks. It does not look as if much effort was made to integrate these new buildings with the rest of the little town architecturally, which is regrettable. The main street runs straight through Cenicero and in the old centre it is so narrow that two lorries can barely pass one another. In this same street there is the always-thronged restaurant and bar of Conchita, where you can enjoy a nourishing, honest and inexpensive meal. A few dozen yards along in the Haro direction there is a small park where a much-reduced copy of the American Statue of Liberty has been set up.

The biggest bodega along the main street is that of Bodegas Riojanas. On the little square in front of the entrance there stands a gateway dating from 1799 which for many generations formed the entrance to one of the Riojanas vineyards.

Bodegas Riojanas

A wine-growing family

The Bodegas Riojanas first came into being through the initiative of an enterprising Catalan, Rafel Carreras Picó, in 1890, the year in which Montecillo and La Rioja Alta were among other bodegas established. After the death of Carreras his heirs sold the business to two wine growers from Cenicero, the cousins Román and Fortunato Artacho. Under their direction the bodega was considerably enlarged. Román remained childless, but Fortunato did have children and Bodegas Riojanas has remained in the possession of the Artacho family. Marcelo Frias Artacho is now managing director and five of his nephews hold other positions in the company.

A maze of passages and cellars

All kinds of certificates for prize-winning wines hang on the wall in the reception hall at Bodegas Riojanas. Wines from this house have been loved by some controversial heads of state – I saw a framed letter from the Argentinian leader Juan Perón ordering wine in 1947 as well as one from Mussolini in 1939. In the spacious boardroom there is a medal on display that was awarded to a wine at Barcelona in 1888 – two years before the foundation. It was for a wine made by the Artacho family. Directly behind the offices lies the oldest part of the bodega, dating from the year of establishment. All subsequent extensions have been built on to this section, resulting in a complex warren, quite beyond the grasp of outsiders, with four storeys, cellars, passages and halls, linked by staircases and a few lifts. The whole maze is at least 220 yd long – "or perhaps even more", according to Marcelo Frias. That this extended oblong layout should have been chosen has to do with the location of the bodega between the street where the railway station stands and the bed of a stream that runs right across Cenicero.

A lot of its own land

Given the fact that the Artachos were wine growers by origin – and reasonably prosperous ones – it is hardly surprising that Bodegas Riojanas should have a good deal of land of its own. Altogether it owns 495 acres of vineyard within the boundaries of Cenicero itself, to which a number of signboards bear witness – as in the Monte Real, close to the Berberana buildings. About 80% of this is planted with black grapes (mainly Tempranillo, with some Mazuelo and Graciano) and the remainder with white (Viura). The bodega's own vineyards meet around one-third of its requirements. Of the rest, one-fifth is bought in the form of grapes (from Cenicero) and four-fifths as wine (chiefly from Rioja Alta and Rioja Alavesa). Bodegas Riojanas produces between 440,000 and 660,000 gallons (US 520,000 to 780,000 gallons) annually, a quantity that is expected to increase further. In this context there was a considerable extension

As a reserva *the Viña Albina is given 1 year in tank, 2 in cask and at least 2 in bottle, so it clearly has maturity. Nearly always, however, this elegant wine also has a hint of freshness, with sufficient tannin not to taste dull or tired. Wood and vanilla are present, but not obtrusively. The grapes for this sound Rioja are 80% Tempranillo, 15% Mazuelo, 2% Graciano and 3% other varieties (including Viura). The* gran reserva *receives an extra year in cask and sometimes 8 to 9 years in bottle.*

Monte Real, reserva *or* gran reserva*, is a stronger type than the Viña Albina. All elements, from colour to aftertaste, are more powerfully present. The ageing periods are the same as for the Viña Albina, but the grape mix may differ slightly: in some years Garnacha, up to a maximum 10%, can be used. Monte Real* reserva *is undoubtedly a very good Rioja, but the* gran reserva *is slightly better still in quality – including, as a rule, a very fine nose.*

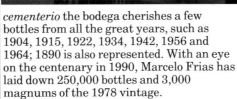

Bodegas Riojanas

of the business in 1985; earlier expansions include those of 1940, 1960 and 1975.

From wood to stainless steel

Getting a clear picture of the way in which Bodegas Riojanas vinifies its grapes is by no means simple, for the firm works with various kinds of vats and tanks. There are, for example, the 22 large open vats of Dalmatian oak still in use. These date from the firm's early period and serve both for fermenting and storing red wine. You also come across open concrete *lagos* here in which, as in the wooden vats, the traditional Riojan style of *macération carbonique* is applied. The black grapes here are tipped in complete with skins, stalks and seeds after being just lightly crushed. But the visitor will also see enclosed tanks of concrete, glass fibre and stainless steel where the must is made into wine in the normal way. A walk through this bodega reveals practically all the types of fermentation plant developed during the last 100 years, all of them still in use. The earliest cellars at Bodegas Riojanas were designed by Frenchmen from Bordeaux, and French wine technicians were active here until 1936. A fairly recent acquisition is the plant for the cold stabilization of all the white and rosé wines, as well as the red Rioja that is to be sold as wine of the year. All types of wine, with the exception of one *gran reserva*, are usually filtered twice, through earth and through cellulose plates.

An ample stock of bottles

There are plenty of casks at this bodega: some 15,000, all of American oak. About 500 of them are replaced by new ones every year. The firm has no central cellar for casks, but a number of different areas, some long and narrow (such as the off-white-coloured galleries from the early days), others wide and high. The wine is normally racked twice a year. During my visit this was still being done by hand and not by means of a pump, as in many other bodegas. There is a stock of about 3 million bottles of wine, stacked up in cases. In its dimly lit

cementerio the bodega cherishes a few bottles from all the great years, such as 1904, 1915, 1922, 1934, 1942, 1956 and 1964; 1890 is also represented. With an eye on the centenary in 1990, Marcelo Frias has laid down 250,000 bottles and 3,000 magnums of the 1978 vintage.

Variations in rosé and white

The wine that Bodegas Riojanas produces in the smallest quantity is rosé, this type accounting for only about 5% of the total volume. Two kinds are made, both based on the Garnacha. The Canchales, like the comparable Puerta Vieja, is given just four months in tank and is then bottled and sold. It is a rather orange-coloured, decently fresh wine, without much vitality or fruit, and with sometimes a touch of *terroir*. The Monte Real rosé spends a year being aged in wood, as well as a year in tank. Its taste is purer, its colour browner, and it is otherwise unimpressive. A rosé like this without fruit is simply out of date. The white Riojas – 15% of production – divide into dry and sweet wines, and also into those with and without cask ageing. All of them are made solely from the Viura grape. The sweet Viña Albina is totally uninteresting, and I did not find any of the dry wines really memorable. Here, too, it was a matter of a lack of vitality and fruit. They had sufficient freshness, but beyond this it was mainly a stony hint that manifested itself in nose and taste. The Purta Vieja and Canchales whites are given four months in tank; the Monte Real has a year in tank and a year in cask. The must for all the Bodegas Riojanas white wines goes through a centrifuge.

Differences in style

It will be clear by now that this wine house has built its reputation principally on its red Riojas, and in particular on *reservas* and *gran reservas*. The bodega uses two

brand names for wines at this level, Viña Albina and Monte Real. The former type has as its basis about 80% Tempranillo, 15% Mazuelo, 2% Graciano and 3% of various grapes, including the Viura. The proportions used in the Monte Real are not much different, although some Garnacha often goes into it – 10% at most. The Viña Albina is made up from the more elegant wines, the Monte Real from the stronger ones, with usually 1% more alcohol. The difference in style is symbolized by the design of bottle: the Bordeaux model for the Viña Albina, the Burgundy for the Monte Real. The two kinds mature for the same length of time. As *reservas* they stay for a year in tank, two in cask and at least two in bottle. If they are selected to be *gran reservas*, ageing in the wood continues up to three years and sometimes they rest in the bottle for eight to nine years.

Traditional Riojas

I am familiar with the Viña Albina *reserva* from various years. For me it has always been a sound, elegant wine, most often with a slightly fresh tone, a light aroma of vanilla, sufficient tannin and a pleasing ripeness. The Monte Real usually has more colour, more wood, more strength and more tannin. It is a more rounded Rioja that can last well: traditional in style and therefore with a good measure of vanilla, and with some fruit in the background. I have been equally charmed with the Monte Real as a *gran reserva*: an almost always fragrant, splendidly matured wine that may taste mellow after something like a decade, but never in any way dull or tired.

Compared with quality wines like these the young red wines from Bodegas Riojanas come over as almost thin. The Canchales (100% Tempranillo and four months in tank) possesses some meatiness and tannin, but little depth or other distinct characteristics; and I have tasted a vintage in which the nose and taste were not

Bodegas Riojanas

entirely pure. The Puerta Vieja *crianza* (also 100% Tempranillo, with 12 months in tank and 12 in wood) has more maturity, body and wood to offer. This decent wine is in considerable demand in Denmark. That *reservas* and *gran reservas* are very much the speciality of the Bodegas Riojanas was emphasized once more in November 1980 when more than 300 cases of its older wines were auctioned at Sotheby's in London.

A firm of contrasts

At this bodega they are proud of the fact that Frenchmen worked here for more than four decades; and the original building was designed on the French pattern. Partly to emphasize this French influence, it was decided at the end of the 1960s to build a reception area behind the bodega in the form of a château. The result is a curious building, looking like an old fortified tower, complete with battlements and Gothic windows. As it is wedged in among the rather untidy cellars, it forms a great and unnatural-looking contrast with them, and also with the nearby flats. Since its completion in 1968, however, intensive use has been made of this mock castle, especially for groups of visitors. There they

can taste the wines, eat and even watch a video film presenting the bodega. In this and in all other aspects Bodegas Riojanas is a business full of contrasts. Authentic wooden vats function alongside all the kitsch of the reception 'château'; traditional techniques are in use beside the very modern; and none-too-successful wines co-exist with very good ones. This bodega could almost be seen as a symbol of the Rioja as a whole.

Right:
Front view of the modern-looking bodega. The offices and laboratories are here.

Below:
Side view of the bodega with carts of grapes ready for unloading.

Other brand names employed by Berberana are Bodegas Mariscol (used, for example, by the Wine Society in Britain) and the Grants of St James's own brand. One used by grocery chains is Viña Canda.

About 85% of the wine is sold in the bottle. Berberana has some 1,230 acres of vineyard under contract.

Bodegas Abalos, in place of that name, is a subsidiary. Its wines correspond with those of Berberana. Brand names include Fino d'Avalos and Castillo d'Avalos.

There are various old bottles on display in the tasting room, including a Berberana Rioja that was put in an Osborne brandy bottle during the Spanish Civil War and its attendant shortages. The oldest bottle bears the legend "Martinez Berberana – cosechero Exportador".

Bodegas Berberana

Anyone walking through Cenicero on a sunny afternoon is likely to see small groups of housewives who have brought their chairs out into the street and sit exchanging news and gossip. Some of them sew, some play cards, but always there are some who are busy twisting wires into *alambrados*, the open metal meshes that are wrapped round some bottles of Rioja. Even the woman in the tobacconist's shop does it in her spare time. That so many Cenicero women are kept busy with this activity is due to Bodegas Berberana, for this local concern uses vast quantities of these nets. They go on all bottles of Carta de Oro, as well as all the *reservas* and *gran reservas* – more than 5 million bottles a year altogether. In the bodega the nets are placed over the bottles by hand and then pulled tight. This keeps at least seven staff constantly occupied, and from early morning onwards the men regularly moisten their throats with jets of wine from their *porróns*.

Of Ollauri origin

The figures quoted show that Berberana is one of the largest bodegas of the Rioja. This has not always been the case; nor was the firm originally set up in Cenicero. It was in Ollauri in 1877 that a certain Martínez Berberana started a small bodega, against the hill where the Federico Paternina cellars were dug out. The little firm remained in the hands of the Berberana family until 1967. It was then sold to Melquíades Entrena who in that same year had merged his own bodega with the AGE group. After working in Ollauri for a few years the very enterprising Entrena decided to build a new, modern and enormous bodega. For its location he chose a site close by the station at Cenicero. The new installation came into service in 1974. The cellars in Ollauri remained in use; there are still some 6,000 casks there. In August 1981, after the death of Melquíades

Berberana sells three types of Rioja, red, white and rosé, under the Carta de Plata name. The red is a crianza 3 years old (1 year in cask) with a supple taste and a somewhat loose structure. The Tempranillo accounts for 75% of it. The white is fresh, juicy and pure (85% Viura). The rosé is also refreshing, but without a great deal of fruit in the taste (100% Garnacha). The white and rosé are given only a little ageing in tanks.

Berberana makes its white Carta de Oro from 90% Viura and 10% Malvasía. The colour is less pale than that of the Carta de Plata white and the wine has a more substantial taste, with also a slight touch of wood and vanilla. This is due to its 6 months in oak casks. It also has 12 months in tank and 6 in bottle (which is a clear glass one of the Bordeaux type, with a mesh on it).

One year in tank, two in cask and two in bottle: this is how Berberana matures its red Carta de Oro. It is sold as a crianza – it would be called a reserva at many other bodegas. Not a really intense, richly-nuanced Rioja, but it fills the mouth, is well balanced, with more colour, maturity, wood and vanilla than the red Carta de Plata.

Berberana sells some 85,000 cases of reserva and gran reserva a year. The former type has 1 year in tank, 3 years in cask and at least 2 in bottle. It is quite an elegant wine, clearly with a good deal of wood and vanilla, together with an agreeable maturity. The grapes are the same as for the Carta de Oro: 60% Tempranillo, 20% Garnacha and 20% Mazuelo and Graciano (very little of this last variety).

It is only from exceptional vintages that Berberana selects the wines that are later to carry a gran reserva label. Before this they will have aged for 1 year in tank, 3 in cask and a minimum 3 years in bottle. Up to and including 1973 it had 2 more years in cask. But not now: and rightly so, for the 1975 had more class than the full-bodied, rich, almost sleek 1973.

Below:
Statuary in Cenicero symbolizing the grape harvest.

Bodegas Berberana

Entrena, the bodega passed into the hands of the Rumasa group. After being temporarily nationalized, Berberana was sold to various shareholders in 1985.

Former grape-growing estate

At the end of the 1970s Berberana was the great vineyard owner of the Rioja. The firm bought an estate of 2,224 acres at Aldeanueva de Ebro, in the Rioja Baja, and planned to plant it in phases with Tempranillo and other grapes. It was called the Monte Yerga, after the nearby mountain on whose gentle spurs the vineyard was planned. However, the property had to be sold and at present Berberana has just 136 acres of its own. The 86 acres planted with black grapes (mainly Tempranillos) provide about 2% of the requirements for red wine; and the 50 acres with white grapes (Viura and Malvasia) some 6% of those for white wine. The rest is bought in, with wine and grapes in roughly equal parts. Must is sometimes purchased for making white wine. A good proportion of the grapes regularly comes from the Monte Yerga estate, which is now a separate company. Tempranillo grapes from the Rioja Baja mostly give one degree more alcohol than those from the other two districts. According to Berberana's cellarman Gonzalo Ortiz Peña, who has been there since 1971, the Baja wines help to reinforce those from Alta and Alavesa, "which goes well with our natural way of making wine".

Great processing capacity

As soon as the grapes arrive in Cenicero they are processed with great dispatch. The bodega's capacity is about five tons a day. Metal tanks painted rust-red and of the self-emptying type are used for fermenting the grapes. At Berberana the fermenting temperatures are kept low: at 16 to 24° C for red wine and 14 to 18° C for white and rosé. There are metal tanks available for malolactic fermentation and for storage; a number of them stand out of doors. The bodega is built in three storeys; the surface

Bodegas Berberana

area of the different levels varies from 64,800 to 86,400 sq ft. Also at Berberana there is a large dining hall where groups are entertained and where, in September, a great banquet is organized for the inhabitants of Cenicero during the annual fiesta.

A picture of neatness

The cask cellar is very impressive. It is a dimly lit area of grey concrete where some 26,000 *barricas* are stacked in rows five high. The wines that end up here are first filtered through earth (and again later, when they go through a membrane before bottling). All the casks are made of American oak. At Berberana they do not want too much tannin in the wines, so the rule is that no wine stays more than six months in new casks. After this the wine is racked to a used cask. But Bodegas Berberana has no really old casks in use, for after about ten years they are sold on to other bodegas. Three coopers are kept perpetually busy repairing damaged casks. The whole bodega is of an exemplary tidiness, even though there are 130 people at work there.

Variation in white

Visitors to Spain will undoubtedly have seen the advertisements on hoardings for Carta de Plata and Carta de Oro, the two most important brands from Berberana. They have been put up right across the country, at some 315 strategic points. Both brands have a red and a white variant. The white Carta de Plata has as its basis 85% Viura grapes and 15% Malvasia. It is stabilized by the cold method, like all the other whites and rosés from Berberana. Its taste is fresh and pure and it is very pale in colour. Whereas the Carta de Plata white goes into a slender green bottle, a plain glass Bordeaux type (with a metal mesh) was chosen for the Carta de Oro. The latter contains rather more Viura (90%) and is also aged for 12 months in tank, 6 in wood and 6 months in bottle. It is a rather substantial white Rioja with a slight

suggestion of wood, fruit and a most genial taste. There is a big demand for it in Spain. Most of the grapes (and sometimes must too) for white Carta de Oro are supplied by the Najerilla cooperative in Arenzana de Abajo. Berberana produces around 440,000 (US 520,000) gallons of white wine a year.

Red wine brands

Red Carta de Plata is a *crianza* made from 75% Tempranillo grapes, 15% Garnacha and 10% Mazuelo plus Viura. The wine perhaps lacks a little concentration, but offers wood and vanilla in both nose and taste. A mildly fresh note can also be present. This supple wine goes on developing in the bottle, even though Berberana ages it for 18 months in tank, 12 in cask, and 6 in bottle. The red Carta de Oro is also a *crianza*, but spends less time in tank (12 months) and longer in cask (2 years) and the bottle (also 2 years). This Rioja has rather more colour, maturity, wood and vanilla than the Carta de Plata, tastes somewhat broader and possesses a good balance. Its grape varieties are Tempranillo (60%), Garnacha (20%) and Mazuelo plus Graciano (20%). Taking the red and white together, Berberana sells some 350,000 boxes of Carta de Oro a year.

Pure and harmonious

Although the red Carta de Oro could actually be sold as a *reserva*, the bodega employs this term only for a wine that has had not two, but three years ageing in wood. The other two ageing periods are identical, as are the grape varieties. It is a likeable wine, well provided with wood and of irreproachable quality. Since 1975 the *gran reserva* from this house has been given three years in wood; it had been five years before. The 1973 (still from the old bodega at this date) seemed rather too fat and smooth to me, but the 1975 was a sound, mature Rioja, a pleasure to taste. The red wines from Bodegas Berberana are recognizable by their purity, their harmony and their taste, which is never rough, heavy or aggressive. Despite the great

quantity – 1.5 million (US 1.8 million) gallons annually – these are carefully made products that offer good value for money.

A lot of rosé

Berberana also makes a good deal of rosé – around 660,000 (US 780,000) gallons a year – under the Carta de Plata brand name. It is a most pleasant Garnacha wine, orange-pink in colour and with considerable freshness. When I was given this wine to taste, Gonzalo Ortiz, the cellarman, said that he had made an even better rosé ten years earlier, a wine of a really exceptional standard. It was not marketed, however, but blended with the ordinary rosé. "Because", said Ortiz, "I knew for sure that I could not go on achieving this quality. We want our brand names to guarantee a quality without peaks and troughs, a quality that is constant."

The Cenicero cooperative makes its red wines (the white and the rosé are uninteresting) from 90% Tempranillo and 10% various types. Because of their strength and their rather rustic character, these are wines that demand bottle age – to wear down the sharp corners a little. I had pleasurable encounters with the 8-year-old wines, such as the Valdemontán and the even somewhat better, rather more refined Reserva Especial with the black Santa Daría label.

The Santa Daría Cooperative

Cenicero's patron saint is Santa Daría and the local cooperative is named after her. The building stands practically at the end of the main street, in the Fuenmayor direction. The front of the building suggests that this cooperative sets little store by outward show. The Cooperativa Vinícola de Cenicero was set up in May 1963 and numbers around 530 members. These cultivate a total of some 2,220 acres, mostly in Cenicero itself, with a small area in the neighbouring hamlet of Torremontalbo. Production hovers around 725,000 (US 858,000) gallons a year, three-quarters of which is red wine; the rest is mainly white Rioja, with just 11,000 (US 13,000) gallons of rosé.

A gradual rise in bottled wine sales

After they have been weighed the incoming grapes are destalked and crushed. Fermentation then takes place in large concrete tanks, which in fact are also used for storing the wine. Since the 1984 vintage the bodega has had reasonably modern equipment for controlling temperature during fermentation; before then it sometimes used to rise to 37° C with red wine. Since the arrival of nine stainless-steel tanks the maximum for white and rosé has been 20° C. All wines are filtered twice. The cooperative delivers most of its production to other bodegas in bulk; only about 20% of it is bottled here and marketed under Santa Daría's own label. However, this percentage is gradually increasing.

Rather rustic

The white wine – made from 90% Viura grapes and 10% Malvasia – proved to be a simple, somewhat fat, run-of-the-mill wine; and the rosé did not even taste pleasant. The red wine was a different matter. In contrast to many other cooperatives, Santa Daría has a reasonable number of oak casks at its disposal – 500 – in which its own *crianzas* are matured for a year. The same wines are then also rested in bottle. The average number of bottles in stock lies between 250,000 and 300,000. I was given the *crianzas* from various vintages to taste. All of them were deep-coloured, firm of taste and rustic rather then refined, with just enough wood and vanilla in nose and taste. These are wines that have to be allowed to mature. This was clear from the tasting, for the most mature bottles showed best. My preference was for the Reserva Especial eight-year-old, which had in fact more class to offer than the Valdemontan of the same vintage. The cooperative uses only the Bordeaux type of bottle for its wines.

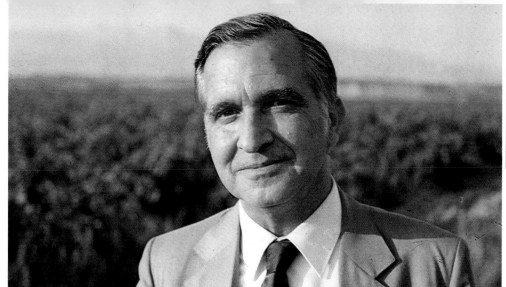

Bodegas Marqués de Cáceres

Cenicero

At the start of the Spanish Civil War the Republican deputy Forner found himself obliged to flee to France with his family. He had lived in the neighbourhood of Valencia, where he produced wine, selling part of the vintage to French importers. His sons Elisée and Henri also went into the wine trade – but in France in their case. They acquired the management of a large table wine business with sales of 18.7 million (US 22.1 million) gallons a year. In time, however, this hectic existence, which was of little interest in qualitative terms, began to please them less and less. They left this massive commercial operation and in 1964, together with some friends, bought the totally neglected estate of Château de Camensac in Bordeaux. A year later, and in the same Médoc *commune* of Saint-Laurent, they purchased another decayed property, that of Château Larose-Trintaudon. With expert help, sustained investment and sheer hard work, the Forner brothers succeeded in wholly restoring both estates and making very good wines that received general praise. Elisée by this time felt totally French, but Henri wanted to return to Spain; in particular to the Rioja, a region that in his view had enormous potential for the production of wine of great merit.

Counsel from Bordeaux

Henri (called Enrique in Spain) was not the sort of man to take chances. Alone, or in the company of Professor Emile Peynaud, the eminent oenologist who had also given advice in the Médoc, he went on reconnaissance in the Rioja, for he wanted to build his bodega where the best grapes were cultivated. In the end his choice fell on Cenicero in the Rioja Alta, where not only did the black grapes appear to offer the best quality, but the whites had just that little more fruit than in other districts. Under Peynaud's supervision a bodega was built, and was ready by 1970. It was given the name of an old friend from Valencia, the Marqués de Cáceres. Buying vineyards

proved impossible for all kinds of reasons and so as early as 1966 Henri Forner had gathered a group of 16 growers around him, with whom he formed the Unión Viti-Vinícola. For a long time too the bodega had close ties with the cooperative in Cenicero, where an increasing quantity of wine was made for Marqués de Cáceres – to strict instructions from Forner and his staff. In 1974, however, the two concerns went their separate ways. At present Forner obtains a lot of wine from the neighbouring cooperative in Huercanos. The Unión Viti-Vinícola continued in existence; its members own between 170 and 200 acres of vineyard.

A ceiling reached

In 1975 the bodega began to sell its first wines – 28,000 cases. Less than a decade later the figure had grow to 350,000 cases, nearly two-thirds of them destined for export. Henri Forner does not want to let his business grow much more: at most he

Bodegas Marqués de Cáceres

anticipates an increase of some 10%. Any further increase of production would, according to Forner, endanger the quality of his wines – and in his view this is what the success of the bodega was based on. In fact Henri Forner is not just concerned about the quality of his own wines, but about those of Rioja in general. When he arrived in the region he discovered to his dismay that while there was a very good system of wine legislation in existence, it was put into only limited effect. He therefore urged stricter control by the Consejo Regulador. He was not thanked for this and in the end Forner, with six like-minded bodega owners, even had to go to law to compel the Consejo to adopt a more stringent supervision. The legal and political skirmishing lasted for about seven years, but Forner and his allies won at the end of the day. It is partly thanks to them that the Rioja now has some of the strictest and best wine legislation in Europe.

Total control

According to Henri Forner, good vinification was his first concern in setting up Bodegas Marqués de Cáceres. His assessment was that principles for the making and nurturing of red wine that had long been applied in Bordeaux had hardly reached the Rioja. Lack of temperature control during fermentation and an excessive use of old wooden casks were two examples, and in his view the situation with white and rosé was even worse: these types of wine were nearly always left to age in wood, whereby fruit and freshness were lost. Right from the start Forner needed to prevail upon the growers to use new methods and abandon the traditional ways. This took a great deal of effort. In countless, often long-drawn-out conversations he had to try to convince the growers that his view was better than that of their fathers and grandfathers. And he succeeded: none of his growers now starts picking without the bodega's permission, and the *cosecheros* vinify the red wines under its supervision. How carefully things are done is evident from the fact that Henri Forner usually has

the sugar content of the grapes measured practically every day from two weeks before the harvest in order to be able to fix the exact moment for all the suppliers to start. With most of them – about 30 altogether, not including the cooperative – the bodega works on a contractual basis. They receive a price per kilo for their grapes set at the average rate for all the villages of the Rioja Alta, plus a premium agreed beforehand. Hardly any grapes are bought in the Rioja Alavesa and the less than 10% obtained from the Rioja Baja is mainly destined for Rivarey and Costanilla, subsidiary brands of a simpler quality.

A balance between wood and fruit

None of the red wine is made by the *macération carbonique* method; all black grapes are destalked and crushed. Fermentation takes place at a low temperature, usually between 22 and 25° C. In the cellars malolactic fermentation is allowed to follow as quickly on the alcoholic as possible. The wines are then transferred to the bodega in Cenicero where maturing in the wood begins. Henri Forner does not advocate too much wood in his red Riojas. The Marqués de Cáceres *crianza* stays 16 to 18 months in cask and the *reserva* about 24 months. "In a good Rioja the wood should not dominate," says Forner, "but should be in balance with the fruit." In the large insulated, 170 × 223 ft *chais* the bodega has some 10,800 casks. In the early 1980s particularly the stock of casks was greatly increased, doubling almost between 1980 and 1984. Half of these *barricas* are made of American oak and for most of the remainder the bodega bought French oak that was made into casks in the Rioja. Casks of Yugoslav and even Spanish oak were also purchased. The first Spanish barrels, made in Santander, arrived in the autumn of 1984. According to Forner Spanish oak is somewhat softer than American and harder than French.

A vast store of bottles

Although the Marqués de Cáceres reds do

not spend an excessively long time in wood, they are given a long period in bottle, and the bodega therefore has an enormous stock of bottles – from 3 to 4 million. A couple of vast halls have been specially built for them – again these are insulated – where the bottles are stored in palletized containers, which are stacked five high. Each of these boxes holds some 680 bottles. The *crianza* stays here for about 15 months, the *reserva* usually for 6 to 7 years: for example, the bodega did not start selling the 1975 *reserva* until September 1984. A wine such as this could, of course, be sold as a *gran reserva* without any problem, but in Forner's view this is not necessary. After long being urged to, however, he did make an exception for his Danish importer, who was given a *gran reserva* label for exactly the same type of wine. Given the rising prices for Rioja it would not surprise me if other markets did not follow this example.

The distinguished 1975

On my visit to Marqués de Cáceres I made the acquaintance of seven vintages of red wine, including three *reservas*, the 1970, 1973 and 1975. Just from these wines it was clear that in its quite short existence this bodega had been making steadily better wines. I thought the 1970 somewhat lacking in body and strength; the 1973 had more taste and character to offer; and the 1975 was one of the best Riojas I have ever tasted. It proved to be a very complete wine, with a deep colour and a full and exquisite taste with ripe fruit, noble wood and a distinguished quality to it. I had tasted the same wine a year earlier. It was then still very closed in; that last year of bottle ageing had made sense. The 1975 *reserva* will undoubtedly enhance the reputation of Bodegas Marqués de Cáceres greatly. And if the Rioja succeeds in producing wines of this class on a bigger scale, then it will be time for certain famous French regions to start worrying in earnest.

Omitted vintages

The red *crianzas* from this bodega also

My favourite new-style white Rioja is the one from Marqués de Cáceres in which, thanks to a slow, low-temperature fermentation, the fruit of the Viura is perfectly conserved, and no wood is involved. Juice, freshness, substance and purity are the other characteristics of this successful product; along with 12% alcohol and a fragrance of flowers. Enchanting.

Marqués de Cáceres produces about 20,000 cases of dry rosé a year – half the quantity of the white Rioja. Tempranillo and Garnacha provide half each of the juice. The Garnacha, too, comes from Rioja Alta, from the higher vineyards on south-facing slopes. The rosé has a vital, refreshing, mouth-filling taste and an orangey colour. After bottling it is given two months' rest (like the white wine). No cask ageing at all.

Marqués de Cáceres red wines are usually made from about 80% Tempranillo 10% Viura and 10% Garnacha, Mazuelo and Graciano together. In the March after the harvest the red Riojas go into the casks, the crianza for 16 to 18 months. For the latter wine this is followed by at least 15 months in bottle. It is a first-rate product, neither too heavy nor too light, with a sound balance between wood and fruit, and with enough tannin for further development.

The reservas receive about 2 years' cask ageing and 6 to 7 years in bottle. After this they still have enough "breath" to evolve further; like the splendid, distinguished 1975, the best wine this bodega had so far brought out – and one of the very best Riojas I have ever tasted. Again there was a masterly balance between mature fruit and noble wood. In some countries the same wine carries a gran reserva label.

Bodegas Marqués de Cáceres

deserve much praise. Naturally the best wines in the best years are selected for the *reservas*, but for the younger kinds, too, very stringent standards are maintained. Thus the vintages of 1972 (unripe fruit), 1974 (too thin, not enough taste), 1977 (unripe) and 1979 (rot prevalent) were not considered good enough for the Marqués de Cáceres label. On the other hand a great deal is invested in good years, as just one figure makes clear: in 1981 the bodega bought at least 1.76 (US 2.08) million gallons of red wine. The *crianzas* are somewhat lighter than the *reservas*, but here too you find a good balance between wood and fruit. In another respect, too, these are balanced wines, for they taste neither too light nor too heavy. Other characteristics are their purity, their sound colour and their tannin, which is not aggressive but enables the wines to go on developing in bottle. The Rivarey and Costanilla brands mentioned earlier are at a simpler, but always decent level. These wines are given six months in cask. Henri Forner will hardly talk about them; his heart lies with wines of real quality.

An exemplary white

While the example of Marqués de Cáceres has been followed as far as red wines are concerned – other bodegas are introducing more fruit and less wood in their wines – thanks to Forner a new school has emerged with regard to making white wine; a school that postulates fruit and freshness and has wholly forsworn the use of wood for white Rioja. As white wine is more sensitive than red to the correct fermentation temperature, this type is vinified in the bodega itself. Only the Viura grape is used and the fruit is picked only when it is absolutely ripe, not under- or over-ripe. After pressing, the must is filtered in an advanced Italian apparatus that Marqués de Cáceres was the first to introduce into Spain. The clear juice is then fermented in metal tanks at a temperature of 16 to 19° C. The process takes a long time – about six weeks – and close attention is paid to it. For the first 14 days and nights there are even two alternating shifts who check the course of the fermentation. Once ready the wine is cold-stabilized and bottled soon afterwards. The bodega then keeps this white Rioja in stock for two months before dispatch to protect it from disturbance. Then it goes out into the world: rather pale, rich in fruit, fresh, juicy, a wine to fill the mouth, uncommonly pure with the same element of wild flowers in its perfume that you find in Sauvignon wines. How successful Marqués de Cáceres is with its white Rioja is clear from the greatly increased production, from 11,000 cases in 1978 to 45,000 six years later.

A refreshing rosé

Forner uses practically the same techniques for his rosé as he applies to

Bodegas Marqués de Cáceres

white wine. This wine, made from 50% Tempranillo and 50% Garnacha, is also vinified at the bodega at a low temperature and stabilized cold. Wood is tabu. The Marqués de Cáceres rosé ranks among the few in the Rioja with a vital, refreshing taste that is fresh without being acid. You can also taste some fruit there; the colour has an orange tint. This wine is also bottled in the spacious hall that was completed in 1984. This area is washed down with hot water every morning and evening. The tank from which the bottles are being filled has to be completely empty before the line is stopped: this is to prevent any residue being left that could oxidise overnight. When Henri Forner had shown me this bottling hall, his bottle store, his casks in their cellar and all his modern plant he said that there was one thing the bodega still lacked, namely a suitable entrance. At the end of 1984 you still had to reach the complex of buildings via a simple roadway. Forner said that there was going to be a gateway, that flowerbeds would be laid out and that – for the first time – the name of his bodega would be painted on the wall.

Fuonmayor

Bodegas Lan

In the various books published about the Rioja the foundation year of Bodegas Lan is usually given as 1972 or 1974. In fact this bodega dates from 1970, when the Basque families of Elorriaga and Valdés decided to set up a wine business. During the early years they operated from various small cellars, in Haro and elsewhere, but their need for a single bodega with modern equipment grew rapidly. Such an investment, however, demanded more capital than the families had available and so in 1973 the *sociedad anónima* Bodegas Lan was created, which brought in other shareholders. At the end of 1973 the firm bought a large piece of land – about 17 acres – in a broad valley between Fuenmayor and Cenicero. The site lay beside the provincial road linking Logroño and Haro, and not far from a junction with the A68 *autopista*. The hard work began straight away; *lan* in Basque means "work" – and also stands for the three provinces of the Rioja, *L*ogroño, *A*lava and *N*avarra.

An austere design

The bodega was built in accordance with the ideas of an extremely talented oenologist, José Manuel Aizpurua, who had earlier earned his spurs at Olarra (q.v.) He chose a very functional, technologically advanced design for the complex, with buildings that were without fuss or ornament, but austere in form and efficient in layout. The new bodega was ready in 1974 – just in time to make wine that year. Its construction had cost 125 million pesetas. The building soon proved to be too small and had to be extended. This work was finished in November 1975 at a cost of another 125 million. For a third time, and again for the same cost, Bodegas Lan was enlarged in December 1980. It now has a covered surface area of 183,000 sq ft and still has more than enough room for any future expansion.

A Roman bridge

Of Lan's average annual production of 440,000 (US 520,000) gallons of red Rioja,

about one-eighth comes from its own vineyards. These are in one block of land and lie near the hamlet of El Cortijo. I drove there one sunny afternoon. The surfaced road from Logroño to El Cortijo goes no further and to reach the Lan estate you have to traverse several miles of bumpy gravel road, strewn with stones of various sizes. The road follows the course of a very winding stretch of the Ebro that lies a good way below. I knew that I had reached the Bodegas Lan vineyards when I saw the remains of a Roman bridge in the river, for this ruin is depicted on the firm's labels. A great deal of work must have been put in on this rough, stony terrain, for the soil here is anything but easy to cultivate. In the early 1970s the property comprised 150 plots belonging to 60 different growers. Bodegas Lan acquired all the land, grubbed out all vines where necessary and made the soil workable and then, in 1974, planted the vines. At present the firm has 173 productive acres. On 99 of these the Tempranillo is grown, with the Viura on 30

acres and Mazuelo grapes on the rest. According to Bodegas Lan these 44 acres of Mazuelo represent the largest planting of this variety in the whole Rioja.

Modern installations

What Lan buys elsewhere in addition to its own production consists chiefly of grapes: four times as much grapes as wine in the case of red and rosé Rioja, and grapes only for the white (one-seventh of the fruit for white wine comes from the bodega's vineyards). The bodega is equipped for the speedy processing of large quantities of grapes and the reception points have a capacity of 60 tons a day. The grapes for red wine are immediately destalked and crushed, then pumped into the metal fermentation tanks. These are self-emptying, of the same model as those at Olarra. They are extremely efficient in their operation and cleaning them is child's play. The red wine ferments for eight to ten days at no more than 27° C. The fermenting

Bodegas Lan

juice is cooled by passing water over the outsides of the tanks – not ice-cold, but at tap temperature (15 to 16° C). In 1974, the first year, Aizpurua carried out an experiment with *macération carbonique*. The results were not bad, but so many practical problems arose in the bodega that the experiment has not been repeated.

All reds aged in wood

In principle the white and red wines are made from free-run juice that is pressed out by the weight of the grapes themselves. Juice from the first pressing is added to the red wines. Occasionally – and this depends on the vintage – Lan also adds juice from the second pressing; but never, however, from the third, which in any case amounts only to 3 to 4% of the total. Underground tanks are available for the malolactic fermentation of the red wines. The grey, concrete cellar for the casks is also underground; with its dimensions of 98 by 433 ft it is longer than a soccer pitch. Here there are some 14,000 casks, stacked five high. This is a relatively large number, but then, Bodega Lan sells no red wine that has not had at least 18 months in cask. As with most of the Riojan houses, all the casks are made of American oak. Two *toneleros* (coopers) are on the permanaent staff to maintan them. At Lan it is not only the number of casks that is comparatively large; it normally holds a stock of around 2 million bottles.

A fresh core to the taste

The white wine, of which there is just one type, is usually put on sale in the February or March after the vintage. The Viura is its sole grape. A pale colour, a soft, slightly fruity perfume and a clear taste with a fresh nucleus to it are its most important features, and it has an alcohol content of around 11.5%. Although this was not an exceptional wine, I nevertheless had the impression that its quality had gradually been improved over the years. This wine is not aged in wood, but at the bodega I was told that they were experimenting with

this. I prefer Lan's white wine to its rosé, a 100% Garnacha wine, the grapes for which come mostly from the same two suppliers. I find the taste of this pale pink, fairly supple wine has just a little too much acid and not quite enough fruit. Both the white and the rosé wines are cold-stabilized, the red never.

Elegant style

Lan's red *crianza* has the same composition as the older red wines, namely 80% Tempranillo, 10% Garnacha and 10% Mazuelo. It is a good Rioja, elegant in nature and very pure. Neither in nose nor

in taste do the wood and vanilla elements assert themselves, but they are discreetly present. In general I prefer this wine when it is three to five years old. It is matured for 12 months in tank, 18 in cask and 6 in bottle. The *reserva* is called Viña Lanciano and is particularly well-known in Spain itself. Wood and vanilla are more strongly present, which is logical since the wine spends half a year longer in the cask. It has 18 months in tank first, then at least $2\frac{1}{2}$ years in bottle after its period in wood. This, too, is a quite elegant wine of its kind, although with rather more body and, of course, greater maturity. The Viña Lanciano *gran reserva* usually has a taste

Both the white and the rosé Riojas from Lan carry this label with the Roman bridge against a background – slightly distorted – of its own vineyards. Although the rosé has perhaps a little too much acid and too little fruit, the white is a pleasant, refreshing, pure wine with a judicious amount of fruit and not too much alcohol. Made from 100% Viura, the wine usually spends a year in tank before bottling.

The wood in Lan's red crianza, with its accompanying vanilla, is refined, not assertive or too "old established". The wine itself is elegant with some fruit and a decent quality. It is given 12 months in the tank, 18 in cask and 6 in bottle. I prefer to drink this Rioja within 12 to 24 months after it goes on sale.

Viña Lanciano reserva has the same blend of grapes as the other Lan reds: 80% Tempranillo, 10% Garnacha and 10% Mazuelo. Rather more strength, maturity

and wood plus vanilla can be expected than from the crianza – but without the wood being dominant. Of its kind this, too, is a quite elegant wine, not really deep or nuanced, but carefully and expertly made. It is matured for 1½ years in tank, 2 in cask and 2½ in bottle. There is also a tall, narrow label in use.

I think the Bodegas Lan wines are best when they still possess youth and vitality – but this is a question of personal taste. Others may prefer the firm's well-matured, brown-coloured gran reserva: quite simply a good wine that is aged for 1½ years in tank, 2½ in cask and at least 5 in bottle (and possibly more – up to 8 years).

Bodegas Lan

that is obviously well matured, and has a lot of brown in its colour. Bodegas Lan sells it after ageing it for 18 months in tank, 2½ years in cask and 5 to 8 years in bottle.

José Manuel Aizpurua was the first to abandon the traditional method of storing bottles stacked on slats, giving up this labour- and cost-intensive system for one using large wooden trays that can be moved like pallets. At Lan these are stacked four high.

Changes of ownership

For most of the time since the new buildings came into use the firm has been run by the same manager and the same oenologist. This has undoubtedly contributed to the consistent quality Bodegas Lan has offered over the years. Things could have been otherwise, for the business has changed owners several times. In 1982 it was taken over by the powerful Rumasa group, which acquired a majority of the shares. For seven months Lan belonged to this concern. Then Rumasa was nationalized and the bodega had the government as its owner. Early in 1985 the government transferred the Rumasa holding to Marcos Equizábal Ramirez, the Madrid entrepreneur who also bought Bodegas y Viñedos, Franco-Españolas and Paternina. This meant that Bodegas Lan had had four owners in three years; and Aizpurua has left in the meantime. Fortunately, however, the wine has not suffered.

It should be mentioned that the firm also trades under two other names, Bodegas Landalan (with the Lancorta trademark) and Bodegas del Señorio de Ulia. In neither case are the wines in any way different from those in the Lan range. The most important markets for Bodegas Lan are Spain, West Germany, Denmark, Britain and Canada.

Right:
The stock of bottles fluctuates between 500,000 and 1,000,000.

Below left:
The coat of arms that appears on some labels.

Below right:
The whole bodega complex, dating from 1975.

Lagunilla supplies Rioja to the Peter Dominic chain in Britain, also part of the IDV group.

There are usually 8,000 casks in their underground cellar, but there is room for 2,000 more.

La Rioja Viticola and Alterra are subsidiary brands of Lagunilla.

Bodegas Lagunilla

Fuenmayor

The Bodegas Lagunilla buildings are in the same wide valley as those of Lan, and practically next door. They are painted white and from a distance almost suggest a grain silo rather than a wine firm. The founder of the bodega, Felipe Lagunilla, would no doubt view them with amazement. The business he started at the end of the previous century was small and located in Cenicero. Lagunilla was born in 1863, the son of a farmer. As a 20-year-old he decided to apply himself wholly to the making and selling of wine, and so two years later, in 1885, he registered his trademark of La Rioja Viticola with the Chamber of Commerce in Logroño. Bodegas Lagunilla still uses this trademark from its foundation year, but as a subsidiary brand. After a further five years, Felipe built the bodega in Cenicero, on the road to the station.

A work of rescue

After the *Phylloxera vastatrix* had destroyed or damaged vineyards in Bordeaux and other French regions, the parasite was reported in the Rioja. The effect was equally disastrous. When in France a remedy was at last found (grafting European vines on to American rootstocks) it was Felipe Lagunilla who first used this method in the Rioja. Many other wine growers subsequently asked him for help and advice, which Felipe offered in a totally disinterested way – even to the extent of giving away ready-grafted vines. This made him famous, but not rich; for he did

all this simply to save viticulture in the Rioja and not to earn anything for himself. To mark the esteem in which he was held he was decorated by King Alfonso XIII in 1916.

The family pulls out

Joaquin Lagunilla, Felipe's son, was given a thorough training in the wine trade, studying at the school of viticulture at Haro and then for a further three years in Bordeaux. In 1927 Joaquin took over the bodega after the death of his father. It grew strongly, the Lagunilla wines enjoying an increasing reputation in northern Spain in

Lagunilla Tinto (the "Valle" has recently been dropped from the label) has the Tempranillo as its main grape. Of its kind it is a quite colourful, firm wine with a correct aftertaste. Nose and taste have a clear touch of wood. Ageing: 12 months in tank, 6 to 12 in cask and 6 to 12 in bottle. Grapes for this and the other Lagunilla wines are bought throughout the Rioja.

The Viña Herminia enjoys a good reputation; the 1975, for example, was judged the best reserva in Spain. The wine usually has a good deep colour, a not particularly exciting perfume (with some wood plus vanilla) and a concentrated taste with body and tannin – one that demands some time in the cellar. It will already have had a year in tank, 2 to 3 in cask and 1 to 2 in bottle.

Like all the Lagunilla reds the gran reserva comes chiefly from the Tempranillo. It is given a year in tank, 4 years in cask and 2 to 4 in bottle; thus the 1973 did not appear on sale until early 1984. A robust, mouth-filling taste with fruit, body, wood and tannin; not tired as a rule but still fully vital. Sometimes particular consignments are given less time to mature in the bottle than others from the same year.

Bodegas Lagunilla

---

particular. The Viña Herminia, Vallezarza and Valderrin became very well known and the equipment in the bodega could gradually be modernized. Joaquin had three sons, who all became involved in the bodega. In 1941 they officially became shareholders and the name of the firm was changed to Joaquin Lagunilla y Cia. The brothers continued the business after their father's death. In 1956 they altered the name to Bodegas Lagunilla. The family remained as owners until 1967. Then one of the three brothers died, after which all the shares were made over to the Basque firm of Vinicola Montañesa from Santander. It was this new owner who started on the

building of the large new bodega on the present site. A year later – when the building was not yet completed – there followed a bid for 80% of the shares by the British group International Distillers and Vintners (IDV). At the beginning of 1974 the parties came to an agreement whereby not a majority but all the shares were sold and included in the sale was a stock of 2.2 million (US 2.6 million) gallons of wine. Since the IDV port and sherry firm of Croft had led the negotiations this received 50% of the shares and IDV itself the rest. In practice Croft now runs the business under the close supervision of IDV.

No processing of grapes

Whereas at most bodegas the grape harvest is an important and hectic time, this season at Lagunilla is one of relative peace. No tractors pulling cartloads of grapes are to be seen here, no weighing machines, destalkers or fermentation tanks. For Lagunilla has no vineyards of its own and, moreover, processes no grapes. The bodega buys in only wine, from cooperatives or individual owners. What you do find in this great complex of tall structures is tanks – with a total capacity of 3.3 million (US 3.9 million) gallons. Most of them are of concrete. I saw storage tanks, blending tanks and heavily insulated tanks in which the wines – 90% of the production – undergo cold treatment. Various filtering equipment is also installed. Wines that are sold young are first filtered through earth, then fined and thereafter filtered once more. By this time these wines are "super-stable": whether there remains much character to their taste is, of course, another matter.

Red predominant

I found the white and rosé wines rather disappointing. For its white Rioja the bodega selects only wines from the Viura grape. They do not come into contact with wood and after six months in the tank they are bottled and sent out. The samples I tasted were fairly smooth, supple and short,

and had no distinctive characteristics to offer. The grapes used for the rosé are the Tempranillo and the Viura. Although the firm itself says that its rosé enjoys a good reputation, I thought it was too lacking in fruit and vitality for commendation; which is not to say that this somewhat orange-tinted wine is not very acceptable when well chilled. For me the strength of Bodegas Lagunilla lies not in its white or rosé wines but in its red, and this accounts for by far the greatest part of its production: at least 440,000 (US 520,000) gallons, against 22,000 (US 26,000) gallons of white and 44,000 (US 52,000) rosé.

Solidly structured

The youngest red wine is the Lagunilla Tinto, made chiefly from the Tempranillo. If this Rioja contains wine from other grapes it is simply because many growers still have a mixture of varieties in their vineyards. The Lagunilla Tinto is matured for 12 months in tank, 6 to 12 months in cask and 6 to 12 in bottle. It is not therefore a *crianza*, for which 12 months in wood plus 12 in bottle are the minimum required. The wine is characterized by a strong colour and a firm taste, with its alcohol at about 12.5%. In it you can distinctly taste and smell some wood. The next wine in the range is the Viña Herminia which spends 12 months in tank, 2 years in cask and 1 to 2 years in bottle. As far as nose is concerned this wine is not usually very interesting, but its taste is concentrated, substantial and well endowed with tannin. This Rioja will generally age well – including in the customer's cellar at home. The strength by which all the Lagunilla red wines can be recognized is also there in the *gran reserva*, a Rioja that is usually put on the market only after eight or nine years – and will still be very vital, again with plenty of tannin.

AGE Bodegas Unidas

The story of AGE begins in 1881, when Félix Azpilicueta Martinez set up a wine business, calling it Bodegas del Romeral. The site he chose was just outside Fuenmayor, beside the railway station. Azpilicueta was progressive and enterprising, and when he expanded his bodega he did not hesitate to install the latest devices. Quite early on he started using glass-tiled fermentation tanks and a semi-automatic system to pump the wine from tank to tank. In 1926 a new wine concern was built opposite Bodegas del Romeral by Cruz García Lafuente. It was given the name Bodegas Las Veras and the two firms competed with one another for several decades at home and abroad. In 1964, however, they decided to collaborate in the export field. This combining of their capacities proved to be a wise decision: they could now for the first time develop the important Cuban market and had the possibility of opening up altogether new markets. Three years later, in 1967, the firms decided to merge and to bring in a third firm, Melquíades Entrena of Navarrete. The name AGE was chosen, from the initial letters of the three surnames, *A*zpilicueta, *G*arcía and *E*ntrena.

American participation

Partly due to the strong emphasis on export, the "united bodegas" grew vigorously. Straight away in 1967 the building of a new cellar complex in Fuenmayor was begun, and a large bottling hall with an underground cellar for casks was completed in 1971. Scarcely two years later the American drinks firm Schenley made an offer for 49% of the shares, which was accepted. At present the remainder of the shares are in the hands of the Cruz García Lafuente y Banesto family (38%) and the Banco Español de Crédito (13%). Production of Rioja rose to 3.4 million (US 4 million) gallons a year. Most of this – 2.8 million (US 3.28 million) gallons – is sold bottled. The remaining 616,000 (US 728,000) gallons of bulk wine goes abroad (as does 45% of the bottled wine). In total therefore AGE exports 55% of its extensive production. Repeatedly this bodega has been the top Rioja exporter for the year. In many countries AGE has fulfilled the role of market pioneer for Rioja. At the time this book was being written, the AGE brand Siglo represented almost half of Rioja sales in Japan. The firm also makes a large amount of sangria, but in an entirely separate set-up.

Grapes and must

AGE owns only 124 acres of vineyard (in Rioja Alta, planted solely with black grapes), so it is largely dependent on its suppliers. For its white wine (about 25% of production), the bodega buys mainly grapes, which it then has vinified under supervision at cooperatives. It also buys some must, which it processes into wine at Fuenmayor. Red wine (70% of the total) is made at various places; and wine is also purchased. In principle, however, purchases are restricted as far as possible to grapes and must. A tour of the great complex at Fuenmayor reveals various kinds of fermentation tanks, of stainless steel as well as of concrete. In addition there are large wooden enclosed vats. These, however, are used only for storing *reservas* and *gran reservas*.

Three years in the cask

With the bottled wines from this bodega the accent lies on the wood-aged types. This is why there is a stock of 35,000 casks available; and there are three coopers on the staff to maintain and repair them. This goodly number of casks does not mean that the wines spend a great length of time in them. No Rioja here stays more than three years in wood.

At the end of the 1970s there was a temporary shortage of oak casks in the region. This explains the presence of a small number of whisky barrels; AGE received special permission to import these from Scotland.

AGE Bodegas Unidas

Three hundred kilometres of jute

The best-selling AGE wine is called Siglo, and its bottle comes wrapped in jute sacking. The firm itself refers to Siglo *saco*, as there is a different quality sold under this brand name, but without the little sack. I have stood and watched with fascination the working of the small bottle line for the *saco* wine. This processes a maximum of 3,500 bottles an hour, while the ordinary line can fill and label about 12,000 an hour. Up to 15 people were involved in providing the bottles with their jute wrapping and appropriate labels. One woman was there just to press the hot wax into the punt of each bottle. Bearing in mind the great success of Siglo I asked how much jute AGE used a year. Apparently it is at least 300 kilometres – 186 miles, with a width of 4¾ ft.

Fairly generous

The worldwide success of Siglo *saco* is not only explained by the striking packaging, but also by the quality of the wine. It is one of the best Riojas that AGE produces. It possesses quite a generous character, with a well-rounded taste and nose, a mature wood aroma and 12.5% alcohol. It is marketed as a *crianza*, after a year in tank, two years in cask and six months in bottle. The grape varieties are listed as 50% Tempranillo, 35% Garnacha and 15% Mazuelo. Given the limited amount of Mazuelo grown in the Rioja, it seemed to me that this 15% was very high, particularly as all the other red wines that AGE bottles are said to contain at least 15 to 25% Mazuelo. The oenologist Eulogio

AGE's bestseller is the Siglo packed in jute sacking and referred to as saco. Partly because of its good amount of Garnacha (30%) it is a quite generous red wine, with a mild, mature wood component in nose and taste, with some fruit. It usually has 12.5% alcohol. It spends 12 months in tank, 24 in cask and 6 in bottle. The same wine is also called Agessimo (also in a sack) or Credencial (from the Bodegas del Romeral subsidiary).

No jute packing for the Marqués del Romeral gran reserva, but there is a mesh over the bottle. The wine stays for a year in tank and then 3 years in cask, which explains the considerable vanilla aroma. A pleasant, well-matured taste, a reasonably deep colour and as a rule 12.5% alcohol. The same wine is also sold as Siglo etiqueta negra. At 60% the Tempranillo is the most important grape (10% more than in the Siglo saco).

AGE Bodegas Unidas

Perez Pardo assured me, however, that the percentages were correct. This was later confirmed in writing in answer to a letter I sent to the bodega on the subject. I was also informed that the Mazuelo content will be reduced eventually in favour of the Tempranillo.

Another marquis

Another much-sold red Rioja is the Marqués del Romeral, a *gran reserva* named after a vice-president of the bodega (and a former Spanish ambassador to Denmark). Its grape varieties are given as 60% Tempranillo, 25% Mazuelo and 15% Graciano; in this wine there is no Garnacha at all. It generally tastes very pleasant. It is a well-matured Rioja with a good deal of vanilla and a firm taste. I prefer this wine to the Siglo *saco*. The Marqués del Romeral spends a year in large wooden vats, three years in oak casks and at least two years in bottles. It, too, is filtered twice, like all the other AGE wines.

I also became acquainted with the 1er Centenario, a *gran reserva* that was brought out in 1981 for the centenary celebrations. This was a 1964 wine – from before the merger and out of the Azpilicueta vaults – that even 20 years after its making still proved full of life, a wine in the grand manner. All the 132,000 bottles of this rare wine have long since been sold.

Various brands

The younger red wines from AGE are fairly simple in type and hardly merit a description. I found the ordinary Siglo, for example, rather less attractive than the *saco*, and the same held for the Romeral in relation to the Marqués del Romeral. The ordinary Siglo is made from 50% Tempranillo, 30% Garnacha and 20% Mazuelo. It is given a year in tank and a year in cask. The Romeral is a *sin crianza*, made from the same mix of grapes. At AGE all the red wines are fermented in the normal way; the *macération carbonique* method is not used at all. The bodega carries various brand names for the same wines: Viña Tere, for example, is the same as Romeral; Agessimo *saca* the same as Siglo *saco* (also Credencial) and Siglo *etiqueta negra* the same as Marqués del Romeral.

Not wholly successful

That AGE bestows a lot of care on its white wines is clear from its purchase of only grapes or must, and from the modern plant (stainless-steel tanks and a unit for cold stabilization). The products themselves are, therefore, somewhat disappointing. It should be possible to produce fresh, fruity wines here, but the bodega has not been altogether successful so far. I found the Siglo *saco* to be the best dry white Rioja, offering rather more taste than the ordinary run. None of the white wines comes into contact with wood and the Viura is the only grape used. The rosés made even less of an impression; the Siglo *saco* of this type even had a sweet element to its taste. The bodega generally makes this wine of the year from 60% Tempranillo and 40% Garnacha. The AGE range is no exception to the rule that in the Rioja red wine is predominant in both quantity and quality.

Below left:
Grape picker near Fuenmayor.

Below right:
The name López Agós y Cia is still displayed at the entrance.

Right:
But the visitor will also see the sign Marqués del Puerto.

Of the 175 shareholders, there are 10 who between them have a majority interest.

A cooper is employed to look after the casks, which remain in use for an average 15 years here.

Bodegas Marqués del Puerto

In 1968 a group of wine growers in Fuenmayor decided to collaborate. They formed a limited company, the Bodegas López Agós y Compañía. It was named after Federico López Agós, a shareholder and at that time manager, and the man who had taken the first initiative. A completely new bodega was built, just outside Fuenmayor and on the provincial road to Logroño. This was in 1972, a disastrous year for Rioja wine, and the firm found itself obliged to sell the whole of its first vintage in bulk. The fact that "marquis" has a certain ring in the marketplace had something to do with the change of name to Bodegas Marqués del Puerto in October 1983. The name López Agós is still used, but on a limited scale in certain markets and chiefly for young wines of the simpler sort. The plan is that this name will eventually disappear. Marqués del Puerto is no fictitious name. King Philip V bestowed the title on an 18th-century diplomat who had served as ambassador in Denmark, Sweden and the Netherlands. The present bearer of the title, Rafael Martínez de Pison y Gaztelu, is a shareholder in the bodega.

Export oriented

Roughly 40% of the grapes required are supplied from the vineyards the bodega owns or leases. Of the remainder, half is normally bought in the form of grapes, half as wine. Practically all of this comes from the Rioja Alta; only in poor years are purchases made in the Rioja Baja. Bodegas Marqués del Puerto produces an average 220,000 (US 260,000) gallons a year of red wine, 22,000 (US 26,000) gallons of white and the same of rosé. The firm is very export-oriented; some 60% of the total volume goes to West Germany, the Netherlands, Denmark, Britain, Switzerland, the United States and other countries. All wine is sent out bottled.

Relatively few casks

Although the bodega looks not unattractive from outside, sheer functionalism has triumphed inside. The firm operates with concrete and metal fermentation and

Bodegas Marqués del Puerto

storage tanks, with modern de-stalking and pressing machinery for the black grapes, with plate filters through which all the wines go twice, and with a cooling plant that stabilizes at low temperatures the rosés, the whites and the red wines for bottling young. The casks stand in whitewashed underground galleries. The average stock of these *barricas* numbers around 2,000, which is relatively few. If you take any other Fuenmayor bodega at random you find a much greater number of casks. Relatively speaking Lagunilla uses twice as many, Lan three and a half times as many. This means that Marqués del Puerto specializes in wines with little or no cask ageing, not in those that spend a long time in the wood. It follows from this that the stock of bottles is also relatively modest: around 300,000. During my visit, however, I was repeatedly assured that in the future the bodega will turn increasingly to *crianza* and *reserva* wines.

White wine aged in wood

I went through the range of wines in the bodega's narrow reception area, screened off in one of the cask galleries, with pennants from Logroño's soccer team and other sports clubs on the walls. The ordinary rosé (90% Garnacha, 10% Viura) and the white (100% Viura) proved to be hardly worth much attention: they were supple wines, but rather tired in taste and nose. Both are bottled after first being given a year in the tank. The white Agós Oro was rather more interesting; after a period in the tank it spent 6 months in wood and 12 in bottle; this is also 100% Viura. Although this Rioja did not excel in freshness, I did taste and smell some subtleties, together with a little vanilla. The example I tasted was nearly eight years old. The name Agós Oro obviously dates from the bodega's López Agós period and it will not remain in common use.

The older the better

Of the red Riojas neither the wine of the year nor the *crianza* made much of an impression; I thought their quality just bordered on the adequate. Fortunately the standard improved with the Marqués del Puerto *reserva*, a wine that like the two previous ones was made solely from the Tempranillo. Its characteristics included a dark-red colour, a taste that was not overwhelmed by wood, a certain maturity and a decent aftertaste. Before it goes on sale it is matured by 12 months in tank, 2 years in wood and at least 2 years in bottle. I was also given a glass of *gran reserva*; this had spent a year longer in cask and a year longer in bottle. This was the best Rioja of the whole tasting, again with a dark colour of a brownish tint, and a delightful taste, well-matured without being exhausted. Its year was 1973, the first successful vintage from this bodega. It is to be hoped that Bodegas Marqués del Puerto will make more wines of this calibre; wines worthy of a noble name.

Bodegas Montecillo

Fuenmayor

Like many others at the time, the Navajas family, which has lived in Fuenmayor for many generations, set up its own bodega in 1874. After all, an enormous demand for Rioja had developed, thanks to the French. The little firm was managed by Alejandro Navajas, who had had training in wine in Bordeaux. Alejandro's son José Luis was also to have part of his schooling in France, at Beaune. It was he who called the firm Bodegas El Montecillo, after a hill of vineyards with this name near Fuenmayor. José Luis was also one of the first in the Rioja to install cooling plant in his bodega, as well as fitting out a reception and tasting area for visitors. Montecillo earned a good reputation, especially in Spain. And it was because of this good name that the bodega was bought in 1973 by Osborne, the 200-year-old sherry and brandy firm. That Montecillo was taken over simply for its reputation is evident from the fact that a start was made almost immediately with the building of a new bodega a few miles

outside Fuenmayor, not far from a junction with the *autopista*. The work was completed in 1975. The old vaults in Fuenmayor are still there and have a historical value. Some wine remains stored in them and people from Montecillo work there for one day once a year. After the Osborne take-over the Navajas family withdrew from the business altogether. José Luis Navajas died in September 1984.

Stringent grape selection

Everything points to the fact that Osborne has invested a great deal in Montecillo, the aim being optimum quality. A tour round the bodega speaks volumes in this respect. The principle of buying only grapes, and no wines, was decided upon – so that the firm could have the whole wine-making process from beginning to end completely within its control. The bodega has no vineyards of its own. It was also resolved that the selection of grapes should be stringent. So stringent is it that no fruit of the 1983 vintage was vinified; the grapes that year were thought to be too inconsistent (the firm had sufficient stocks to avoid running into commercial problems). Of the 330,000 to 440,000 gallons (US 390,000 to 520,000 gallons) that Montecillo produces in an average year, about 85% is red, 12.5% white and 2.5% rosé. Only bottled wine is sold.

Bodegas Montecillo

Carbon dioxide in the white

For fermenting the wine the bodega is equipped with metal tanks of the modern self-emptying type. The temperature in them is kept deliberately low. The red ferments at a maximum of 24° C, the white and rosé at 17 to 18° C. The bodega retains a minimal dose of carbon dioxide in its white Rioja, so that the wine keeps its fresh quality longer. White and rosé wines are always stabilized cold; red occasionally – and then only the youngest type. After fermentation is completed all the wines are given 6 to 12 months' rest in concrete, white-tiled tanks. The rosé and white wines are then bottled; the reds are transferred to oak casks. This is sometimes preceded by filtering the wines through earth.

A functional, efficient concern

Bodegas Montecillo is a very efficient firm. It has a staff of only some 25 people. The functional principles on which the bodega was constructed are clearly demonstrated in the cellar where the casks are stored. In most other bodegas one man fills one cask; at Montecillo one man fills two casks. A pump is not needed here as gravity does the work. In addition, the casks are not rolled about one at a time by hand, but four at a time on a trolley. Something else I found remarkable was the ingenious way in which a mobile hoist has been fixed below the ceiling of the cellar, which makes it possible to haul casks up or let them down from the five-high rows with very little manpower.

An increasing proportion of French casks

There are normally 10,000 casks in the Montecillo cellar, maintained by the firm's own cooper. Besides the casks of American oak there are also some of French wood, from Limousin. Thirty per cent is the present quota, but the bodega hopes to increase this: for experience has shown that French oak has a less aggressive influence on the wine. Montecillo does not want the wood aroma to be too dominant in its wines; and a relatively long period maturing in the bottle is preferred to prolonged ageing in the cask. All the French casks bought have been used ones. I was told, too, that casks have even been purchased from the famous Château Margaux in Bordeaux.

The bottle vault

Even the red *crianza* Viña Cumbrero is given 6 to 12 months' bottle ageing before being sold. This is preceded by 6 to 12 months in the tank and 12 to 18 months in

Use of Malvasía (30%) for this white wine makes it more aromatic than most. Viura is the other grape. Also characteristic is the discreet presence of carbon dioxide, which produces the merest tingling on the tongue and keeps the wine fresh. You can also taste some fruit. The bodega also sells this wine under the Montecillo name.

Suppleness, a pleasant, not too raw aroma of wood and a degree of fruit are usually present in this crianza, along with a strong colour. Ageing: 6 to 12 months in the tank, 12 to 18 in cask and 6 to 12 in bottle. Occasionally (depending on the vintage) the wine is given a cold treatment. The same quality is also sold simply as Montecillo.

Viña Monty is Bodegas Montecillo's best wine: a balanced, beautifully matured, charming reserva that is deliberately and to an important extent matured in French oak casks (for 3½ to 4½ years). It also receives 6 to 12 months in tank and 1½ to 3 years in bottle. Vanilla and wood are present in a refined way in both perfume and taste. It is made exclusively from Tempranillo.

Right:
Montecillo has its own laboratory with a permanent staff.

Below left:
One of the two large bottle stores. About 900,000 bottles are stacked here and there are about 600,000 in the other gallery opposite.

Below right:
The mature glow of a Viña Monty, the best red Rioja from this quality bodega.

The bodega's tanks have a total storage capacity of 1.76 million (US 2.08 million) gallons.

There is a cooper in permanent employment to maintain the firm's 10,000 casks.

Bodegas Montecillo

---

the cask. It is a supple, substantial Rioja, with a lot of juice, a beautiful touch of wood in it and considerable colour. I thought the 1982 one of the very best of this type that the bodega has made. The usual grape varieties are Tempranillo (70%), Garnacha (15%) and Mazuelo (15%). This last percentage is possible according to the bodega because quite a lot of Mazuelo is grown around Fuenmayor. The firm has about 2.5 million bottles of *crianza* and other types in stock; part of this array is in a 330-ft long vault, stacked one at a time by hand – the only area in the bodega where efficiency has not penetrated.

A winning reserva

Where the *crianza* has three grape varieties as its basis, the *reserva* Viña Monty is made from the Tempranillo alone. Once out of the tank the wine is aged for 30 to 40 months in cask and for 18 to 36 in bottle. It is an exquisite Rioja, deep in colour, with plenty of vanilla (but without a strong element of wood) and a pleasant, almost generous taste. The 1975 was the first vintage of this wine produced in the new bodega. Montecillo also brought out a *gran reserva* in 1973, but this came from the old bodega. It was a wine in which the wood

predominated as it had been matured in what were then new casks of American oak. The 1975 was different; more refined in style. How refined was shown at a great blind tasting of Rioja and Bordeaux wines held under the supervision of notaries on 17 September 1983 in Amsterdam. Although not too much weight should be attached to comparative tastings of this sort, given the great variation of vintages and other factors, it was nevertheless remarkable to find the Viña Monty 1975 awarded the most points – more than, for example, the Château Brane-Cantenac 1979 and Château Léoville-las-Cases 1979 (both Bordeaux *deuxièmes grands crus classés*).

An aromatic white

That Montecillo makes a rosé seems to be merely a matter of form: it was barely mentioned during my visit, and I was not given any to taste. The white Viña Cumbrero, on the other hand, is regarded as a serious product. They make it from 70% Viura and 30% Malvasia grapes. Some carbon dioxide is retained in the wine which you cannot only smell, but also taste from a slight tingling on the tongue. For the rest it is a quite aromatic, refreshing wine with some fruit. This Rioja does not go straight out into the world after bottling but stays in the cellars for three to six months first.

Bodegas Montecillo already exports half of its production and it is hoped that this will grow to about 70%.

Bodegas Corral

The establishment of Bodegas Corral was set in train in the second half of the last century by Saturnino Daroca. Back from the Third Carlist War, which ended in 1876, he made up his mind to become a wine grower. He planted vines on his estates in Sojuela, Entrena and Medrano, three villages lying close together just south-east of Navarrete, and also bought a house with a cellar in Sojuela from the monastery of Santa Maria La Real. Daroca's work was later taken over by Martin Corral, his son-in-law. It was he who in 1898, at the age of 17, named the little firm the Bodegas Corral. Corral's two sons, Gregorio (died 1980) and Florencio,

further expanded its activities. They no longer sold their wines just in Rioja but in other parts of Spain, and even abroad. Production grew and so did the bodega; so much so that eventually serious problems of space had to be contended with. Then in the early 1970s it was decided to build a completely new bodega, in Navarrete, on the road that leads into the town from Logroño. The whole complex was completed in 1974.

The dynamic and the modest

Four years later the Corral family engaged a young general manager, Javier Martinez

(born 1951). He did not belong to the family, but had been closely associated with Florencio in particular. He came from a family of wine growers in Cenicero. Javier is a most dynamic man who not only manages his bodega in a go-ahead way, but also took the initiative in setting up the ARBOR association, holds an important office with the Consejo Regulador, and is master of ceremonies for the regional wine fraternity. The contrast between him and his chairman could hardly be greater. All his life Florencio Corral has conducted himself as a modest, simple man; someone who is averse to outward show, who has no interest whatsoever in interviews ("I've

The Don Jacobo *crianza* is a red wine with about 12% alcohol, given 18 months in tank, 18 in cask and at least 4 in bottle. Tempranillo (70%) and Garnacha (30%) are its grape varieties. The supple, rather full-bodied taste has fruit with a measure of maturity and a modest amount of wood and vanilla; a correct aftertaste.

The quality level rises with the reserva, a wine from 80% Tempranillo, 15% Garnacha and 5% Mazuelo. A Rioja with just that little extra strength, wood and character – very pleasing. It has also won awards (the 1978, for example, took a silver medal at Bordeaux). Ageing: 1 year in tank, 4 in cask, 2 in bottle.

It was 1984 before Florencio Corral allowed this 1975 to be sold as a *gran reserva*. Before then it was a reserva – after the same ageing period as the wine just described, except for more time in the bottle. It has rather more maturity and an extremely attractive and very good taste which appears to be just right after about 10 years.

Bodegas Corral

always simply done my job, and now I'm old I've suddenly become interesting") and has never even attended a party in his own bodega. But he is certainly involved in all the important decisions. Thus for years Don Florencio did not consider the 1975 *reserva* to be mature enough to be sold as a *gran reserva*, even though there would have been no legal reason not to. Not until the autumn of 1984 (when his 61st grape harvest had been gathered in) did he give permission for the wine to be sold from 1985 onwards with a *gran reserva* label.

On the pilgrim way

As it happened the site picked for the new bodega was quite a special one, for it faces on to the old pilgrim route to Santiago de Compostela and with no other bodega is this the case. In addition there used to be a hospital to care for sick pilgrims situated on what is now a bare field behind the premises. It was built in 1185 and Joan of Arc once rested there. In 1875 the people of Navarrete removed the remains of its Romanesque porches to the churchyard, where these weathered relics still stand. The route to Santiago de Compostela was called the "James Way", the object of pilgrimage being the tomb of the apostle that had been discovered there in the 9th century. This explains why Bodegas Corral has Don Jacobo as its most important brand name; the illuminated advertisement for it can clearly be seen from the nearby motorway.

Experimentation

Bodegas Corral produces around one

million bottles a year, of which about 90% is red wine. The firm has its own vineyards – 100 acres in Sojuela – but has to buy in a lot of grapes. Its own harvests meet only one-fifth of the requirements for black grapes and half of those needed for white and rosé. Not included in the total is a plot immediately behind the bodega where experiments with various types of grapes are carried out. After destalking and crushing, the grapes for red wine are fermented in concrete or metal tanks. As these tanks are quite small there are hardly ever any problems with temperature, which seldom rises above 25 to 28°C. Javier Martinez has also experimented with *macération carbonique*: for the first time in 1983, with 50 tons of grapes. The experiment was a success, so a wine of this type may possibly be given a permanent place in the Corral range. I tasted this 1983 almost a year after it had been made. It had a supple, almost rich taste with a distinct fresh tone to it and ample colour. It had been made mainly from the Tempranillo. The intention was to give this wine some more ageing in cask in order to fix these characteristics.

Besides grapes Bodegas Corral also buys in wine, but in very limited quantities. It is done mainly to reinforce red wines that are somewhat weak in colour and strength – which is not of course necessary every year.

Three kinds of oak

A spacious cellar was built underground for maturing wines in the wood. There are around 6,100 casks in this vault. Javier Martinez said that 300 to 500 new *barricas* were bought before every harvest. Not all the casks are made from the American oak that is everywhere present in the Rioja, for you also find here some 1,500 of French oak, together with about 1,000 of Yugoslav. In the future, however, the accent will be put more and more on American wood, partly because of the price factor. There is a cooper on the payroll to maintain the casks. White and rosé wines are never aged in the wood, but in

Bodegas Corral

principle the reds always are – for a minimum of 18 months. During its period in the casks the wine is usually racked twice a year. Except for red Riojas of *gran reserva* standard, all wines go through membrane filters before bottling, having been filtered through earth or cellulose earlier. Whites and rosés are stabilized by the cold method. Once bottled the red wines are given at least four months' rest. The stock of filled bottles at Bodegas Corral generally varies between 300,000 and 400,000.

Primary aromas protected

When I asked Javier Martinez what he thought distinguished Corral's red Riojas he replied, "ageing in the cask, controlled in such a way that the primary aromas of the wine are not driven out." Martinez wants to avoid having the wood predominant, so the wine is not left too long in new casks. On racking, wine from a new, or relatively new, cask goes into an older

cask as a matter of policy, and subsequently remains in older wood. Only young wine comes into contact with new wood, and for a limited timespan. With 18 months in tank, 18 in wood and at least 4 in bottle, Don Jacobo *crianza* is the youngest of the red wines. It is supple in taste, and has some degree of maturity, juice and substance, is correct in its aftertaste and is only moderately affected by the wood. The grapes used are the Tempranillo (70%) and Garnacha (30%).

The older wines

With the Don Jacobo *reserva* the Tempranillo content rises to 80%. The rest is made up of 15% Garnacha and 5% Mazuelo. After a year in tank this wine is given four years in cask and two in bottle and therefore an aroma of vanilla and wood is clearly perceptible, but without being dominant. The wine does not make a "dried-out" impression but usually retains a good deal of juice in its taste. It is an

extremely pleasurable Rioja, albeit not strikingly rich in character and subtleties. It is somewhat more substantial in the mouth than the *crianza*. In the *gran reserva* the vanilla and wood are not really much more prominent for its period in the cask is the same as for the *reserva*; it is just given a longer time in bottle. I have greatly enjoyed this wine on repeated occasions – with game dishes, for example, which it partners excellently.

White and rosé

Corral's white Rioja has as its basis 90% Viura and 10% white Garnacha. The wine tastes fresh, dry and juicy, but rather lacks the fruit and class that would make it really enthralling. The white Don Jacobo is a product of average quality: there are worse white wines in the Rioja, but better ones too. The same applies to the rosé which this bodega makes from 90% Tempranillo and 10% Garnacha. This wine possesses a quite firm, supple taste with a fresh element to it, but appears somewhat short of fruit, breeding and length. The firm decided on a low Garnacha content quite deliberately in order to avoid any hint of sweetness and to limit the alcohol at the same time (generally to 11.5%). The pink-orange tint does not come from letting the skins soak in with the juice but from pressing the whole fruit vigorously. By this means just the right amount of colour passes into the must.

It is not easy for a medium-sized, wholly independent bodega to maintain itself in the Rioja, let alone grow. At Corral, however, they are looking forward to the future with confidence – and the sound quality of their red wines gives them every reason to.

The red wines the bodega bottles itself are mostly given this label. As a rule three different vintages are available. The 2-year-old wine (a few months in tank, 8 to 10 in cask, 12 in bottle) often comes across as the most pleasing, with a vital, quite full-bodied taste with fruit, and a beautiful vanilla perfume. Grape varieties are: 70% Tempranillo, 30% Garnacha. The white and rosé merit little attention.

Bodegas A. Navajas

Just outside Navarrete, behind the Guardia Civil bureau, stands Bodegas A. Navajas. It is an unspectacular building that from the outside suggests a hangar rather than a wine business. Immediately on entering, however, you see an excellently equipped fermentation hall with tall, stainless-steel tanks throughout. There are in the Rioja many larger and better-known bodegas whose plant could not come anywhere near this small firm's installations, and it was with some pride that the owner, Antonio Navajas, showed me them. They date from 1979.

Until 1983 Antonio Navajas worked in partnership with the son of Alfredo Arjona, who founded the bodega in the centre of Navarrete in 1918, and Bodegas Arjona was the name of the firm. This had to be changed when the two partners separated. Not only did the name go, but also certain of the wines, such as the Viña Clara and Viña Tursey. All the labels used by the firm now have Bodegas A. Navajas printed on them.

The red wine best

About a quarter of production – 66,000 (US 78,000) gallons a year and rising – comes from the firm's own 12 acres of vineyard. The rest has to be bought in and, given the bodega's facilities as much as possible of this is in the form of grapes (70 to 75%). Most of the wine made here is sold to other bodegas, including Marqués de Cáceres and AGE. Antonio Navajas handles only 5,060 (US 5,980) gallons of bottled wine a year. Most of this is red wine, although the bodega also sells some rosé (from 40% Tempranillo and 30% each of Garnacha and Viura) and, in good vintages only, a little white (100% Viura). The rosé and white made no impression on me in terms of quality, but the red did. I was given three recent years to taste, all with a good deep colour, a beautiful vanilla perfume and a quite substantial taste with a gratifying measure of fruit, freshness, wood and

tannin. I thought the nicest of them was the wine that had had a year's rest in bottle in addition to its eight months or so in wood. The bodega has some 600 casks, 500 of them bought new in 1979. At Navajas the wines that the bodega bottles itself are filtered twice, once before going into the casks and once before bottling.

This modest family concern has as yet done little exporting. Its bottles are sold chiefly in Madrid, Barcelona and via a mail order business that specializes in wine.

Sociedad Vinícola Laserna

About halfway between Logroño and Laguardia the Ebro makes a narrow loop that runs almost due north. On the eastern side of this loop there is a broad, flat-topped hill called La Mesa ("The Table"). On the level ground between hill and river lie vineyards, including the 111 acres of the Sociedad Vinícola Laserna. This bodega is one of the few that processes only grapes from its own land. The buildings stand at the foot of the hill, a few hundred yards from the hamlet of Laserna. The firm was founded in 1974 by Cune (which has half of the shares) and a group of private individuals. Wine was, however, made on this site long ago; during alterations to the ancient cellars a stone fermentation vat of early date was discovered, and demolition work led to other finds being made. There was, for example, a stone from 1483 with an unfortunately badly worn inscription, a baptismal font set in the wall – and the skeleton of a woman with a hole in her skull, the evidence, immured and silent, of a murder committed centuries ago.

A vineyard renewed

The collaboration between Cune and the other shareholders (mostly growers who brought their land with them) did not happen overnight. They had known each other since 1940. That the establishment of the Sociedad Vinícola Laserna made sense is clear from the work done since to restore the vineyard and bodega. The wine growers separately had never been able to manage any of this; in 1974 the vineyard covered only 57 acres, mainly planted with very old vines. Some dated back 90 years and yielded only 10 hectolitres per hectare. So there had to be grubbing out and replanting, and additional vines had to be put in – in stages of course, otherwise the vineyard would consist entirely of young plants. All the equipment in the bodega had to be totally renovated and added to; horses were still in use there in 1975, and part of the premises was reserved for making olive oil. It says a lot for the new owners that as far as possible they left the character and appearance of the buildings intact, rather than simply imposing a new, wholly modern structure on the site. The latter course would have been cheaper, for restoring and adapting old buildings is an expensive business. Just the treatment of the stonework of the outside walls cost the sum of 4 million pesetas.

Sociedad Vinícola Laserna

Dry soil

The vines planted on the Laserna estate consist of 80% Tempranillo, 10% Garnacha and 10% Mazuelo. In addition the firm has 5 acres of Gamay but this grape, familiar from the Beaujolais, does not do well here and will probably be replaced. The bodega seldom achieves a yield of 20 hectolitres per hectare. One of the reasons is the very dry soil: the rain that falls runs off straight away and into the river. However, the situation of the vineyard also means that the fruit ripens quickly and well. Laserna therefore often harvests relatively early. Waiting too long means that the sugar content rises too high and, indirectly, the subsequent alcohol percentage. In 1983, for example, two tankfuls proved unusable because the alcohol content of the wines had reached 18% unaided.

The grapes are fermented in stainless-steel tanks after being destalked and crushed. Fermentation lasts 9 or 10 days.

The malolactic fermentation takes place in concrete tanks, after which the wine is immediately transferred to wooden casks. All the wine that the bodega bottles itself is aged in the wood. The simpler qualities are sold to Cune.

Half American, half French oak

Of the thousand or so casks the bodega has in various parts of the premises, about half are of American oak and the rest are of French wood. The view at Laserna is that both types of wood contribute something to the wine. That is why when wine is racked – every six to seven months – it not only changes casks, but also the variety of wood. In the early days the wines were bottled directly from the casks, by hand. Then Cune did the bottling. Since 1985, however, Laserna has had its own modern bottling area where an annual 80,000 to 120,000 bottles are filled. The wine is filtered before bottling. Laserna has on average 350,000 bottles in its cellars, both stacked and on large wooden trays.

A delicious taste

Laserna's policy is to sell only *reservas*. Once, in 1979, it did market a younger wine, but never since. Each *reserva* receives at least 6 months in tank, 18 to 20 months maturing in cask and 2 years in bottle. I have been able to taste various vintages. It struck me that the quality seemed to improve from 1980; that appears to have been the year when the stainless-steel fermentation tanks came into use. I thought the 1980 itself was an enchanting wine: creamy, vital, stylish, and with a taste of vanilla. The 1981 also tasted good, albeit a shade less noble. And the 1982, sampled from the cask, seemed most promising. There is no doubt in my mind that the Laserna estate is among the very best of the producers in the Rioja. At the same time this bodega demonstrates that it is fully possible in this region to make outstanding wines from a single vineyard – if people are prepared to take great pains.

Oyón

Bodegas Faustino Martínez

The bottles that Bodegas Faustino Martínez sells its best-known wines in – those of the Faustino brand – are recognizable from a distance. The glass is usually tinted and always frosted, and on the outside they seem to have been gone over with sandpaper – like many bottles in the French Cognac region. The labels, too, are striking. Those on both the Faustino I and the Faustino V have a portrait of a gentleman in a historical costume, which rather gives people the idea that these must

be ancestors of the Faustino family. This is not at all the case. The rather sombre-looking figure in a hat on the Faustino I label is in fact the Dutch painter Rembrandt; the original of this portrait hangs in Brussels. And the man in the wig over the name Faustino V is the German composer Gluck. No one in the bodega now knows where this picture came from. The use of these striking bottles and their curious labels might give rise to the idea that Faustino Martínez is not really a

serious wine firm. The converse is actually the case: this is a thoroughly quality-orientated bodega. Good Riojas are there behind Rembrandt and Gluck.

A family concern

The founder of the firm was Eliuterio Martínez Arzac. This wine grower started his own small bodega in the centre of Oyón, which is not quite two miles north of Logroño. His son expanded the business

The white Faustino V comes in a
slender, frosted glass bottle. It is
made from the first-pressing
juice of the Viura, fermented at
low temperature and stabilized
cold. It is quite a pale Rioja,
fresh, sound and with a delicious
taste, albeit rather limited in its
fruit and perfume. It is a better
Rioja than the ordinarily correct
Faustino V rosé, made chiefly
from the Tempranillo grape.

The latest addition (since the
early 1980s) to the Faustino
range is the Viña Faustino. This
is made from Tempranillo
grapes only, by the macération
carbonique method. It is a Rioja
for drinking within a year, or at
most two: of a deep, purplish
colour, full bodied with juice and
fruit (tending to blackcurrant)
in its taste. Serve it cool.

A considerable proportion of the
3.5 million bottles this bodega
keeps in stock is for the reserva
and gran reserva qualities. The
former type is the Faustino V,
made from 80% Tempranillo and
20% Graciano. It is a quite
rounded, almost creamy Rioja
with good colour and wood and a
hint of freshness: an absolutely
sound product. It is given 14
months in tank, 12 in cask and a
minimum 24 in bottle.

The Faustino I is the gran
reserva, kept for 16 months in
tank, 2 years in cask and at least
3 in bottle. This aristocratic
Rioja nearly always has a robust
colour, a well-matured, full-
bodied taste, a distinct aroma of
vanilla and wood and a vital
character that hardly shows
tiredness after two decades. The
grapes differ slightly from the
reserva: 70% Tempranillo, 15%
Graciano and 15% Mazuelo.

Bodegas Faustino Martínez

and in 1931 it started bottling its own wine.
The biggest growth, however, has taken
place under the management of the
grandson, Julio Faustino Martínez, the
present owner. He has built a new, modern
bodega on the road linking Oyón with
Logroño. Now the next generation is alrady
active there in the person of José Miguel
Martínez Zabala, one of Julio's five sons. It
is clear therefore that this bodega is going
to retain the character of a family business,
for the present at least.

Much land of its own

One characteristic of Bodegas Faustino
Martínez is the importance that has always
been attached there to having its own
vineyards, and generation after generation
their area has been increased. It is now
more than 865 acres. The most important
plots lie a few miles west of Oyón in the
area of Laguardia. All the properties lie in
the Rioja Alavesa. Those near Oyón are
particularly impressive: the pale-coloured
limestone soil goes on over hill after hill.
There has been no hesitation about
replanting large areas. Old, scarcely
productive vines have been replaced by
young ones, by Tempranillos and Gracianos
especially. About 80% of the vines are
black varieties, the remainder are
all Viuras. There is a white vineyard
directly behind the bodega. And on the
bodega site itself there is also a small
vineyard. Here new varieties are
experimented with, "so as to be ready when
the regulations regarding grape varieties
are revised".

Diversification

The bodega vinifies around 352,000 (US
416,000) gallons of red wine, 154,000 (US
182,000) gallons of white and 88,000 (US
104,000) gallons of rosé. For these its own
vineyards supply 47%, 50% and 47%
respectively of the grapes required. In
addition about 440,000 (US 520,000)
gallons of ready wine are bought in, which
brings total production to 660,000 (US
780,000) gallons a year. This will not grow
by much; a possible increase of at most 10%
is foreseen. More than this and the quality
of the Faustino range could be at risk. To
increase turnover despite this, a separate
bodega is planned for the secondary
Campillo line. In fact the idea of
diversification is by no means strange to
the Faustino Martínez family. Their
Bodegas Vitorianas is already in
existence, producing table wines under the
apellation Alto Ebro; and in Oyón the
making of sparkling wine is getting under
way.

Juice shaken out

The first fermentation tanks that the
bodega obtained, in the early 1970s, were of
steel glazed on the inside. Later, stainless-
steel tanks, connected with a cooling plant,
arrived. In these the Faustino V, the best
white Rioja from this bodega, had its birth.
It is made in a very special manner. On
arrival the grapes – Viura only – are not
pressed but only bruised. They then go into
a machine that shakes 40 to 45% of juice
out of the grapes in a very short time. This
juice has therefore hardly been in contact
with the skins at all, and it is given
separate treatment. The remaining must,
obtained from pressings, is used for simpler
qualities of wine. The Faustino juice goes
first into ordinary tanks and then enzymes
are added. These ensure that any solid
contents – such as stalks, any skins that
have got through and the yeast cells
present – sink to the bottom within a day or
two. The clear must is then drawn off and
taken to the fermentation tanks.
Fermentation is induced by adding
specially selected yeast cells from the
Oenological Institute at Haro. During
fermentation the temperature is kept low
so as to retain the primary aromas as much
as possible. Finally the wine is further
stabilized by the cold method and filtered
through a membrane before bottling. Three
to four months later it goes on sale.
Naturally this is not a cheap way of
working, but the result is fine – and likely
to improve still further.

Wine of the year with substance and fruit

Besides the traditional kinds of red wine
the bodega also makes a macération
carbonique type, called Viña Faustino. This
is another wine firm that has come to the
conclusion that the Tempranillo grape
lends itself excellently to this method of
intercellular fermentation. It is only a pity,
according to the bodega, that the
Tempranillo grown in Rioja Alavesa is
probably the most expensive grape in the
whole of Spain. However, this Viña

Left:
Gift box with tempting contents. The bodega puts its Faustino I and other Riojas in frosted-glass bottles.

Below:
Palletized consignment of Faustino V, with a portrait of the composer Gluck on the boxes.

The firm has a modern, stainless-steel bottling plant with a capacity of 12,000 bottles an hour (only half of which is used at present). Although the bottles arrive sterile from the factory they are still washed once more. During bottling the corking machine blows away any dust that may have collected on the corks.

The Viña Faustino is often stabilized by the cold method, like the white and rosé wines.

Bodegas Faustino Martínez

Faustino may be regarded as a successful product: a Rioja with substance and good fruit; a wine to be drunk cold, in its youth. Apart from this red wine, the white that has already been mentioned, and the usually correct rosé, the bodega brings out few other young wines under the Faustino label. Of the remainder of the range only the *reservas* and *gran reservas* are exported. On the Spanish market there are still small quantities of the one-year-old Don Faustinos, a brand that is going to be dropped, and the Faustino VII, a *crianza*. The 1981 vintage of this latter wine was selected to be served at all Spanish government functions and state enterprises (including the *paradores*). The bodega supplied 8,000 cases of it in 1984.

Clarity and cleanliness

The grapes for the normal red Faustino wines are destalked and crushed. They are then fermented in tanks, the temperature of which is measured every six hours and reduced if necessary. During fermentation the wine is not left for the whole period in contact with the pulp of skins and seeds. At a particular moment the wine is pumped into a clean tank where fermentation continues slowly until all the sugar has been converted into alcohol and carbon dioxide. Bodegas Faustino Martínez keep the fermentation area as clean as possible. The walls are painted white before every harvest and the floor is treated several times a year with a powerful cleaning agent. Malolactic fermentation takes place in another cellar, where the wine is also fined. The next stage for these wines is ageing in wood.

Older wines the speciality

The firm has about 11,000 casks at its disposal, practically all of American oak; there is also a negligible number made of French or Yugoslav wood. Old casks are replaced by new ones after 15 to 16 years and there is always a cooper on permanent staff to maintain them throughout. Bodegas Faustino Martínez is an advocate of a long period in the bottle rather than lengthy cask ageing, and so both the *reserva* and the *gran reserva* are treated accordingly. Thus the Faustino V *reserva* (the one with Gluck on the label) is given a year in cask and 2 in bottle, after having 14 months in tank. It is a quite rounded, almost creamy Rioja that does not, however, taste heavy thanks to a slight element of freshness; and, given its good amount of wood in the taste, it would not have been improved by a longer time in the cask. Tempranillo (80%) and Graciano (20%) are its grapes. In the Faustino I *gran reserva* (with the Rembrandt label) the Tempranillo content is down to 70% and the rest is made up of equal parts of Graciano and Mazuelo. This wine is given 24 months in cask and at least 36 in bottle. I have tasted four vintages. They were firm-tasting, nicely matured wines that seemed to keep their vitality for a long time, as was shown by the 1964 and the truly delicious 1968. Faustino Martínez is probably the biggest exporter of *reservas* and *gran reservas* in the Rioja. It is to be hoped that this family concern will be able to continue supporting the heavy financial burden involved in these kinds of wines for many years to come.

Bodegas El Coto

Just past Mendavia, which lies 14 miles east of Logroño, stands the Imaz hunting lodge. It dates from the 16th century and its grounds stretch to the north bank of the Ebro. This *mansión* is not permanently occupied, but all the salons and bedrooms are well furnished and equipped for entertaining guests. Numerous hunting trophies, some from Africa, hang on the walls along with paintings and family photographs. And in one of the wings a vast room has been set aside for grand receptions and dinners. The owners of this lodge are also shareholders in a bodega that was built in Oyón in 1970. How it got its name can readily be deduced: El Coto is Spanish for 'hunting ground'; and Coto de Imaz was chosen as the name for the best wine.

Capacity doubled

At Imaz you can sense the atmosphere of generations, if not centuries, past, but the bodega in Oyón is cool and modern. It was designed by Jesús Martínes Bujanda Jnr, who 14 years later built another bodega on the same industrial estate (*see* the following chapter). The Martínez Bujanda family still has a share in El Coto, along with the Bankunión. The firm has 297 acres of vineyard, which were already planted in 1970. A further 222 acres has also been bought for planting. The land is at Cenicero and Mendavia. More than 85% is planted with Tempranillo and the rest practically exclusively with Viura.

The first El Coto wines were launched in 1975. Their success was so great that two years later the doubling of the bodega's capacity had to be decided on. This possibility had been allowed for in building, so there were no problems of space and no violence was done to the appearance of the bodega. With a present annual production of 330,000 (US 390,000) gallons the desired volume has been reached; further expansion would not be regarded as sensible from the standpoint of quality.

Technological care

Bodegas El Coto works on the basis of vinifying most of the wine on the premises. Its own vineyards supply 57% of the grapes required for the red wines – 264,000 (US 312,000) gallons – and all the grapes for the white – 22,000 (US 26,000) gallons. Outside purchases are in the form of grapes as far as possible. The *macération carbonique* method is generally not applied here. The grapes for red wine are destalked and crushed, and then fermented in concrete or stainless-steel tanks. By adding industrial carbon dioxide gas at the start of fermentation, oxidation is restricted and

EL COTO
RIOJA 1983
Denominación de Origen Calificada

BODEGAS EL COTO, S.A. OYÓN · RIOJA · ESPAÑA

This bodega's white wine ferments at low temperature and is made from the Viura. It is a fairly austere Rioja with a considerable degree of acid. Rather more fruit and body would be welcome. Alcohol content is about 11%. The rosé is of lesser quality and tastes somewhat flat; the Garnacha is its grape. Both wines are given 6 months in tank; the white only is cold stabilized.

COTO VINTAGE
RIOJA 1981
Denominación de Origen Concretada

BODEGAS EL COTO, S.A. OYÓN · RIOJA · ESPAÑA

In the October 1983 issue of the influential British magazine Decanter the Coto Vintage crianza of 1978 received the highest commendation. Coto Vintage is a Tempranillo wine with a pleasantly correct amount of wood and vanilla in it, a good colour and a fairly slender kind of taste. Ageing: 6 months in tank, 12 in cask and 12 in bottle.

COTO DE IMAZ
RIOJA 1978
Denominación de Origen Calificada

The engraving on the label shows the hunting lodge this wine takes its name from. It is not a full-bodied, deep or generous kind of Rioja but is refined and mature, with ample wood and vanilla, together with a brown tinge to the colour. This reserva receives 12 months' maturing in tank, 24 in cask, 24 to 36 in bottle. Coto de Imaz is fined with fresh white of egg.

Right:
Director Juan Narvaiza Echaurre holds a book with samples of El Coto's unique type design. The commercial director Julián Diéz Blanco looks on.

Bodegas Laturce is a subsidiary brand, for which the trademarks Laturce, Casa Mayor, Viña del Canonigo and Aurelio are used.

The average stock of bottles is one million, with room for as many again. Total storage capacity of the tanks is almost 880,000 (US 1.04 million) gallons.

Bodegas El Coto

---

the development of volatile acid is kept to an absolute minimum. This way of working demands some well-thought-out technology – and this was installed in 1983, when the stainless-steel tanks with their perfect temperature control were also put in. A walk through the bodega shows that this firm is most insistent on order and cleanliness; for example, all the vinification areas are tiled and every day that the bottling plant is in use it is sterilized with steam at 105°C.

Its own alphabet design

The cask cellars (one was deliberately built on the north side of the site and the other is underground) contain 8,000 *barricas* of American oak. Most of the rows here are stacked four high instead of the usual five. I was told that this was done to save the bottom row of casks, which carry all the weight: these then last longer and need fewer repairs. Consequently there is no cooper on the staff. If Bodegas el Coto wants to install more casks in the future this will present no problem, for there is room for another 2,000. Next to this underground vault there is a reception room. Visitors can see a book in which the alphabet that El Coto has had designed specially for its own use is reproduced in large format. This unique, if slightly "bitty" looking typeface is employed consistently for everything from bottle labels and plates in the bodega to the directors' business cards.

On the slender side

The youngest wine from this bodega is called simply El Coto. It goes on sale after 6 months in tank, 6 in cask and 6 in bottle. The Tempranillo is the only grape used, as in the other red Riojas from this firm. Besides some fruit, this wine has a measure of wood in its nose and taste, but beyond this it comes across as rather light. The Coto Vintage *crianza*, too, could do with more concentration, although it does possess more colour and strength as well as more wood, plus vanilla. It is given 6 months longer to mature in both cask and bottle; it is a well-balanced wine, pleasant but without a lot of depth. The Coto de Imaz *reserva* is matured for a year in tank, 2 years in cask and 2 to 3 in bottle. Wood and vanilla are more to the fore in this Rioja, which also gives evidence of its considerable maturity. In Spain this is a highly regarded wine that you see in many good restaurants, in specialist wine shops, sometimes on Iberia flights and regularly on menus in the Senate. The better wines from Bodegas El Coto show refinement. They are made with care but all are rather on the slender side; they lack real fullness, depth, generosity. With most meat dishes this characteristic presents no problem at all – except perhaps with game.

Ōyon

Bodegas Martínez Bujanda

Bodegas Martínez Bujanda's new vinification centre was completed in October 1984. It was built on a low hill on the industrial estate at Oyón and it is undoubtedly the most progressive wine business that the Rioja has; a bodega that must represent the dream of every wine maker or oenologist. All possible types of wine making can be carried out here under perfect conditions. The bodegas was in fact built around this requirement. It all starts with the arrival of the grapes. In the harvest period 1,500 to 2,000 tons can be processed here, each variety separately. Obviously this means that efficient destalking and crushing equipment is available, as well as a set of modern presses. In addition it is possible to heat up, cool down or filter the must. The white wine is always filtered. All the fermentation tanks are made of stainless steel and the temperature in each of them can be programmed separately from the impressive panel in the control room. The same panel also enables the wine to be moved to any desired point in the bodega via a network of pipes, which are also of stainless steel.

Family concern

The new bodega was built by the present Martínez Bujanda. It was his great-grandfather Joaquín Martínez Bujanda, who founded the original bodega in 1890. This stood, and still does today, in Oyón itself. Joaquín's successor was his son, Marcelino. He expanded the business further, in particular so as to be able to mature an increasing quantity of wine in casks. The next generation, in the person of Jesús Martínez Bujanda, together with his children, formed the family concern into a limited company. Under his management a large acreage of land was bought and planted. It was his son, Jesús Martínez Bujanda Jnr, who designed the new bodega. Earlier, in 1970, this industrial engineer

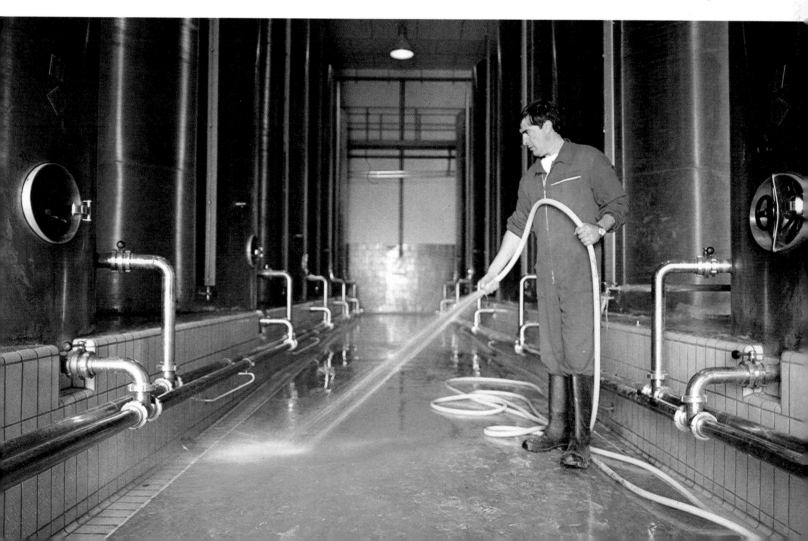

Left:
The crushing and destalking machine.

Below:
The impressive winery control panel.

had been in at the birth of a new wine business: El Coto, on the same industrial estate. The Martínez Bujanda family is still a part owner of El Coto (*see* the previous chapter). The financing of its new complex was made possible through interests that the family has in other firms, including some outside the wine trade.

Beaujolais tanks

Jesús Martínez Bujanda, who in appearance could be Peter Seller's brother, is a perfectionist. He laughingly told me that his wife accuses him of having a mistress – the bodega! He thinks about it all the time, and holidays are devoted to visiting wine businesses. One of the subjects he has gone deeply into in his quest for perfection is the correct vinification of *primeur* wines, to which the Tempranillo lends itself excellently. The method that is usual in the Rioja Alavesa is not to his liking, for in his opinion the wines lose just too much of their colour or aroma. He therefore turned repeatedly to the Beaujolais for advice and he had a dozen tanks made on the pattern used there. He also studied the vinification of the Beaujolais Primeur, even during the weekend before the opening of the bodega. Another detail: he suspected that ordinary mains water would be too hard for cleaning his plant, so the bodega acquired a water-softening installation.

Experiments

When the new complex came into use a number of interesting experiments were carried out. In one, intact black grapes were successfully separated from crushed grapes and their juice. The eventual aim was as perfect as far as possible a *macération carbonique* on the Beaujolais model; for the same reason no sulphur dioxide was added to the intact grapes, but carbon dioxide was (*see* the chapter "Making the Wine"). What was also remarkable was the fact that "indigenous" yeast cultures from the firm's own vineyards were used for the fermentation. By these means a very

successful "Rioja Primeur" was achieved, a *vino sin crianza* with a lot of fruit for drinking young. Both this and the ordinary red wine ferment at 25 to 27°C. For white and rosé the firm works with fermentation temperatures of 15 to 16°C.

Order and cleanliness fundamental

A year before the vinification centre was ready another part of the bodega, also totally new, had been opened. This building was designed for the treatment, storing, ageing and bottling of wines. It lies to one side of, and downhill from, the fermentation hall. This complex, too, was fitted out to perfectionist standards. Not only was the whole building efficiently

insulated, but special equipment was put in to change the air at regular intervals in the cask vault. One of the areas serves as a cold chamber where white, rosé and young red wines can be stabilized at low temperature if desired, in stainless-steel tanks. Everything in this building looks spotless, as in the vinification centre. The floors, for example, are tiled where appropriate. "For me, order and cleanliness are fundamental", says Jesús Martínez Bujanda. That he really means this is obvious from the boxes of cleaning materials that stand in every room.

Martínez Bujanda's white Rioja is made from 80% Viura and 20% Malvasia. It is bottled quickly and does not come into contact with wood. It has a fairly pale colour, a good dry enjoyable taste with fruit. It is also a very pure wine, among the Rioja's best for quality.

This bodega's crianza is a usually very sound wine with plenty of colour, a pleasant wood-vanilla aroma, a vital, slightly fruity, quite full-bodied taste and a good aftertaste. After a few months in tank it matures for 2 years in cask and about 1 year in bottle. Tempranillo is the only grape used – as for the reserva and gran reserva Conde de Valdemar, which are also of a good standard.

Bodegas Martínez Bujanda

Growth allowed for

In the area where the wines mature all processes are carried out with the greatest possible care. So is the filtering of the wines (twice: first after fining and again when the wine is bottled) and the bottling itself. The bottles are first washed, then sterilized, and then filled in a screened-off, totally hygienic area. A little nitrogen goes into the space between cork and wine as a protection against the effect of oxygen. The bottling plant has a capacity of 3,000 bottles per hour.

The bodega has around 8,000 casks, all of American oak, and these are maintained by a cooper on the staff. There is a stock of about 800,000 bottles. These numbers will increase, for production at Bodegas

Martínez Bujanda is rising. Space for more casks and bottles is already available.

Only its own grapes

The future increase in volume is related to an extension of the firm's own vineyards. At present it has 494 acres of vineyard, of which 445 acres are fully productive. Eventually, however, the productive area is to grow to more than 620 acres. The rule is that grapes or wines from other producers are not processed in the new bodega. It was built solely for the vinification of the firm's own grapes. Present production lies around 209,000 (US 247,000) gallons a year (roughly 80% red, 10% white and 10% rosé), but there is the capacity for at least 110,000 (US 130,000) gallons more. Land is owned in the three Riojan districts. About 250 acres (not all of it yet planted) are in the Rioja Baja, near Tudelilla. The most prevalent grape variety there is the Tempranillo; Garnacha and Viura have been planted only on the higher slopes, so that in this warm, dry district they do not produce wines that are too heavy and alcoholic. Something over 170 acres is cultivated near Cenicero in the Rioja Alta. The rest of the land is mainly around Oyón, in the Rioja Alavesa. The bodega has also conducted interesting experiments with non-Spanish grape varieties, such as the Cabernet Sauvignon (one or two small tanks a year), the Riesling and the Müller-Thurgau.

White and rosé

The normal dry white Rioja this bodega produces is made up from 80% Viura grapes and 20% Malvasia. The latter rather delicate variety has been planted near Cenicero. The grapes are fermented slowly at a low temperature, so that they retain their fruit. Martínez Bujanda's white wine is therefore a fruity, juicy, exceptionally pure Rioja that for quality is among the best of the region. It is not aged in the wood and has to be drunk young. The rosé, composed of Garnacha and usually some

Tempranillo, also has fruit and juice, and is a very successful wine that quenches the thirst in an excellent manner.

Tempranillo only

In principle only the Tempranillo grape is used for the red wines. Jesús Martínez Bujanda restricted the tasting to his younger wines, which he thought best represented the course the bodega has been following in recent years. The wines I was given to taste were still maturing in tank or cask and took in three different years. What was striking about all the wines was their sound colour. Those that had some cask ageing also presented a lesser or greater measure of good vanilla and wood, together with an amount of fruit, a substantial structure and a decent aftertaste. All were successful wines with considerable ageing potential. At Bodegas Martínez Bujanda the *crianza* matures for a few months in tank, followed by around 2 years in cask, and finally about a year in bottle.

No folklore

The *reserva* and *gran reserva* from this bodega are sold under the name Conde de Valdemar. There are no fixed rules regarding their ageing: Jesús Martínez Bujanda lays down the length and manner of maturing for each wine in each vintage – generally preferring to leave the wines longer in bottle than cask. A *reserva* is given a minimum of four years' ageing, at least 18 months of this in cask. For the *gran reserva* the minimum is six years, with at least two to three years in cask.

Although Bodegas Martínez Bujanda is not a publicity-conscious firm, fond of the limelight, it is likely to receive its due attention. Not because of a glorious reputation built up over the generations, or unique vaults and reception rooms full of atmosphere, but simply because of its advanced plant and sound wines. The bodega spends no time on trappings of the folklore kind, devoting all its attention to its wine-making techniques.

Logroño

Bodegas Franco-Españolas

There are two bridges linking Logroño to the north bank of the Ebro, one of stone and the other of iron. Directly opposite the latter, which runs from the old town centre, are the buildings of Bodegas Franco-Españolas. As the name indicates the business is partly of French origin. In 1890 the Frenchman Frédéric Anglade Saurat arrived in Logroño as the representative of the house of Anglade in Bordeaux. He bought not only wine but also land to plant with vines. Years later, with his vineyards in full production, Anglade Saurat started a bodega with Spanish capital. Franco-Españolas was set up in 1901, but the firm regards 1890 as its actual foundation year: 60,000 bottles of a special Rioja have, for example, been laid down to celebrate the centenary in 1990. The Franco-Spanish collaboration was to last until 1922, when the connection came to an end, all the shares passed into Spanish hands and the French technical staff departed. The name of the bodega, however, remained unaltered. Its Spanish character was further underlined by the visit that King Alfonso XIII made to the firm in 1925.

Growth in size and reputation

Later, too, the bodega was able to boast of the interest shown by heads of state. Framed menus in the reception area show that wines from Franco-Españolas were regularly drunk at the Spanish court. The white Viña Sole was even served at the coronation banquet of the present Spanish monarch. The firm is also proud of the letter sent from the White House by President Eisenhower in 1959: "I greatly enjoyed partaking of this excellent wine when I had the honor of being Generalisimo Franco's guest last December, and I am more than pleased by your kindness in wanting me to have a generous quantity for my own use."

Since its foundation the firm has grown into one of the larger ones of the region. It produces about 1.1 million (US 1.3 million) gallons annually, of which 70% is red wine, 25% white and 5% rosé.

Enterprising owner

In 1973, after a long period of independence, this bodega was bought by the Rumasa group. With the nationalization of this organization, Franco-Españolas was for a time state-controlled. This episode came to an end in 1985 when a contract was signed in Madrid that transferred all shares to Marcos Eguizábal Ramirez. This businessman had been active in the building world since 1955, and in addition had created in Almeria one of Europe's most progressive agricultural concerns. His interest in the Rioja went back a long way, for this is where he was born – at El Villar de Arnedo, in Rioja Baja, where his father and grandfather had been in the wine trade. The first bodega taken over by Eguizábal, who lives in Madrid, was Bodegas y Viñedos at Ollauri, in 1982, and at the beginning of 1985 Lan and Paternina as well as Franco-Españolas became his property.

Hardly any vineyards

The vineyards that Franco-Españolas formerly owned have been sold. It now possesses only a couple of plots immediately behind the bodega but these are of no importance. It buys in only grapes for its white and rosé Rioja, and mostly wine for the red. About 80% of this wine comes usually from the Rioja Alta: the cooperative at San Asensio is an important supplier. In the hygienic halls at Franco-Españolas part of the red wine is given its first contact with wood by being stored in very large, closed wooden vats for three to six months. These are of American oak and date from the beginning of the century. It sometimes happens that wines undergo their malolactic fermentation in them. These enclosed vats, 30 in number, have a combined capacity of 211,000 (US 250,000) gallons. To this stainless-steel and other tanks add more than 1.54 million (US 1.82 million) gallons.

Cellar noises

The bodega is built on three levels. Underground there are the casks, on average 25,000. Generally it is quiet down here, but when the wine is being racked the air is full of noise. Racking is still done by hand at this bodega, with a man ceaselessly hammering with a wooden mallet on the empty cask as it fills. He does this not only to bang the air out of the cask, but also so as to be able to hear when it is nearly full. At the same time, elsewhere in the large vault you may encounter men cleaning the empty casks with steam, which provides an

Whereas other bodegas make their dry white wine from the Viura only, Viña Soledad consists of half Malvasía. This gives the wine a friendly, slightly aromatic mellowness: it tastes fresh but never acid. There is also a touch of fruit, suggesting apples, together with great purity. This is a Rioja for chilling well and drinking young.

This traditional, aged-in-the-wood white Rioja has won awards in competitions in Britain, Hungary, Russia and Yugoslavia. It has a pale colour, vanilla and wood in its nose and taste, and a refined, mellow yet lively freshness. An interesting wine, given a year in tank, 4 years in cask and 1 to 4 in bottle. Viura (50%), Malvasía (25%) and Garnacha Blanca (25%) are its grapes. The wine used to be called Viña Sole.

Of the four kinds of wines in the Diamante series (dry white, semi-sweet white, rosé and red) the first and the last types are the most attractive. The red is a crianza with a decent depth of colour, some discreet wood, and a touch of freshness and fruit. It is matured for 12 months in tank, 18 in cask and 6 in bottle. With a probable 50 to 60% the Tempranillo is the most important grape, followed by the Garnacha. The white comes from 50% Garnacha Blanca and 50% Malvasía.

A bestseller in the Franco-Españolas range, the Rioja Bordón crianza is given 1 year in tank, 2 to 3 years in cask and 2 in bottle. Vanilla is unmistakably present in perfume and taste, along with a certain generosity and 12.5% alcohol. This pleasant Rioja, not really deep nor with a very long aftertaste, has in it 20 to 40% Garnacha and some Mazuelo in addition to the Tempranillo.

The Royal is sold as a reserva or gran reserva according to its age and its year. Or, sometimes, the same wine is sold in both categories with an interval between – as with the 1975. The reserva matures in tank for a year, in cask for 4 years and in bottle for 2. The gran reserva has more bottle age. These are good wines, somewhat more elegant and mature, and with more noticeable wood than the Rioja Bordón. The Tête de Cuvée is a rare and beautiful gran reserva with 6 years in cask and 4 in bottle.

I had some difficulty in obtaining any Excelso gran reserva to taste, for the bodega is sparing with this rare wine, made only in exceptional years. Like the Royal Tête de Cuvée it spends 6 years in cask, but then has longer in bottle. I know only the 1964: a very well-matured, albeit not really old Rioja that after 20 years proved to be extremely drinkable, with a good deal of tannin in its aftertaste.

Bodegas Franco-Españolas

infernal spectacle in the dim half light. In another area of the bodega three coopers are continually busy repairing damaged casks. Normally the casks are kept in service for eight years.

Uncertain mixtures of grapes

Bodegas Franco-Españolas produces a fairly lavish range of wines, consisting of about ten different types. In addition it also bottles "own brands" for chains at home and abroad (including Sainsbury's in Britain). Hardly any wine is sold in bulk. A noticeable feature of the red wines is their

Bodegas Franco-Españolas

relatively low Tempranillo content, which rarely exceeds 50%. In fact the information the bodega gave me concerning grape varieties was of a rather contradictory nature. I presume that the percentages are not known exactly because the red wines are nearly always bought outside in ready-made form. The three grape blends that I was given for the Rioja Bordón will serve as an example. In these the percentage of Tempranillo was 20%, 40% and 50% respectively. In one of the blends the Graciano was not mentioned, although it was in the other two. It therefore does not make a lot of sense to give the proportions of the grapes for each of the red Riojas from Franco-Españolas; I will simply mention the varieties that are definitely used.

Bordon the bestseller

The Diamante *tinto* is the youngest red wine of the standard range. Tempranillo (probably more than half) and the Garnacha are the most important grapes

used, with some Mazuelo. This is a very acceptable *crianza*, with a fresh tone to it and even a dash of fruit. It is given 12 months in tank, 18 in cask and 6 in bottle. The Rioja Bordón undoubtedly contains more Garnacha in its make-up. This wine, which matures for twice as long in cask and bottle as the previous type, has a mellow, almost generous taste with a distinct vanilla aroma. It is not a wine with a great deal of depth or length, but is most pleasantly drinkable. This brand represents about one-sixth of the red Rioja that Franco-Españolas produces. It has two variants of its Royal brand, a *reserva* and a *gran reserva*. There is little difference between the two in their blend of grapes: probably 40 to 60% Tempranillo, 20 to 30% Mazuelo and 30% Graciano. The wines are often slightly lighter in colour and constitution than the Rioja Bordón, while at the same time they possess more maturity, a few tenths of a point more alcohol and more wood and vanilla. The Tête de Cuvée is a very special Royal *gran*

reserva, always a splendid wine, but selected only in great years. An even older and rarer *gran reserva* is sold in a bottle adorned with a seal. This is the Excelso. I am familiar only with the 1964 and this, 20 years on from its vintage, made a very well-matured impression in both perfume and taste, and lingered on in the mouth with a good deal of tannin. This wine had been six years in the wood.

Traditional and modern white

The white wines are, as has already been mentioned, vinified at the bodega. After pressing the must is filtered and it then ferments at 18 to 19°C in stainless-steel tanks. One of the white Riojas receives the traditional ripening in wood: the Viña Soledad (formerly the Viña Sole) Tête de Cuvée. This wine stays in the cask for four years and as a result acquires a pronounced vanilla aroma. The taste certainly does not suffer from this: it is gently fresh and refined. This interesting Tête de Cuvée has as its counterpart the ordinary Viña Soledad, which is sold under a different label and in a slender brown bottle; it is a new-style white Rioja, on the market since 1980. A colour tending to pale, a fragrant bouquet, a lightly fruity, fresh (but not at all acid) taste are some of its features. The Viña Soledad Tête de Cuvée is made from 50% Viura grapes, 25% Malvasia and 25% Garnacha Blanca; the ordinary Viña Soledad is composed of half Viura and half Malvasia. Other white wines from this bodega are the dry Diamante (which tastes fresh without being thin) and the semi-dry Diamante. There is also a rosé in the Diamante series, a 50% Garnacha, 50% Viura combination with a supple, somewhat oily tate that soon palls.

Bodegas Franco-Españolas is a concern that makes no really exciting wines, but Riojas of a generally reliable quality.

Bodegas Olarra

Logroño

It is a pity that the "cathedral of Rioja", as the Olarra bodega has been nicknamed, was not placed somewhere out in the countryside, for this would do the revolutionary form of this complex rather more justice. The bodega actually stands on a dull industrial estate just east of Logroño, on the north bank of the Ebro. The main building comprises three wings joined to form a letter Y. They symbolize Rioja's three districts: Alta, Alavesa and Baja. The visitors' entrance is situated where the two short wings join; the grapes come in on the other side. The broad, pointed roofs with their semicircular brown pantiles are interrupted along their whole length by a row of windows, and above are four raised glass sections. By these arrangements a pleasant, somewhat indirect light falls in the bodega. This can be regarded as exceptional: the working areas in most other wine businesses in Rioja are rather cut off from the outside world and its light. Another striking feature of the Olarra complex is formed by the 111 hexagonal pointed roofs at ground level beside the Y, also covered with semicircular pantiles. They cover an underground cask cellar and their design is reported to have a regulatory effect on the temperature and humidity there.

An oenologist of authority

The Olarra bodega was ready in 1973 and was named after one of the shareholders, Luis Olarra. He had acquired a minority holding not long before in what was then still called Bodegas Guiloche. Olarra, a steel magnate and inveterate cigar smoker, was not involved in the design of the bodega. Those who were included José Manuel Aizpurua, later the technical director at Bodegas Lan, among other things. He was the second man to enter the service of the concern that was to be built. Aizpurua brought the famous Ezequiel García into his team, an oenologist who had been trained in Spain and France and had previously worked for CVNE for 18 years. Señor García (born in 1930) still works for Olarra and has contributed in no small

measure to the excellent reputation this bodega enjoys. Honour is also due to the architect Juan Antonio Ridruejo, for he was the most important designer involved. Before there was any drawing or building he and other members of the team made an intensive inspection of French, German and Californian wineries. By the time the new bodega was at last opened it had demanded an investment of 3 billion pesetas. In the autumn of 1984 Luis Olarra sold his 30% shareholding to the Guibert-Ucin family (José Maria Guibert and Jesús Ucin), who alrady held the same percentage and thus acquired a majority interest. Olarra disposed of his steel interests at the same time; the Guibert-Ucin family is big in steel in the Basque country. It is said the Luis Olarra has gone over entirely to the production of preserves (but also that he has started a wine business in Navarra).

All grapes bought in

Bodegas Olarra possesses no vineyards of its own but does have some 1,850 acres under contract. These provide the grapes for the 770,000 (US 910,000) gallons it produces annually (73% red, 14% white, 13% rosé). The grapes for red wine are destalked and crushed and then ferment for 9 or 10 days in steel tanks of the "self-emptying" type. There are 52 of these, each with a capacity of 11,000 (US 13,000) gallons. Their temperature is carefully checked and reduced if necessary. The red wines usually ferment at around 15°C. Care is taken that the wine is regularly pumped over the top of the cake of skins that forms (the *sombrero*) in order to ensure the greatest possible extraction of colour, tannin and aroma. After the first fermentation has run its course the wine drains down into concrete tanks for the malolactic fermentation. The next phase is the first ageing of the wine in large wooden vats, to which it is transferred after filtering. The red Riojas usually stay here for five or six months. This contact with wood, early and minimal, has an intensive sequel in the casks.

The processing of the grapes and the

Below:
Aerial view of the Olarra bodega. Its three wings symbolize the three Rioja districts. The 111 tent-shaped roofs covering the cask cellar can clearly be seen. The small building to the right is for the reception of specially-invited guests.

Opposite page, above:
Ezequiel García, a winemaker who has trained in Spain and France, has been called the "wizard of the Rioja".

Opposite page, below:
Olarra will ship a proportion of its wines in wooden cases on request, especially to the United States.

The bodega's buildings occupy nearly 4½ acres of a 13-acre site.

Olarra has many visitors. In the reception hall they can see a 15-minute video about the firm.

The bodega can store more than 2.2 million (US 2.6 million) gallons in its tanks.

Occasionally Olarra bottles some wine in magnums – the 1973, 1975 and 1978 being examples. Magnums of crianza go to the United States.

In 1985 Bodegas Olarra launched a new reserva, the Añares, matured for 2 years in oak casks. The first vintage was the 1981. The wine is comparable with the ordinary reserva (see opposite page).

To mark the soccer World Championships held in Spain in 1982 the bodega brought out a special label. It was black and bore the World Cup logo. The wine was a 1975 red.

The firm has three subsidiary brand names. Otoñal is a crianza (of a slightly simpler quality) sold chiefly in Spain. La Catedral is used for exactly the same qualities as Olarra itself. Only Sweden takes wine in bulk, and what is bottled there is called El Molino.

The great majority of the grapes the bodega processes come from the Rioja Alta, followed by the Rioja Alavesa.

The white Reciente (Spanish for "recent") is a pale Rioja with a green tinge in its colour. It tastes pure, bright and fresh, with some fruit. Only the Viura grape is used and the juice ferments at low temperature. The wine is not aged in oak casks, only in large wooden tanks. It is cold stabilized. This Rioja should be drunk young, within two to three years at most.

BLANCO SECO

The Olarra blanco seco is this bodega's best-known wine; sales are significantly greater than for the Reciente. Besides the 60% Viura, 20% each of Malvasía and Garnacha Blanca go into this Rioja, which is given 5 months in tank, 6 in cask and 6 in bottle. Features are a definite aroma of vanilla, a reasonably substantial taste and a suggestion of fruit. After 4 or so years the Olarra white is still extremely drinkable and satisfactorily fresh.

ROSADO SECO

The light pink colour of Olarra's rosado is obtained by leaving the black skins of the Garnacha (70%, supplemented by 30% Viura) in contact with the must for a short time. Like the white wines the rosé ferments at low temperature and is stabilized cold. It is then matured for 5 months in tank, 6 in cask and another 6 in bottle. Of its kind this is an attractive wine: fresh, juicy, vinous and slightly fruity. Ideal for drinking on a hot summer's day.

Bodegas Olarra

The youngest red wine sold with the Olarra label is this *crianza*. It matures for 6 months in tank, 12 in cask and 12 in bottle. Not a Rioja with a lot of bite or depth, but it has fruit, and is a pure wine with vanilla in perfume and taste. Its grapes are 50% Tempranillo, 20% Garnacha, 15% Mazuelo and 15% Graciano, and they come largely from Rioja Alta.

Wines with the Olarra label are sold in Bordeaux bottles, those with the Cerro Añon name are bottled in the Burgundy type – indicating that the latter are a firmer, more powerful kind of Rioja: rather deeper in colour, heavier in perfume, fuller-flavoured, richer in alcohol. The grapes for all the Cerro Añons are 70% Tempranillo, 20% Garnacha, 5% Mazuelo and 5% Graciano. The *crianza* is aged for the same length of time as the equivalent Olarra.

The Olarra *reserva* is made from the same grapes as the *crianza* (and the *gran reserva*). The maturation period is increased to 6 months' tank, 24 months' cask and at least 24 months' bottle. The wine is more mature and rather more complex than the *crianza*, but otherwise clearly related. This stylish Rioja has a counterpart in the form of the Cerro Añon *reserva*, which is matured for the same time but offers more colour and robustness, and sometimes has an element of ripe fruit suggesting cherries.

Bodegas Olarra also has two kinds of wine in the *gran reserva* category: the Olarra (beautifully aged and graceful) and the Cerro Añon (also well-matured, but more robust of structure). These mellow Riojas possess style and have less wood than similar wines from other bodegas because they never stay longer than four years in the casks. Besides this they have half a year in tank and a minimum three years in bottle.

Bodegas Olarra

movement of the wine around the plant is automated to a great extent. The bodega possesses modern machinery for pressing, directing and blending the grapes, all controlled from an enormous, futuristic-looking panel. This is why only four or five people are needed to handle the harvest as it comes in.

An allowance for growth

There are around 25,000 casks in the cellar, where the temperature is always at 14 to 15°C, and they are stacked five high in rows. There is no doubt that this number of *barricas bordelesas* will increase as production increases: the bodega has the capacity for a further 220,000 (US 260,000) gallons. Most of the casks are made of American oak, with just 300 of French wood. There are two coopers on the staff to maintain them all. The bodega keeps the casks in service for an average 10 years. Ezequiel García is no advocate of an exaggerated wood flavour in his wines, and so none of the Riojas stays more than four years in the cask. After bottling (and a second filtering) the red wines rest for a time in bottle, this period varying from one year for the simplest kinds to three or more for the *gran reservas*.

Two brands and styles

The Olarra *tinto* is a red Rioja that goes on sale after 12 months in tank, 12 in cask and 12 in bottle. It is a slightly fruity, tasty, albeit rather over-refined wine with a modest amount of vanilla in nose and flavour. It is made from 50% Tempranillo, 20% Garnacha, 15% Graciano and 15% Mazuelo. the Cerro Añon is the same age but has a somewhat different blend of grapes: 70% Tempranillo, 20% Garnacha, 5% Mazuelo and 5% Graciano. This Rioja has rather more colour, strength and alcohol; its character explains why it goes into a Burgundy bottle, which also applies to the *reserva* and *gran reserva*. The Olarra line, on the other hand, has a Bordeaux bottle.

Exemplary purity

The Olarra *reserva* is made from the same grapes as the ordinary *tinto*. The two wines do not differ greatly in their personality, although the *reserva* takes on a mellow refinement with its maturity and comes across as rather more complex. It spends 6 months in tank, 2 years in cask and at least 2 years in bottle. Here, too, the comparable Cerro Añon offers more colour and strength, with a solid aftertaste and a good balance. There can sometimes be a suggestion of ripe cherries in the taste. The *gran reservas* from this bodega receive 6 months in tank, 4 years in cask and at least

3 years in bottle. Both the Olarra and the Cerro Añon are mellow, nicely matured wines, the one graceful, the other sturdy – and both are still very vital in their taste after 10 to 12 years. All the red Riojas from this house have style, refinement and an impeccable purity.

White and rosé

Grapes for white wine are pressed immediately on arrival in one of the six fully automated horizontal presses. Directly afterwards the must is separated from the skins, stalks and seeds. This still cloudy must then goes to the steel tanks for 48 hours, during which time any remaining solid elements can settle. Once clear, the juice is sent on to a clean tank where the selected yeast cells are added to it. These set off fermentation. All the white Riojas here are stabilized by cold treatment, as are the rosés. Usually, too, both types are given a short period – six months – ageing in the wood. They are filtered twice. The white Reciente is a pure Viura wine, refreshing and pleasantly provided with a measure of juice and fruit. It stays in the tank for just six months. The Olarro *blanco seco* is matured in the cask; it is a sympathetic, reasonably substantial wine with a little more colour, and vanilla distinctly present. Its grapes are 60% Viura, 20% Malvasia and 20% Garnacha Blanca. The rosé usually possesses a pale pink colour and a splendidly vinous taste, with juice and freshness at the same time. It is composed of 70% Garnacha and 30% Viura grapes.

The first wines from Bodegas Olarra were on the Spanish market in 1977 and a year later they were also being sold abroad. At present about a third of production is exported, the most important markets being the United States, Britain, Denmark, Germany and France. There can be no doubt that exports will increase still further, for international interest in the stylish wines from this model concern is growing steadily, and justifiably.

Right:
Church tower in Alfaro, where the firm was originally founded.

Below:
Old horse wagon with comportas *in front of the modern Palacios bodega in Logroño.*

Below right:
Antonio Palacios Muro, a French-trained oenologist who runs this bodega in go-ahead fashion.

Reservas and gran reservas from this house are identical as wines, differing only in the time spent in ageing.

The average stock of bottles is 200,000.

All the wines are filtered and the young reds as well as the whites and rosés are stabilized by cooling.

Two other brands from this firm are Utrero and Eral.

The Remondo brand already represents more than a third of total turnover, and this proportion is still increasing. Changing the firm's name to Bodegas Remondo is being considered.

Denmark, the Netherlands and West Germany are the biggest foreign markets.

The wine museum beneath the Hotel Palacios in Alfaro has some ancient bottles, including one from the year of birth of Antonio's grandmother: 1865. One wall of the museum is wholly taken up with signed bottles. The idea is that the people who have signed them will return here to drink them.

The bodega has sponsored the San Sebastián professional basketball team.

Bodegas José Palacios prefers grapes for its white and rosé Riojas to be picked early in order to obtain the optimum freshness in the wines.

The firm has tanks with a combined capacity of 1.32 million (US 1.56 million) gallons.

Bodegas José Palacios

The history of the Palacios family has for generations been linked with the town of Alfaro, deep in the Rioja Baja. One piece of evidence is the find made a number of years ago when the family home was being rebuilt. Six bottles were discovered between two of the walls, wrapped in parchment with a medallion around the neck of each. The medallions gave the name of the vineyard and the year – 1651. The text on the parchment proved to be a will indicating how the vineyard should be divided among the children: the Palacios family was already making wine. This tradition was continued for generation after generation. The cellar where wine was made until well into the first half of this century is still there near the centre of Alfaro. There was capacity for 11,000 (US 13,000) gallons, a large quantity for the time, all from the family's own land. In 1947 José Palacios started a serious commercial wine business; and this is regarded as the founding year of Bodegas José Palacios. In the meantime José has passed the management on to one of his sons, Antonio. He studied oenology in both Spain and Bordeaux and has worked for the bodega since 1970.

The hotel

Back after three years in Bordeaux, Antonio carried through a number of sweeping changes. He was one of the first in the region to cease wood-ageing white and

Left:
Vinification is carried out behind these doors. The building is in Alfaro, next to the Palacios hotel.

Below:
José Palacios Remondo, who established the present firm in 1947.

A pelota court has been laid out beside the firm's buildings in Alfaro.

In Alfaro temperature control during vinification is vitally important. Particularly as it can still be quite warm here in November, in contrast to Rioja Alta and Alavesa.

Bodegas José Palacios

rosé wines. In addition a number of technical improvements were brought in, including the control of fermentation temperatures. Then in 1971 the bodega started to bottle on a big scale. José had moved the firm to a spot close by the road leading into the town from Logroño and in 1970 the family had built a hotel next to the bodega, with 86 rooms, two restaurants, a large bar, various public rooms and its own swimming pool. Also, in the cellar, the Museo de Viños Rioja has been set up. This contains a charming collection of bottles from all over the region, old wine-making apparatus, a *pellejo* (a large bag made from a whole goatskin in which wine used to be carried), a wooden fermenting vat, together with a bar and casks of wine marked with the names of José's nine children and their years of birth. The hotel is doing very well and enjoys a good reputation for its cuisine – and, of course, serves large amounts of Palacios wine. There are other respects in which it comes in handy to have a hotel next door. For example, the kitchens can make good use of the egg yolks which are left after the wine makers have used the whites to fine their *reservas*.

A second bodega

In 1974 Bodegas José Palacios reached a new phase of its existence. An agreement was arrived at with a group of growers which resulted in the building of a second bodega in Logroño. This was to be used exclusively for the storing and bottling of Riojas, with vinification, cask ageing and so on remaining in Alfaro. The new bodega was occupied in 1978 and the offices were also moved here. The angular, not very imaginative building lies almost opposite Bodegas Olarra, in the same industrial quarter. Collaboration with the growers soon came to an end and Antonio Palacios in fact regrets taking this considerable step. For the moment, however, Logroño remains the registered address of the bodega.

Other links with growers

Although the family used to cultivate quite an area of vineyard, it now possesses not a single vine. Everything for the annual 440,000 (US 520,000) gallons is bought in the form of grapes or wine – roughly in the proportion of 2 to 1. For his grapes Antonio has made agreements – always verbal, never written – with around 120 growers who between them work 1,360 acres. The contact with these growers is close; it is usually the bodega that indicates the exact moment when picking should start. In the period before the harvest the ripeness of the grapes is continually checked by Antonio and his assistants. Most of the growers are established in and around Alfaro; and Bodegas José Palacios vinifies half of all the grapes raised around here. The Garnacha is predominant, but the Tempranillo is given preference in new or replacement plantings. One of the examples Antonio showed me was the vineyard of the Torres brothers. Its very clayey and gravelly soil was planted throughout with Tempranillo in 1980, plus a little Cabernet Franc. The vineyard covers 49 acres, in one piece of land, and the vines are trained along wires. An irrigation system has even been installed. All the grapes go to Bodegas José Palacios, where they are vinified separately. The wine is also matured separately so that the best possible assessment of the result can be made. So far this has been followed by blending with Riojas of equal standard, but it is not impossible that the bodega will one day bring out an 'estate-bottled' wine. However, the vines will have to be a good deal older before any decision can be taken about this.

The bodega obtains about 60% of its grapes and wines from the Rioja Baja and the rest from Alta and Alavesa. It has only purchased in the two last districts since 1968.

Grandfather's rules

A great deal has changed in the making of wine over the last few generations in the Rioja, including in this firm. Anyone who walks through the insulated vinification area of Bodegas José Palacios in Alfaro, with its steel tanks that can be cooled by water sprinklers, who sees the modern presses, who looks at the equipment for cold stabilization and the filters in Logroño, will be hard put to it to imagine how different it all used to be. It was in this context that Antonio gave me the rules that his grandfather set down for the making of good wine:
– To give the wine a good colour the addition of tartaric acid is recommended.
– After fermentation is complete the wine should be fined by adding blood from a billy goat or a boar in the proportion of 1 *cantara* (16.5 litres) of blood to 150 of wine.

Bodegas José Palacios

(*Author's note*: There is nothing extraordinary about using blood for fining. It contains a lot of albumen and can therefore function in the same way as the customary egg white.)
– To preserve the wine Metabisulfito should be added after fining (this is the preservative sold at the Moderna druggist's shop in Logroño, owned by Alejo Martinez, who will indicate the proper quantities). Wine fined and treated in this way will never deteriorate.
– Putting fine sand from the Ebro into the vats is recommended to separate out the wine lees.
– After brushing the vats clean it is best to wash them out with hot water and soda.
– For filling in cracks in the vats a mixture of blood and lime is best.
– To see whether a wine is keeping properly, pour some into a glass with a 10 peseta coin in it and let it stand outdoors overnight.

These instructions were drawn up around 1920. The last on the list was presumably intended to check whether the wine had sufficient acids. The low denomination coins at that time were made of copper. The idea may have been that after one night the acid in the wine should have completely cleaned the coin.

Quickly into the casks

The black grapes that come into the bodega are just destalked, not pressed. This gives a kind of semi-*macération carbonique*, a technique Antonio's father started. Immediately after the second, malolactic, fermentation, the red wine goes into the cask; most bodegas wait for up to six months. In September 1983, for example, the 1983 red had already been in cask for 10 months when at many other firms the same vintage was still in the tank or had only just gone into the cask. This swift transfer into the wood is made to protect the young wine from oxidation. In Antonio's experience the tannin in the wood checks oxidation and the wine stays fresher and more vital in the cask than it would in the tank. The bodega has about 2,000 casks, all made of American oak – 500 more than it possessed at the beginning of the 1980s.

While Bodegas José Palacios markets mainly young reds in Spain, it exports a good deal of wood-aged wine. The first bottles were sent abroad in 1980; since then the export volume has grown rapidly to about a quarter of the total. The bodega hopes to sell more and more of the better qualities in Spain as well; and so the number of casks, small now in relation to production, will undoubtedly increase steadily.

The Remondo quality line

In line with this quality policy is the emphasis the firm puts on the range it sells under the name Bodegas Remondo, which brings together all the better wines. The intention is to make Remondo the prime brand; it could even be that the firm's name will one day be changed to Bodegas Remondo. The José Palacios name is reserved for the younger, cheaper wines. There are various white, rosé and red wines in the Remondo range. Relatively speaking the bodega does not make a lot of white wine: around 33,000 (US 39,000) gallons annually, which amounts to 8% of total production. This may have to do with the fact that not very many white grapes are planted in the Rioja Baja. In addition, Antonio Palacios selects very stringently. There are two different kinds of white. The Copa Remondo is made from 60% Garnacha Blanca grapes and 40% Malvasia. It is a gently fresh, juicy and ordinarily pleasant wine. The Herencia Remondo on the other hand is made only from the Viura and offers rather more style and elegance; it is, too, a slightly lighter and fresher Rioja. Both wines are rested for three months after bottling.

Artistic labels

The Rioja Baja has long been a district where a lot of rosé is made; the Garnacha

Copa Remondo
Rioja
70 cl.
BODEGAS REMONDO
LOGROÑO · RIOJA
PRODUCE OF SPAIN

The red Copa Remondo comes in the wine of the year category: it is given just 9 months in tank and 3 in bottle. It is made from about 60% Garnacha from Rioja Baja and 10% from Rioja Alta, and roughly 30% Tempranillo. It is a supple, friendly, slightly countrified everyday wine with a modest hint of ripe fruit. For drinking within 2 to 2½ years.

RIOJA
DISTINCIÓN
BODEGAS REMONDO
LOGROÑO · RIOJA · ESPAÑA

The red crianza Distinción comes from 60 to 70% Tempranillo with the rest Garnacha. It is matured for 3 months in tank, 12 to 16 in cask and 8 in bottle. Characteristics include a mellow, sometimes almost mild taste, a fairly robust core and an agreeable amount of wood and vanilla. The painting reproduced on the label is by the Spanish artist Joaquin Sorolla (1863–1923). A quite powerful rosé carries the same label.

HERENCIA REMONDO
RIOJA
Reserva 1978
BODEGAS REMONDO · RIOJA
70 cl.

While the crianza with this same medallion label is very similar to its Distinción counterpart, with the reserva we reach a different quality level. This type of wine is made only in better vintages and then matured for 12 months in tank, 2 years in cask and at least 9 months in bottle. Here, too, the grape varieties are 60 to 70% Tempranillo and the rest Garnacha. A balanced Rioja, with plenty of colour, firmness in the taste, a good basis of wood and the potential for further development.

PRODUCT OF SPAIN
HERENCIA REMONDO
RIOJA
GRAN RESERVA 1975
BODEGAS REMONDO · RIOJA
70 cl.

In order not to have too much wood in the taste of the gran reserva the bodega restricts its time in cask to 2 years. This is followed by 3 to 6 years in bottle. The wine usually has an attractive, quite mature taste with a full-flavoured core to it, together with wood and vanilla. The aftertaste is nicely sustained and the balance is generally good. The bottle is packed in a facsimile of a family document of 1651 complete with a red ribbon.

Opposite page, above:
Bottles of white Herencia Remondo are labelled by hand in Logroño.

Opposite page, below:
The original of the picture that appears on Herencia Remondo rosé labels hangs in Hotel Palacios' basement restaurant. It was painted by the artist Sellan, who likes to drink rosé with fish.

Below:
Grapes arriving in Alfaro.

Bodegas José Palacios

lends itself most excellently to this purpose. This is no doubt one reason why this bodega produces more rosé than white: about 88,000 (US 104,000) gallons, or 22% of the total. The Copa Remondo comes from Garnacha grapes grown in the Rioja Baja; the Herencia Remondo is made from the same variety, but from the Alta. As has been mentioned elsewhere in this book, Garnacha vineyards on the higher south-facing slopes of the Rioja Alta can yield remarkable wines. The Herencia Remondo rosé generally has some fruit, juice, a certain vivacity and an orangey-pink colour. It is one of the Riojas that has the reproduction of a painting on its label, in this case a work by the artist Sellan, who lives in Bilbao. He immortalized two fishermen lifting a box of Spanish mackerel on to the quay – a fish the painter himself likes to partner with rosé wine. The original hangs in one of the restaurants of the Hotel Palacios.

Mild and firm

Although the Garnacha is present in all red Remondo wines, only the Copa Remondo has a preponderance of it – around 70%. This friendly wine-for-everyday is not aged in the wood. In the other red Riojas the Tempranillo predominates and the Garnacha content varies between 20 and 40%. From *crianza* to *gran reserva* these are all harmonious wines with a mild taste, a firm core, and an adequate dose of wood and vanilla. Antonio Palacios is not in favour of allowing the wood to dominate the wines – and so even the *gran reserva* does not spend more than 2 years in cask, the legally prescribed minimum. And the bottles of this same wine are wrapped in facsimiles of the 1651 document, to underline the fact that after all these centuries the Palacios family is still making wine with the same love and *esprit*.

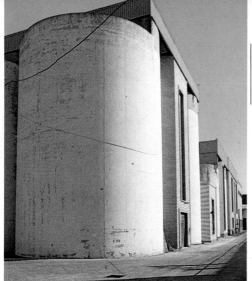

Left:
Outdoor tanks at the bodega.

Right:
Visitors can still see a wooden fermentation vat – as a museum piece.

Bodegas Campo Viejo

In the 1950s relatively little wine was sold in bottle in Spain. This was one of the most important reasons for the establishment of Savin, a limited company that set itself the goal of providing the home market with bottled, labelled wines. The year was 1959 and the place where it started was San Sebastián. In a short time Savin grew into an impressive group of wine businesses, with ten cellars and bottling plants throughout Spain – one of them being Bodegas Campo Viejo in Logroño. This firm was founded in 1963, originally near Aldeanueva de Ebro in Rioja Baja, but then it moved to Logroño in 1965. The site chosen there was an industrial estate separated from the centre of the town by the railway line and the station. Right from the start Campo Viejo grew so vigorously that building and expanding has been going on all the time, which has done the exterior appearance of the bodega little good. This untidy assortment of cellars, offices, large sheds and tanks does not have much to offer visually. How vigorous Campo Viejo's expansion has been can be seen in the production which in just on 25 years grew from nothing to an annual 3.85 million (US 4.55 million) gallons. This makes it by far the biggest producer of Rioja. The firm is also a market leader in Spain and one of the most important exporters.

Experiments in the vineyards

About one-fifth of this production is provided for by the firm's own vineyards. They cover 687 acres, an area that is still gradually increasing. The vineyards are concentrated around five places: Navarrete (Rioja Alta), Torremontalbo (Rioja Alta), Aldeanueva de Ebro (Rioja Baja), Alfaro (Rioja Baja) and El Villar de Arnedo (Rioja Baja). Besides the traditional grape varieties, a limited number of experimental vines have been planted, including the Cabernet Sauvignon, Pinot Noir, Gamay, Merlot, Chenin Blanc, Sémillon and Chardonnay. These and other trials are taking place under the supervision of the Instituto Nacional de Investigaciones

Agrarias, a government body connected with the Ministry of Agriculture. In 1982 the bodega vinified some Cabernet Sauvignon for the first time – 10 casks of it. The first impressions of this and the subsequent vintages was positive where the quality was concerned, but less promising with regard to quantity. With its small grapes, this variety yielded only a little over 35 hectolitres per hectare.

Stainless steel as well as concrete

Normally Campo Viejo obtains up to about a half of the volume it needs to buy from other vineyards in the form of grapes, and the remainder as wine. By far the larger part of the grapes is destalked and pressed in Logroño by the suppliers. The bodega has so far reserved only a small percentage for *macération carbonique* and these grapes, all of the Tempranillo variety, come exclusively from the firm's own vineyards. I have tasted the resulting wine: a supple, substantial Rioja with some fruit and an alcohol content around 12.5%. It would not surprise me if more of this wine were to be produced. Both concrete and stainless-steel tanks are available for fermenting the wine. The latter were specially installed for white and rosé wine; temperature control is automatic. Campo Viejo has a total storage capacity of 7.7 million (US 9.1 million) gallons.

Three kinds of oak

This bodega's growth has taken place chiefly in the sector of the cheaper young Riojas. With the rising prices of grapes, however, more emphasis is being placed on wood-aged wines. By 1983 60% of the Riojas on the Spanish market were of *crianza*, or older, quality, and Campo Viejo was then selling 85% cask-matured wines abroad. The number of casks has therefore been considerably increased in recent years, from 35,000 in 1981 to around 45,000 in 1985. These *barricas* are stored underground, in a spacious, high vault. Most of them are made of American oak, but you also see casks of French (12 to 15%)

and Yugoslav (10%) wood. It has been the experience at Campo Viejo that wines mature quicker in French oak and acquire a different aroma in the process, and so its use is restricted. In principle French casks are selected only for *reservas* and *gran reservas*, and then only during the first year in the wood. These two types of wine are exceptional in another respect, for they are the only Riojas not filtered here before bottling.

Horizontally in boxes

Although Bodegas Campo Viejo does not bottle all its wines (about 15% of production is sold in bulk, mainly to Switzerland and Belgium), it has a considerable stock of bottles, averaging around 7.5 million, and the intention is to increase it further. The bottles come off a double, fully automated line that fills 16,000 per hour. I was struck by the fact that Campo Viejo packs its cask-matured wines in the cases horizontally, so that the corks remain thoroughly moist. Bodegas Campo Viejo is not the only name you see on the labels. A large number of the young, simple wines carry the names Bodegas Castillo de San Asensio or Bodegas Almenar. I have visited the bodega twice, but on neither occasion was I given wines of these subsidiary brands to taste – perhaps rightly so.

A pleasurable rosé

With the arrival of the stainless-steel fermentation tanks the quality of the white Campo Viejo distinctly improved, but as their capacity is still insufficient to process all the must, the optimum has not yet been reached. The wine is made with 90% Viura grapes, supplemented with Malvasia and a very small amount of Garnacha Blanca. I found it to be a mildly fresh, agreeable thirst quencher, and also very pure. None of the white wines from this bodega comes into contact with wood. Campo Viejo produces around 770,000 (US 910,000) gallons of white Rioja a year.

Half this amount of rosé is made. The wine marketed with the Campo Viejo brand

Since 1982 Campo Viejo has fermented its rosé at low temperature in stainless-steel tanks. The wine has gained in fruit and freshness, making it very pleasant. Garnacha (75%) and Viura (25%) are the grapes. Campo Viejo white is now largely fermented in this way, too, and will be entirely so in the future. Viura (90%) and Malvasía plus some Garnacha Blanca are the grapes here. Both wines are given 6 months in the tank and are stabilized cold.

Campo Viejo reserva has distinctly more to offer than the crianza and also has more Tempranillo (80% instead of 60%). A supple, accessible, almost rounded wine with some freshness, good wood and a touch of fruit. Ageing: 1½ years' tank, 2½ years' cask and 2 years' bottle. Various vintages of this wine have won awards in Spain and elsewhere.

Grapes for the Viña Alcorta come from Campo Viejo's own vineyards in Torremontalbo and Navarrete. The Tempranillo is its only grape. This wine is made so as to offer a rather more elegant type of reserva. It develops well in bottle and is given a longer ageing there than the normal reserva (3 years). Vanilla is clearly there in nose and taste; you also taste a certain freshness; and the aftertaste is in harmony.

Standards for ageing the Campo Viejo gran reserva are 1½ years' tank, 3 cask (including a year in French oak) and 3 in bottle: the firm starts shipping this wine after 7½ years. It is quite a generous wine with juice, vanilla, sound structure and a good deep colour. No great refinement or distinction, but altogether a pleasure to drink.

Campo Viejo awards the Marqués de Villamagna title only to the very best wines of the very best years (such as 1970, 1973, 1975, 1978). Grapes for it – 90% Tempranillo, 10% Mazuelo, Garnacha and Graciano – are carefully selected and the wine is usually aged for 1½ years in a large wooden vat, 3 years in cask (French oak, from Limousin) and 4 in bottle. Wood and vanilla can be tasted, maturity alongside freshness, a good aftertaste and unmistakable class.

Below:
The most evocative room at Campo Viejo is the large reception room, where dinners are also organized.

A sum of 400 million pesetas was involved in setting up Bodegas Campo Viejo. The firm is now part of the Savin group, whose 4,500 shareholders own a series of wine businesses, some outside the Rioja. Names include L'Aixertell (sparkling wines), Castillo de Olite (Navarre), Condestable, Villamar (Jumilla), Savin, Monte Alegre, Monte Viña, Santa Cruz, Viña Cruz, Montefiel, Montoro, Elegido and Viña Nerea (table wines).

Bodegas Campo Viejo

name is all vinified at low temperatures and so combines freshness with fruit. It is a most pleasurable rosé, made from 75% Garnacha and 25% Viura. Both the white and the rosé wines are intended for drinking within a year to eighteen months.

Choice in the reservas

Although the ordinary red Campo Viejo, a *crianza*, enjoys great popularity I am not very enthusiastic about it myself.

Repeatedly there seemed to be a hint of oxidation present in both perfume and taste – the 1981 is an example – and it did not have anything special to offer in any case. However, it is generally reasonably deep in colour, reasonably rounded, and reasonable in aftertaste and price. It is made from 60% Tempranillo, 25% Garnacha and 15% Mazuelo plus Graciano. Its ageing programme consists of 18 months in tank, 12 in cask and 6 in bottle. A more interesting level is reached with the Campo

Viejo *reserva* in which, besides a dash of freshness, some fruit and also vanilla can be detected. This wine has more Tempranillo in its make-up, namely 80%, with Garnacha, Mazuelo and Graciano as the complementary varieties. It remains significantly longer in cask (2½ years) and bottle (2 years). A special kind of *reserva* goes under the name of Viña Alcorta. This is more elegant in taste than the comparable Campo Viejo and has a year's extra bottle age. The bodega makes it

Left:
Some of the horizontal presses. The grapes at Campo Viejo come in on four conveyor belts.

Below:
An average 45,000 casks are kept in the cellars, mostly of American oak. There are three coopers on permanent staff to maintain them.

Bottom:
Older bottles are sometimes given a wax capsule.

Bodegas Campo Viejo

entirely under its own control from Tempranillo grapes only, picked in the vineyards at Navarrete and Torremontalbo.

Marqués de Villamagna

The *gran reserva* Campo Viejo is not sold until it has had 18 months in tank, 3 years in cask and 3 in bottle. The grape varieties are exactly the same as in the *reserva*. It is usually a nice-tasting, vinous Rioja, a wine to savour in which juice and vanilla are both present and, in the nature of things, there is a good measure of maturity. There is also an even more special *gran reserva*,

the Marqués de Villamagna. The bodega sells its best selections from exceptional years under this name. The first Marqués de Villamagna appeared in 1970 and for this, grapes from five communities in the Rioja Alta were used, from three in Alavesa and two in Baja. The grapes were 90% Tempranillo, with 10% made up of Graciano, Garnacha and Mazuelo. After vinification the wine spent two years in wooden vats and then about four years in casks of French oak. It was then bottled and launched about four years later. For the 1973 the period in the cask was shortened to three years, as it was for the 1975 and 1978. This reduced the wood element in the

wine somewhat which, given the results with the 1970, seemed the right thing to do. Class is unmistakably present in the Marqués de Villamagna wines. They are *gran reservas* which demonstrate that this bodega, notwithstanding the massive scope of its operation, is also able to work on a small scale and make distinguished Riojas of flawless quality.

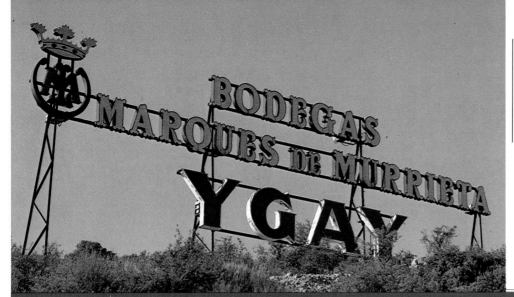

Left:
The autopista just east of Logroño crosses the bodega site. This advertisement for the bodega has been set up on a hill beside the road. It lights up at night.

Below:
On the Marqués de Murrieta estate. The motorway (autopista) is top right in the picture.

In November 1907 Luciano de Murrieta was created a 'Son of Logroño'.

Murrieta wines triumphed at the agricultural show held in 1857 in Madrid.

Bodegas Marqués de Murrieta

The founder of Bodegas Marqués de Murrieta was called Luciano de Murrieta García-Lemoine – he was made a marquis later in life. He was born in 1822 in the then Spanish colony of Peru, where his father had emigrated (and married a beautiful Creole girl). When Peru obtained its independence the Murrietas left for London. Luciano did not associate with the ex-colonial clique there but moved on to Spain and went into the army. He reached the rank of colonel and became aide-de-camp to General Baldomero Espartero, the famous Riojan whose statue stands in the Plaza del Espolón in Logroño. When the first Carlist War broke out Luciano fought on the losing side, that of Carlos de Borbón. together with his general he was obliged to flee Spain and go to London. Exile there lasted from 1843 to 1848. It was at this time that Luciano had the idea of exploiting the potential of the Rioja as a wine-making region, and even of exporting the wines that were then strictly local. His friend the Duque de la Victoria had faith in the idea and promised to make his bodega and his money available. On his return from England, however, Luciano did not make an immediate start on his experiment. He visited Bordeaux first to learn the techniques.

The first casks

In Bordeaux Luciano de Murrieta discovered the importance of ageing in wood, which led him to decide to introduce the system into the Rioja, where it was not known at all. Only the wine of the year was sold there and any that was left over was poured away to make room for the following harvest. Thus there were no skilled coopers available in Logroña and Luciano had to get all his casks from Bilbao: 100 of them, all with a capacity of 4½ cantaras (72 litres). In about 1850 Luciano was back in Logroño again and in 1852 he shipped out his first consignment of wood-aged Rioja

COSECHA 1980

RESERVA
COSECHA 1970

Reserva Especial
Rioja Cosecha 1962

ETIQUETA BLANCA
COSECHA 1980

All Marqués de Murrieta wines are aged in the wood, including the youngest white: a crianza made from 90% Viura and 10% Malvasía. It is given 12 months' tank, 24 cask and 6 to 12 bottle. This wine has a fresh taste with a refined mellowness, suppleness and vanilla. There is also vanilla in the perfume. Colour: attractive with a golden tint and the slightest tinge of green.

The white Rioja this bodega sells as its Reserva usually spends about 10 years in the wood, together with 1 year's tank and 2 years' bottle. Nevertheless there is a freshness perceptible in the taste together with maturity, juice, vanilla and other nuances. A beautiful and interesting wine made only from Viura grapes.

In exceptional vintages the firm keeps not only red wine separate for extremely long wood-ageing periods but also white. Castillo Ygay 1962 is an example, which more than 20 years on proved to be a pleasure to drink. It had depth and nuances in perfume and taste, with a noble maturity and a vanilla aroma that was definitely there, but in this case not obtrusive. Even juice and freshness were still present. Viura is the only grape variety used.

Bodegas Marqués de Murrieta sells no wines without at least 2 years in the wood. This is exactly what the red Etiqueta Blanca – a crianza – is given, together with 1 year tank and ½ to 1 year bottle. It is made up from 50% Tempranillo, 40% Garnacha and 10% Mazuelo. This relatively high Garnacha content gives the wine a quite robust taste, with a good amount of wood and some maturity discernible. Not the finest wine from this bodega, but a sound product.

Bodegas Marqués de Murrieta

(from the Duque de la Victoria's bodega in Logroño). Half of the casks were destined for Cuba, the other half for Mexico. Those for Havana arrived without problems and were there sold for a good deal of money. The batch for Mexico, however, was lost in a violent storm off the harbour of Veracruz.

The general success of the experiment convinced Luciano that he was on the right road. He now began to leave wines to mature in the cask for four years and, around 1860, he started his own bodega. The exact year is not known: at Bodegas Marqués de Murrieta they maintain that theirs is the oldest bodega still functioning in the Rioja, and the earliest but one to have commercialized wine (after that of Marqués de Riscal, opened in 1860).

The Ygay estate

The bodega acquired its present site in 1872, when Luciano de Murrieta bought the Ygay estate. This lies just outside Logroño, beside the Zaragoza road; a slender white gateway marks the entrance. Luciano had always been a liberal and possessed of a social conscience. He expressed this in a practical way at Ygay, one instance being the housing on the estate of 50 families whose poor circumstances would otherwise have forced them to emigrate to South America. This remarkable man, a lifelong bachelor, did good in other ways as well. He financed not only the first maritime school in Bilbao but also the first infant school in Logroño. On the day he handed the building over to the town, 20 October 1906, the street in which it stood was named after him – and still is the Calle Marqués de Murrieta.

Besides grapes the marquis also grew hops (much of the crop went to Britain) and olives, which repeatedly won prizes. Honey of a highly praised quality was also produced at Ygay. Luciano died in 1911, after which his heirs continued the business as a family partnership. This position changed in October 1983 when two of the three joint owners, all members of the same family, sold their share to Vicente Cebrian, the Count of Creixel, giving him a two-thirds majority.

Increasing cultivation

One of the Count's plans is to make the bodega self-sufficient in grapes. At the time of the take-over the 366 productive acres were already supplying a considerable proportion of the grapes required: nearly 60% of those for the red wine – an average 99,000 (US 117,000) gallons, about 80% of the white – 29,700 (US 35,100) gallons, and 20% of the rosé – 19,800 (US 23,400) gallons. The whole estate, however, covers 642 acres, and the rest is to be brought into cultivation.

Planting the young vines and waiting for them to become productive will take a considerable time. For the present the bodega will therefore continue on its current footing. This means that it will go on obtaining the extra grapes it needs from a group of some 15 permanent suppliers. Some of these growers have been supplying Bodegas Marqués de Murrieta for more than 40 years, and none of them lives more than 5 miles away. All the grapes therefore come from the same zone, central Rioja, so that there is no question of greatly varying sugar contents.

The bodega does not make wine every year. Not a drop was produced in 1972, for example – but great efforts were made to find alternative customers for the regular grape suppliers, who also received a money premium, as a token of goodwill and to maintain the close relationship.

Five levels

Luciano de Murrieta's original bodega is still in existence. It is a solid structure, built of large grey stones. There are now also various other buildings on the site, the latest of which date from the beginning of the 1980s. As the bodega acquired its present form in various stages, different types of fermentation tanks are in use. There are glazed concrete and stainless-steel tanks, and the large wooden vats from the early period are also still in service. The

The red Reserva 1970 was specially ordered by the King of Norway when he visited Spain; a firm, distinguished Rioja with a good amount of wood, and the 'backbone' for a long development in bottle. It had 1 year in tank, around 10 years in wood and 2 in bottle. Made from 60% Tempranillo, followed by 30% Garnacha and 10% Mazuelo.

What is amazing at Marqués de Murrieta is the number of very old wines it usually has in its collection. In 1984 it still had some Reserva 1960 in stock, a wine that had spent 17 to 18 years in cask. It then had a deep, dark colour, an obviously well-matured character, a lot of wood (with a slightly bitter tang), a robust taste with a full-flavoured core to it. There was no tiredness here: this wine could have gone on for years more.

The gran reserva Castillo Ygay 1942 did not go on sale until 1983 – to replace the 1934, sold out by then. An exhausted wine might have been expected, but on the contrary it was still vital with none of the infirmities of age. I thought it was a beautiful, majestic Rioja – and it gained in quality in the glass. It had matured for 1 year in tank, about 35 in wood and around 5 in bottle. The grape varieties were described as a 'traditional mixture'.

Left:
True to tradition, bottles from this bodega are wrapped in a metal mesh.

Below:
General view of the bodega buildings. The oldest cellar is in the top left-hand corner partly hidden by trees and in front of the taller, white-walled building.

Below left:
Busy with calculations in the bodega office during the harvest.

Bodegas Marqués de Murrieta

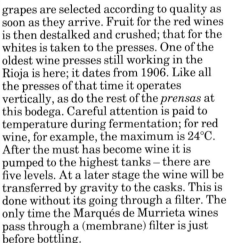

grapes are selected according to quality as soon as they arrive. Fruit for the red wines is then destalked and crushed; that for the whites is taken to the presses. One of the oldest wine presses still working in the Rioja is here; it dates from 1906. Like all the presses of that time it operates vertically, as do the rest of the *prensas* at this bodega. Careful attention is paid to temperature during fermentation; for red wine, for example, the maximum is 24°C. After the must has become wine it is pumped to the highest tanks – there are five levels. At a later stage the wine will be transferred by gravity to the casks. This is done without its going through a filter. The only time the Marqués de Murrieta wines pass through a (membrane) filter is just before bottling.

All wines aged in wood

The founder of this bodega believed in wood-aged wines, and so do his successors. No Rioja is sold without having at least two years in the cask. One result of this consistently applied practice is what is probably the highest cask ratio in the whole region. The bodega has 10,000 casks for an average annual production of 148,500 (US 175,000) gallons. Or for every litre produced, there are 3 litres maturing in the wood. All these *barricas* are made of American oak and are maintained by a cooper. At this bodega they remain in use not for years but for decades. Normally, 300 are replaced every year, which means that each cask is in service for an average of some 33 years. In fact, many of them stay in use for 40 to 45 years. In old casks of this kind the influence of the wood on the wine is at an absolute minimum. A thick layer of crystals forms on the insides of the casks, which prevents direct contact between the

wine and the oak. It also protects the wine from the effects of oxygen. The bodega leaves this layer in place; and that is why even long-matured Riojas keep their freshness and vitality. At Marqués de Murrieta they are also careful to ensure that casks for red, white and rosé wines are never interchanged; the long presence of a particular wine impregnates the casks with its own flavour.

Before the early 1980s this bodega had hardly any bottles of its older wines in stock. They remained in the casks until an order came in and only then were they bottled. There was then a wait of six weeks before these Riojas were delivered. Partly because of the acute shortage of space it was decided to abandon this policy. The bodega now has an average of 600,000 bottles in stock.

Cast-iron reputation

Bodegas Marqués de Murrieta has no need to follow an aggressive sales policy. The customers simply come of their own accord, and in fact their orders cannot always be met. The beginning of this firm's cast-iron reputation goes back to the last quarter of the previous century when at international fairs in Paris in 1879 and 1889 it won one gold and two silver medals, as well as an honourable mention. A Rioja from Marqués de Murrieta also won a silver medal at Bordeaux in 1895. Today the bodega has a great number of admirers. When King Olav of Norway was on a state visit to Spain he asked for a Marqués de Murrieta 1970 to be served with his meals. Graham Greene visited the bodega itself and to mark the occasion three bottles of 1904 – the author's year of birth – were opened. According to those present they tasted delicious.

Three kinds of white

The Marqués de Murrieta range is not large: eight wines, each of them a classic. Three of them are white, the youngest being a *crianza*. This is given 12 months in tank, 24 in cask and 6 to 12 in bottle. I was allowed to taste two versions of this wine:

Bodegas Marqués de Murrieta

very young, from the tank, and from the bottle in the normal way. The first type tasted juicy, rounded, agreeable, but not remarkable. The second, on the other hand, offered character. I found it to be a much more interesting Rioja, with a mild perfume with vanilla in it and a fresh, pure, refined taste. In 1983 The Wine and Spirit Trade's Benevolent Society judged the 1973 worthy of a place at its great annual dinner in London, where it accompanied the *Mousseline de saumon Balmoral*. The grapes used for this Rioja are the Viura (90%) and the Malvasia (10%). The two older wines I tasted were made from the Viura only. The Reserva 1970 had then had a maturing period of one year in tank, around ten years in cask and two years in bottle. Nevertheless this Rioja, too, still had plenty of freshness, together with a light vanilla aroma, nuances in taste and nose, as well as its maturity. For me it was a beautiful wine, with a certain style. The white Castillo Ygay 1962 also proved to be a pleasure to drink. The key signature here

seemed somewhat lower, rather more serious. There was a gleam of gold in the colour and a noble taste which, like the perfume, gave a diversity of impressions. Immediately after this the rosé was served, a *crianza* made up from various years, with 80% Garnacha grapes, 10% Tempranillo and 10% Viura. It was the only wine from Marqués de Murrieta that failed to charm me. I thought it too ripe and too woody – but then I like fruit and freshness in this kind of wine. But in Spain in particular there are many lovers of this traditional-style Rioja *rosado*, a wine that is left for 12 months in tank, 24 in cask and 6 to 12 in bottle.

Very old vintages

The youngest red wine, Etiqueta Blanca, is given the same maturing period as the rosé. Here, too, you find a rather ripe character and a good deal of wood, but in addition there is a fresh core to it. That this *crianza* tastes rather more robust than the other red wines is partly due to its relatively high

percentage of Garnacha (40%, with 50% Tempranillo and 10% Mazuelo). The next red wine in the range, the Reserva, often ten years older, contains 30% Garnacha and 60% Tempranillo, and again 10% Mazuelo. It is a wine with more distinction and more subtleties. I greatly enjoyed the 1970 Reserva in particular. This was in 1984, and whereas a vintage such as 1970 had long been sold out at the other bodegas, Marqués de Murrieta was still offering a pair of even older wines: the Reserva 1960 and the Castillo Ygay 1942. The latter wine had only gone on sale in 1983, after about 35 years in cask and nearly 5 years in bottle – as a replacement for the 1934, which seems almost incredible. Both wines proved to be uncommonly drinkable. They were wholly traditional Riojas with a full-flavoured core, a well-matured, slightly bitter taste of wood, and an unmistakable allure.

No concessions

If you want to put the characteristics of these mature Riojas into words, then concepts such as generosity or fruit are just not appropriate and would contradict the nature of wines that have been so long in the cask. Rather you would associate them with terms such as majestic, elegant, conservative, distinguished. Bodegas Marqués de Murrieta made them with no concessions to changing patterns of taste or temporary trends. The values of the past remain those of today. Therefore anyone who drinks old wines from this bodega has the assurance that they are just as reliable, sound and full of strong character as they were generations ago. In recent decades the Rioja district has undergone many changes, some of them turbulent, but this firm has been subject to hardly any: Bodegas Marqués de Murrieta remains a calm island of tradition and quality. Long may it remain so.

Left:
The weight of a load of grapes is checked on the weighbridge.

Below:
During the harvest grapes continue to come in until dusk.

Members of this cooperative are required to pick Viura (20%) and Tempranillo grapes (5%) before the later-ripening Garnacha (75%).

The cooperative lies alongside the Logroño–Zaragoza road.

The Peña Vieja goes into a 70cl Bordeaux bottle. Its component grapes are roughly 75% Garnacha, 20% Viura and 5% Tempranillo. It is not cask-aged, but does spend a couple of years in tanks. Particulars are: reasonably deep colour, nose not altogether pure, a fresh element in the taste, not too full-bodied yet with a good core of alcohol – very nearly a correct wine.

The San Miguel Cooperative

Below the hill village of Ausejo, nearly 19 miles from Logroño, there is a cooperative where practically all the local community's wines are processed. This is the Bodega Cooperativa San Miguel, set up in 1956 in a far from memorable concrete building. There is also concrete in plenty under its high roof, for all the fermentation tanks are made of this material. About 420 growers are associated with the concern and they cultivate nearly 1,100 acres between them. About 75% of their wines are Garnachas with 5% Tempranillo and 20% Viura. The cooperative produces some 220,000 (US 260,000) gallons of red wine annually and 22,000 (US 26,000) gallons of rosé. In addition wines from the Asociación Rioja Empresas Cooperativas Vitivinícolas (ARECOVI – the association of Rioja Baja cooperatives) are nurtured here.

Casks for wood ageing

Since the early 1970s the San Miguel cooperative has had casks available in which some of the wines are matured. Generally it is these Riojas that the concern bottles itself: a modest selection of their own wines and those of associated cooperatives. The stock of casks numbers around 200. Usually the wine stays in the wood for one year, although this period may be extended. The wines chosen for maturing are the lighter kinds, with 12.5 to 13% alcohol; the wines sold in bulk often have 15% or more.

A not very high standard

The San Miguel bodega used to have its own brand, called Campolosa, but since the collaboration with other cooperatives this has been abandoned in favour of the collective brands Peña Vieja and Viña Antiqua. The former is given no cask ageing but the latter is. In tasting the two kinds my preference was for the Peña Vieja, although even this would score six out of ten only with difficulty. I thought the Viña Antiqua was simply unpalatable. It was an oxidized and also rather acid wine of poor quality – not worthy of the name of Rioja. At this cooperative they obviously have difficulty caring for the wine in the cask. All of San Miguel's bottled Riojas go through earth filters twice, and sometimes even three times. The 80,000 to 90,000 bottles annually are mainly consumed in the immediate neighbourhood.

You probably have to be born in Arnedo really to appreciate the local rosado – I was not and I find it difficult. It is a pale-orange wine with suppleness, some vague fruit, a firm 14% alcohol and insufficient freshness. The red wine from the same Ciencuevas brand lacks colour and class, although this simple Rioja does possess strength – some 13.5% alcohol.

Right:
Entrance to the cooperative. A lot of the wine is sold to the local population.

Far right:
A grower trotting to the bodega on a mule.

Below:
Arnedo is dominated by a high hill with the ruins of a Moorish castle on it.

This cooperative can store 462,000 (US 546,000) gallons of wine in concrete and fibreglass tanks.

The Ciencuevas wine is named after a rock face – directly behind the old centre – where there are at least 100 caves.

The Nuestra Señora de Vico Cooperative

Arnedo

Anyone visiting the bars of Arnedo stands a good chance of coming across wines from the local cooperative, for it delivers around 10,000 litre bottles a month to the *horeca* of the district and a good many 16.5-litre *cantaras* go to private individuals. Rosé is far and away the favourite wine hereabouts; sales of this type in the cafés are double those for red. The cooperative is situated right by the high rock that towers over Arnedo. It was founded in 1956 and since then the members have not invested a great deal in it. Only the most urgent replacements and renovations have been carried out. In autumn 1984 no one here had any idea of how high the temperatures rose during fermentation – not for the red, the rosé or the white. There was no equipment for the cold stabilization of rosé and white wines and no casks had been obtained for maturing red Riojas. There was an earth and a plate filter. But the tide is perhaps turning for I was given to understand that drastic improvements in materials and equipment were being discussed actively as well as an expansion project.

About 750 members

The 750 or so members of the Bodega Cooperative Nuestra Señora de Vico cultivate 1,100 acres between them. Most of the vineyards lie around Arnedo itself but there are also members in Grávalos, a village 10 miles to the south-east. They are planted principally with Garnacha (85%), supplemented by Viura and, to a much lesser extent, by Tempranillo. The intention is that when replanting is carried out the Viura will be replaced by the Tempranillo: which will also give the cooperative the opportunity to stop the production of white wine. At present it is around 42,000 (US 49,000) gallons a year, a little below the annual 44,000 (US 52,000) gallons of red. With its 110,000 (US 130,000) gallons a year rosé is the most important wine here.

Tannin level kept down

To make rosé wine the grapeskins are left in contact with the must for one night. The wine then reaches 14% alcohol by natural means. The result is a supple and, of course, robust wine that could do with rather more freshness. The red wine is simple and seems to lack some colour. Afterwards I heard that the bodega leaves the black grapeskins in contact with the wine for only part of the fermentation period (usually 10 days). This is to prevent the occurrence of too much tannin. The cooperative markets roughly 13,000 (US 15,500) gallons of wine in bottles. It regularly supplies bulk wine, in tankers, to AGE, Campo Viejo and other concerns.

The red Chitón is a crianza from 50% Tempranillo and 50% Garnacha. It stays about 6 months in tank and then has 12 months in cask, followed by 6 to 7 months' bottle age. It is a decent Rioja with a juicy taste, with wood and vanilla, but without much personality, depth or length. Part of the grape blend is pasteurized.

Señorio de Prayla is the name given to a reserva that goes on sale after 2 to 2½ years in wood and at least a year in bottle. It can have rather more colour than the Chitón, but at the same time a rather smooth, over-supple taste and a lack of concentration. Pleasant to drink, yet it leaves no lasting impressions. The grapes are 70% Tempranillo and 30% Garnacha. There is a mesh over the bottle.

Arnedo

Bodegas Faustino Rivero Ulecia

In a sloping, narrow street in the old centre of Arnedo stands the bodega where Agapito Rivero was once established. Its 110-yd vault was dug into a rocky hill and offers a temperature of 13°C all through the year. This bodega has been used by the Rivero family for a very long time; it was back in 1932 that the wooden fermentation vats were replaced by concrete ones. Today, however, it just stores casks of wine, for in 1979 modern premises for bottling and maturing wine were completed just outside Arnedo. This enabled the family to start selling wine in bottle. They already had a vinification centre in Alfaro and another one in the Rioja Baja. The year 1979 also saw the setting up of the Bodegas Faustino Rivero Ulecia, a *sociedad anónima* wholly controlled by the Rivero family. The registered offices are at the bottling plant.

Emphasis on young wines

The bodega owns no more than 23 or 24 acres of vineyard, covering only some 2% of production. The rest is bought elsewhere, principally in the form of grapes, although some red wine is on regular order from cooperatives in the Baja. All the white is purchased ready made, usually from the San Asencio cooperative in Rioja Alta. Faustino Rivero Ulecia produces around 460,000 (US 540,000) gallons a year, roughly in the proportions of 70% red wine, 23% rosé and 7% white. All of it is sold bottled. The bodega puts the main emphasis on the sale of young wines, which also explains the relatively small number of casks – about 2,000. All the wines are filtered twice, and nearly all of them are pasteurized. The *reservas* and a proportion of the *crianzas* are the only ones that are spared this fate.

Not remarkable

The red Rasillo, which is also sold under the full name of the bodega, is made from 70% Garnacha grapes and 30% Tempranillo. It is a simple, readily drinkable Rioja rather lacking in colour and class, and can be slightly oxidized in addition. The Chitón, a *crianza*, has rather more quality to offer, with some wood, vanilla and juice to it; it is partly, not wholly, pasteurized. The proportion of Tempranillo rises to 50% with the Chitón and reaches 70% with the Señorio de Prayla. Nevertheless I did not find the latter to be a better wine: it tasted rather too smooth and lacked concentration. The Señorio de Prayla, a *reserva*, is fined with white of egg. Of the remaining wines only the Rasillo rosé merits any attention. Of its kind it is a better product than that from some of the cooperatives in the Rioja Baja – with juice, some freshness with a controlled 12 to 12.2% of alcohol – yet this is another wine from Bodegas Faustino Rivero Ulecia that could not be termed remarkable.

The San Adrián Cooperative

San Adrián

To find the San Adrián cooperative you have to drive through the village in a westerly direction, then turn off left opposite the Guardia Civil building. It stands at the end of this street, at an intersection, and was built in 1958. The 200 or so members bring in the 800 to 1,000 tons of grapes they normally harvest, and these produce 120,000 to 165,000 gallons (US 140,000 to 195,000 gallons) of wine. It was not so long ago that the cooperative was producing more rosé than red Rioja, but today the proportions have been reversed. Red now accounts for 70% of production, rosé for 30%. White wine is not made here. True to local tradition the Garnacha predominates in the just over 600 acres owned by the members. For replanting, however, the cooperative has laid down a minimum 25% of Tempranillo vines. What is only a recommended percentage elsewhere in the Rioja Baja is mandatory here.

Ageing in the wood still limited

That this was a wise decision was demonstrated at a tasting at the cooperative. I was given different blends to taste in which the Tempranillo content varied. The wines with a preponderance of Tempranillo proved to be clearly the best. The Viña Sansande with 60% Tempranillo and 40% Garnacha tasted much more agreeable than the same wine with the percentages reversed; in the latter form it came across as dull and heavy. However, the cooperative cannot as yet allow the ordinary Viña Sansande to have this larger proportion of Tempranillo. This is done only with a very limited quantity of wine, namely the cask-aged *vino de calidad superior.* How little of this wine has been made is shown by the fact that fewer than 10 casks have been available so far, and only the members themselves have had any. This does not alter the fact that the ordinary Viña Sansande – the *2° año,* is of a very acceptable quality. It is a substantial, warming Rioja with fruit, tannin and a deep colour, a wine that goes with game and winter evenings. The wines I tasted had an alcohol content of 14.5%, but the cooperative plans to bring this down.

The rosé did not appeal to me so much: I thought it was simply too heavy. It was made from Garnacha and Viura grapes.

All the Riojas from this concern are filtered three times, twice through earth and once through cellulose plates, and the wines can obviously do with it. The San Adrián cooperative seems to have opted for the arduous path of quality. It is to be hoped that its efforts will be appropriately rewarded; and that in the future the proportion of Tempranillo in the wines will go on growing together with that of wood-aged wines.

San Adri

Bodegas Gurpegui

In the early years of this century the Rioja had groups of coopers who went round the bodegas making or repairing casks. One such *tonelero* was Primitivo Gurpegui Muro. In Haro on one of his journeys he met a girl called Bibiana Muga (whose family was later to set up the Bodegas Muga) and the two were married in 1921. That same year Primitivo opened his own bodega in his native village of San Adrián. In this he was following the example of his maternal grandfather, who had run a bodega in Haro;

its buildings were taken over in 1896, 24 years after their construction, by what was later to be called Bodegas Carlos Serres. Primitivo's son Luis came into the business at 18 and became its owner seven years later when his father died. Luis expanded Bodegas Gurpegui enormously, "by 90% of the present volume", as he himself says. He is a shrewd, dynamic man, progressive in outlook and greatly interested in new techniques. Besides this he is a man who smiles a lot, enjoys life and appreciates food

and a good glass of wine ("I'm the biggest customer for my own wine").

The King of the Rosé

Although Bodegas Gurpegui started bottling halfway through the 1950s, bulk wine was for a long time the main busines This bodega supplied large quantities of wine to other wine businesses, and until 1975 it was in fact the biggest producer of Rioja. Today there are bigger firms and at

Bodegas Gurpegui

Gurpegui the emphasis has shifted to bottled wine – it is now 70% of the total. This is still an important bodega, however, with a normal production of 1.65 million (US 1.95 million) gallons a year. Over a quarter of this – 440,000 (US 520,000) gallons – is rosé. Luis Gurpegui was the first to make this type on a large scale; he is even known as "the King of the Rosé". Partly with the idea of steadily improving the quality of his rosé, Luis was the first in the region to install plant that would enable rosé and white wines to be fermented at a constant low temperature. This was in place and ready by 1981. In the meantime Luis' four sons had come in to assist him in the business, with Luis Carlos the oenologist and Primitivo in exports; the latter's wife Virginia, who speaks excellent English, looks after public relations.

Vineyards owned or rented

The headquarters of Bodegas Gurpegui are still at the San Adrián premises. However, the firm has also acquired three other vaults: in Andosilla (just under 4 miles from San Adrián and dating from 1950) in Aldeanueva de Ebro (built in 1872) and in Haro (the former family bodega which was bought back from Carlos Serres). Gurpegui has also in addition vineyards of its own, 490 acres at present, all in San Adrián or the immediate neighbourhood at Androsilla and Azagra. When Luis showed me a newly planted plot I was immediately reminded that we were deep into the Rioja Baja, the centre of an enormous canning industry. The young cuttings were not protected from rabbits and other pests in the usual way with plastic or netting, but were covered by tins. The fact that the vineyards lie in the Rioja Baja does not mean in this case that they are mainly planted with Garnacha. In the first place there are 123 acres with white grapes, and at 247 acres the Tempranillo is the most important black variety. Besides its own land Gurpegui also rents 86 acres near Logroño and 37 acres near Baños de Ebro. The combined 617 acres of vineyard produce cover 10% of the red Rioja

production, 20% of the white and 75% of the rosé. Of the remainder that has to be bought in, half is normally in the form of grapes, half in wine. The total area cultivated by the firm's regular suppliers is 2,965 acres.

A street called Gurpegui

The production of rosé and white, and of red wines for drinking young, is concentrated in San Adrián. The bodega there is in the western part of the main street, behind a closed, not very inviting frontage. The site runs through for some distance to another narrower street at the back. On the opposite side of this there is another Gurpegui bodega, where an annual 880,000 (US 1.04 million) gallons of Navarre wine are made. It is little wonder that the connecting street has been named after Luis Gurpegui. Once you are inside the Rioja bodega you find that it has a pleasant reception hall where a pair of old wine presses stand. Next door to this a tasting

area has been set up. The many extensions and additions to the fabric in the wine-making parts of the bodega create a confusing impression, which is reinforced by the obvious problems of space here.

Thermo-vinification

Technically, however, the bodega is well equipped. Rosé and white wines ferment at 18°C in an installation consisting of a battery of cooled stainless-steel tanks, and at a later stage they are also stabilized at a low temperature. There are filters here: rosé and white go through a plate filter before and after stabilization, and through a membrane filter when they are bottled. Sweet white wines can be pasteurized. Then for red wines for drinking young the bodega has the plant for what is called thermo-vinification. In this the must is heated after pressing, it is then passed through the grapeskins and is subsequently vinified separately. The result is a rather rich wine, with fruit and tannin. An

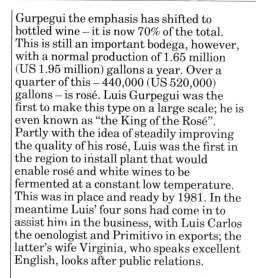

BODEGAS BERCEO · HARO

Bodegas Gurpegui

additional advantage of this method is that good wines can still be made in years when rot is prevalent. Despite the fact that Gurpegui has had a lot of success with this unusual type of Rioja – it always sells out quickly – the Consejo Regulador has forbidden the installation of plant for this kind of wine making anywhere else.

Bodegas Berceo

While operations in San Adrián are modern and on a massive scale, the firm's cellar in Haro keeps the past alive. It is at number 32 in the legendary Calle de las Cuevas and bears the name of Bodegas Berceo. The Gurpegui family has been engaged in restoring this old building since the beginning of the 1980s. This is being done with great taste. The outer doors, ceiling beams, banisters and balusters, for example, are being painted in a splendid, old-fashioned shade of red. In addition the walls are being cleaned down, panelling is being restored and wooden vats brought back. There are seven of these, all built in 1983, with a capacity of 8,800 (US 10,400) gallons each. They are being used for maturing wine, but could also serve for fermentation. Like other bodegas in this street, Bodegas Berceo is built against a steep hillside. The grapes arrive at the top, on a flat area where there are three tall stone shafts intended to bring fresh air to the underground cellars 60 ft below. The Gurpeguis plan to give the above-ground part of the bodega the appearance of a real château: the architect's drawing has already been made.

The Viña Berceo *crianza* is generally a splendid wine with reasonable depth of colour, a pure perfume with vanilla and a lively taste with fruit, wood and, again, vanilla. Bodegas Gurpegui makes it from 70% Tempranillo and 30% Garnacha. The wine is given a year in tank, at least a year (often 2) in cask and a minimum 6 months in bottle.

My impression of the Viña Berceo *reserva* is that it rather falls between two stools: in its own category its quality is less convincing than either the *crianza* below or the *gran reservas* above. Its quality should, nevertheless, be termed correct; and in its taste you encounter some wood, body and fruit. Its ageing phases are 1 year in the large vat, 2 years' cask and a minimum 2 years' bottle.

Like its *crianza*, Gurpegui's *gran reservas* are composed of 80% Tempranillo, 10% Mazuelo and 10% Graciano. This Viña Berceo is a sound, well but not over-matured wine with balanced quantities of wood, vanilla, tannin and fruit. It is kept for 1 year in a large vat, 2 in cask and at least 6 in bottle – all at the Berceo bodega in Haro.

Gonzalo de Berceo is a *gran reserva* Bodegas Gurpegui produces in small quantities and only in the best years. It is matured over a long period: 1 year's large vat, 2 years' cask and about 10 years' bottle. This allows the wine to develop in tranquillity into a very mature, brown-coloured Rioja that retains its vitality – and can be laid down for a further period.

Opposite page, above:
Drawing showing how the Berceo bodega in Haro will eventually look.

Opposite page, below:
Newly planted vines on Gurpegui land near San Adrián. This is the Rioja Baja, with a concentration of canning factories – hence the use of tins rather than netting or plastic sheets to protect the young plants.

Below:
Gurpegui is the only Riojan bodega equipped for thermo-vinification.

The firm's tanks have a combined capacity of 2.2 million (US 2.6 million) gallons. Average annual production is 880,000 (US 1.04 million) gallons of red, 330,000 (US 390,000) gallons of white and 440,000 (US 520,000) gallons of rosé wine.

Bodegas Gurpegui

Fine old presses

After destalking and crushing the black grapes are fermented at Berceo at a temperature of at most 28°C. Besides the large wooden vats already mentioned there are tanks, mainly concrete, for fermenting the wine. *Vin de presse* is obtained from the *marc* here by means of splendid circular presses, of an old type but still functioning well. After the fermentation process the *crianzas* remain for a year in an enormous concrete container that runs the whole length of the building. *Reservas* and *gran reservas* on the other hand are given their first ageing in large oak vats. The next stage for the red Riojas made at Haro is the period of cask ageing. White and rosé wines are not made at all here. Any white grapes coming in here are just pressed, then the must is transported to San Adrián.

Cask ageing limited

Bodegas Gurpegui does not advocate excessively long periods of wood ageing and so none of the red wines normally stays longer than two years in the *barricas*. All of these 7,000 casks are of American oak. There is not enough room for these in the cellars at Haro and so quite a number are stored at San Adrián and the other two premises. The wine is racked two to three times a year during its cask ageing. Before the Riojas go into the casks they pass through an earth filter, and through a membrane type at bottling. Once bottled the wines are given a further ageing period that can vary from six months, for the *crianzas*, to around ten years for one of the *gran reservas*.

Various brands

Bodegas Gurpegui's most important brand of bottled wine is the Viña Berceo; but the name Dominio de la Plana is, however, used for exactly the same qualities. The Viñadrián line is for Riojas at a simpler level. In 1979 the firm started to export and at present about a quarter of the production crosses the frontier. The biggest customers for the bottled wines are Britain, Denmark, the Netherlands, Germany and Canada, and bulk sales are made to various countries. My tasting notes are confined to the bottled Riojas. After I had been shown the excellent plant for fermenting the wines the dry white Berceo came as a considerable disappointment. It was an indifferent wine that needs to be purer and fresher, with more fruit. It is made from 90% Viura grapes and 10% Malvasia, and it does not come into contact with wood at all. The rosé tasted better. This is not one of those light picnic partners but a quite powerful table wine, able to hold its own even with spicy meat dishes or strongly flavoured cheeses. The Garnacha is its only grape variety.

A lively taste

The Viña Berceo red *crianza* undergoes a period of a year's ageing in tank, a minimum year in cask (it can be as much as 2 years) and at least 6 months in bottle. Its grapes are 70% Tempranillo and 30% Garnacha. This wine usually has a reasonably deep colour, a pure perfume with a good amount of vanilla, and a vital taste with fruit, wood and, again, vanilla. The *reserva* by contrast, comes across less convincingly. It is generally a correct, but not very inspiring Rioja, made from 80% Tempranillo, 10% Mazuelo and 10% Graciano grapes. Its year in the wooden vat, two years in cask and two years at least in bottle give it more maturity and wood than the *crianza* – but rather less fruit and not so much charm. It does seem as if the Gurpegui *reservas* form an intermediary class with which difficulty is experienced.

Two *gran reservas*

The *gran reservas*, on the other hand, are of very good quality: the Viña Berceo is quite a robust wine in colour, nose and taste, sound of structure and with a good measure of tannin in the aftertaste. It arrives on the market after about a year in the wooden vat, two in cask and at least six years in bottle. This Rioja is therefore beautifully matured (but not tired) and its wood and vanilla are clearly discernible. The firm is proud of the fact that the 1973 won a silver medal at the Bordeaux Vinexpo 1983. The mixture of grape varieties in the *gran reservas* is the same as for the *reservas*. The bodega attaches most prestige to its Gonzalo de Berceo, a *gran reserva* produced in limited quantities and only from superior vintages; 79,960 bottles were, for example, made of the 1970. This *gran reserva* spends at least ten years in bottle in the cellars at Haro, after having one year in the wooden vat and two in cask. It is a sinewy Rioja that has been able to develop beautifully into a harmonious, outstandingly enjoyable whole. This wine, naturally not cheap, contrasts greatly with the moderately priced wine of the year from San Adrián; contrasts of this order are also encountered between the buildings and the techniques employed inside them; if there is a single term that could be applied to Bodegas Gurpegui, then that term is manysidedness.

San Adrián

Bodegas Muerza

By the crossroads in the heart of San Adrián there is a large café called the Casino. On either side of it are the entrances to Bodegas Muerza, on the left for visitors and on the right for the grapes. In addition, the first floor of the Casino has been used by the wine firm since 1973, Muerza storing its bottles on pallets in what used to serve as the local cinema and dance hall. "It is a happy environment for the wine to mature in", said a spokesman for the bodega. The white-painted buildings with their bright-green shutters are not the firm's original address. It was founded in 1882 by Ricardo Ugalde, a *cosechero* at Haro. He occupied a cellar there, in the centre not far from the Calle de las Cuevas.

Changes of ownership

The business in Haro was passed on from father to son until the family joined with other shareholders. The bodega not only became a limited company but also changed its name several times. In 1939 it was called Francisco Hormaeche y Cia and in 1947 Bodegas Ugalde. Not long afterwards the firm acquired Fructuoso Muerza as a shareholder, after which the name changed to Bodegas Ugalde y Muerza. In 1952 it finally became Bodegas Muerza. The move to San Adrián took place in the same year, into buildings that Fructuoso Muerza had bought in 1941 from an olive oil factory that had only operated for two years. Fructuoso extended them in 1947.

The Rioja Vega crianza is a wine with juice, suppleness, a certain terroir and a fairly long aftertaste. At 50% the Garnacha is the most important grape, supplemented by 45% Tempranillo and 5% Graciano. Despite this it is not one of those heavy, turgid wines: its alcohol is restricted to 12 to 13%. Ageing: 6 to 9 months' tank, 12 to 16 cask and at least 12 months' bottle.

Muerza's reserva contains more Tempranillo than the crianza, namely 70% (with 25% Garnacha, 5% Mazuelo, 5% Graciano). This makes it a wine with more vivacity and breeding, although the same terroir element can be tasted. Its longer time in cask and bottle (2 to 2½ and 1 to 2 years respectively) means it also has more maturity and wood.

The gran reserva has something of the same terroir in its taste as the two wines just described, albeit to a lesser degree. In addition, your nose and tongue pick up impressions of wood, vanilla (neither overwhelming) juice and mellowness. The wine matures for 6 to 12 months in tank, 2 to 3 years in cask, 3 to 4½ years in bottle. Its grape varieties are 75% Tempranillo, 20% Garnacha, 5% Mazuelo, 5% Graciano.

Bodegas Muerza

Subsequent alterations took place in 1952, 1963 and 1974 – or roughly once a decade. At present 80% of the shares are in the hands of four brothers who produce the Montilla aperitif wine in the south of Spain. Besides these, the American Harry Fieldstein has an interest in the business. Since 1984 the Muerza wines have been distributed and exported by Agronavarra, a group with its headquarters in Pamplona.

Land in two districts

Bodegas Muerza has a modest estate of just over 64 acres, planted exclusively with Tempranillo vines. This applies even to the 22 acres in Rioja Baja, on fairly high ground near Aldeanueva de Ebro and planted at the beginning of the 1970s. The rest is in Rioja Alta, near Sotés, a village between Navarrete and Najera. The Muerza land provides grapes for about 20% of the 94,600 (US 112,000) gallons the firm makes annually. The rest is bought in the form of wine (two-thirds) and grapes (one-third) for the red Rioja, and for the 14,300 (US 17,000) gallons of white and the 9,500 (US 11,200) gallons of rosé. A large part of the wine comes from Rioja Alta, the grapes chiefly from Rioja Baja. In the past Muerza sold a good deal of young red wine of the year (as Señorial and also under the Bodegas Ugalde name), but present policy is directed towards bringing out more mature Riojas. This is why the number of casks is rising, from 1,200 to around 2,800 so far. At the same time it is hoped to increase the stock of bottled wine from 300,000 to 500,000 or more.

The Rioja Vega brand

The grapes for red wine are destalked and crushed and then fermented in tiled concrete tanks. The fermentation period is closed with the first filtering, through earth. The wines that are considered suitable then go into the casks to mature for a period that can vary from 1 to 3 years. The firm has casks of American oak only. They remain in circulation for 12 to 14 years and are maintained by a staff cooper.

The wine is filtered for a second time just before bottling, through cellulose plates this time. By far the best-selling brand from this bodega is Rioja Vega. The red crianza version of this contains 50% Garnacha, 45% Tempranillo and 5% Graciano. The presence of the Garnacha grape is obvious in the taste, although fortunately the wine does not possess excessive alcohol. Fruit suppleness and a certain terroir are complemented by a fairly long, almost slightly dry finish. This Rioja is given 6 to 9 months in tank, 12 to 16 in cask and at least 12 months in bottle.

Terroir in the taste

In the reserva the proportion of Garnacha drops to 25%. In this wine the Tempranillo predominates with 70%, with subordinate roles for the Mazuelo and Graciano, with 5% between them. Ageing in wood lasts for 24 to 30 months and in bottle for 12 to 24. This wine is rather livelier and more matured than the crianza, and in addition has more wood. You can, however, taste the same element of terroir in it, the hint of earthiness that tells of its native soil. The same is true of the gran reserva, a wine with a lingering aftertaste that now has 75% Tempranillo in its make-up. It used to be made from equal proportions of Tempranillo and Garnacha – which was still the case with the 1970 wine. Muerza gives this category of Rioja 6 to 12 months in tank (like the reserva), 2 to 3 years in cask and 3 to 4½ in bottle.

Future plans

Only black grapes are selected for the Rioja Vega rosé: 80% Garnacha and 20% Tempranillo. The stalks are removed and the grapes crushed, then they are taken to wooden vats. The juice that is produced by the weight of the grapes themselves serves for the rosé. This juice is then vinified in concrete tanks. At the time of my visit Bodegas Muerza was not yet fermenting the wine at low temperatures and so the rosé lacked freshness and fruit. The same applied to the white, a 100% Viura wine. In the near future, however, the bodega hopes to be able to ferment these wines at 18°C. It already has the plant for stabilizing white, rosé and sometimes young red wines at low temperatures. Bodegas Muerza intends to increase production and sales by a minimum of one-third: this San Adrián concern, now more than a century old, has plans in plenty.

Left:
Until 1984 the name Bodegas de la Torre y Lapuerta was what appeared on the wall beside the entrance – but the bodega has changed its name once more.

Below:
Some of the cellar buildings.

Bottom:
Grapes arriving.

The bodega has a small plaza de toros, where guests can play the part of bullfighter.

Viña Hermosa, Viña Algodi, Monte Placido and Paco Gomez are subsidiary brands.

Average stock of bottles is 70,000, together with 7,000 casks (of which 500 to 700 are renewed each year). Storage capacity in the tanks is 1.1 million (US 1.3 million) gallons.

The meagre sin crianza from this bodega is composed of 50% Tempranillo and 50% Garnacha, whereas the older wines have 80% Tempranillo and 20% Garnacha. They normally mature for a year in tank, 2 years (to a maximum 3) in wood and 6 months (up to 3 years) in bottle. All the wines I tasted were lacking in character. The best was the gran reserva Campo Burgo 1970, with a reasonably deep, slightly brown colour. It had an element of wood and a vague hint of caramel in the taste and a reasonable maturity.

Alfaro

Bodegas Campo Burgo

The firm of Bodegas Campo Burgo, a *sociedad anónima*, must be one of the most spaciously housed in the Rioja, for it is established in the extensive buildings of a former sugar factory behind the station at Alfaro. The site covers an area of nearly 50 acres of which almost 7½ acres is taken up by large, mostly tall industrial sheds. The company moved into the complex in 1984, after purchasing it in December 1983. Bodegas Campo Burgo had previously been situated in the centre of Alfaro, where it had had a site of only 1 acre at its disposal. The bodega dates from 1895 and was founded by Pedro de la Torre Fernandez. He called his firm Bodega de la Torre. The name was to change a number of times: in 1908 it became Torre y García del Moral; in 1930 Torre Hijos SA; in 1957 Andrés de la Torre y Torres; and in 1968 Bodegas de la Torre y Lapuerta SA. It was in this last year that Andrés de la Torre's son teamed up with a certain Lapuerta, the enterprise retaining its essentially family character.

This changed when the Julian Cantarero group, which already had wine interests in Valdepeñas and Navarre, acquired the shares. In 1985 the name changed yet again, this time to Bodegas Campo Burgo.

Mainly bulk wine sales

Until the beginning of the 1980s this Rioja wine house apparently sold almost entirely in bulk. Since then, however, it has started bottling on a considerable scale. Of the 528,000 (US 624,000) gallons it produces annually about one-third is now bottled – 70% of the red, 20% of the white, 10% of the rosé. The bodega has no vineyards of its own and so all supplies have to be bought – roughly half in the form of grapes, half as wine. According to the firm all the wine is purchased in Rioja Alavesa, and about 85% of the grapes in Rioja Alta and Alavesa: not much comes from the immediate neighbourhood.

Characterless wines

All the wines from this house are stabilized at low temperature and in addition are filtered at least three times. Wines for drinking young are even pumped four times through filters (twice through earth, once through cellulose plates and once through a membrane). This notably intensive treatment results in notably characterless wines. The only wine that gave me some faint satisfaction was the Campo Burgo *gran reserva*, but this dated from 1970 and had therefore been made by the previous owners. The other red wines had one unwanted undertone or another and did not impress at all. The *sin crianza* (a 1983) I considered to be a mockery of the quality standards the Rioja represents; nor did the white and rosé wines leave any positive impression. The bodega has good plant and equipment and some 7,000 casks of American oak. One can only wish that it was better used.

Other Bodegas

Here are brief descriptions of five lesser bodegas that merit a mention.

Bodegas Velazquez (Cenicero)

This firm was set up by a family that has been active in the wine business for more than a century. Until 1973 it processed only grapes from its own vineyards in its cellar at Fuenmayor; the wine was sold in bulk. In that year the new bodega in Cenicero (next door to Bodegas Riojanas, on the road to the station) was ready for occupation and the firm started maturing and bottling wine. Some of the wine still comes from its own 123 acres of vineyard and in addition it buys in both grapes and wine. Bodegas Velazquez puts about 92,000 (US 109,000) gallons of wine on the market annually, of which more than half goes abroad. Ignacio García Asensio, the manager and joint owner, has around 2,200 oak casks at his disposal and keeps an average stock of some 625,000 bottles. The wines – all red – are not remarkable but are certainly of a correct quality, both the wine of the year and the *crianza*. The firm sells under the names Campo Blanco and Monte Velaz as well as Velazquez.

Bodegas Ribera Alta (Haro)

This wine is among the region's oldest, for it dates from 1886. Its founder was Ángel Gómez de Arteche, Duque de Moctezuma. In 1916 it was taken over by the brothers Agustin and Jesús Gómez Cruzado and was given the name of Bodegas Gómez Cruzado. This was changed to the present name after another take-over. The bodega lies in the middle of Haro's Barrio de la Estación district, wedged between Muga and La Rioja Alta. Besides the cellar at this site it also has an underground vault across the road which runs for 130 yards into the hillside. Here the casks and bottles of *reserva* wines are stored. The Rioja wines produced by Bodegas Ribera Alta come largely from the vinification centre in Cenicero, for space at Haro is too limited and the equipment too old-fashioned. This centre, officially called the Bodegas Porres y Montaña, stands beside the railway, not far from Bodegas Berberana. Here grapes from the firm's own 25 acres and from other vineyards are processed. In addition wine is also bought in. There are 4,500 casks available for wood-ageing the wine.

The San Vicente de la Sonsierra Cooperative (San Vicente de la Sonsierra)

The white, multi-storeyed buildings of the local wine cooperative are in the main street of San Vicente de la Sonsierra, just outside the actual centre of the village. It was founded in 1962 and numbers about 225 members. In addition to its bulk wines it also sells bottled Riojas, some of them cask-aged. For this the cooperative has more than 100 *barricas*. The wines are of a decent quality and are quite elegant in structure. Among the brand names used are Sonsierra, Fino Sonsierra and Viña Mundiarte.

Bodegas La Primicia (Elciego)

In 1981 a new bodega was created in Elciego out of existing buildings and vineyard plots, with the Banque de Bilbao as the major shareholder. This little firm, given the name of Bodegas La Primicia, works on the principle of processing only grapes from its own 44 acres (all in Elciego, but divided up). The vineyards are planted with 70% Tempranillo, 15% Viura and 10% Garnacha vines, with Mazuelo making up the rest. The fruit is neither destalked nor crushed: the traditional Alavesa method of vinification is followed here. Production amounts to an annual 33,000 (US 39,000) gallons and may rise to 44,000 (US 52,000). The rule for ageing the wine is 12 months in tank, 14 months in cask and 12 in bottle. There are 550 casks available. The first wine to appear on the market was the 1981, which came out in 1985. This Rioja had a reasonably deep colour and a supple, friendly taste. I also tasted the 1983 from the tank. It seemed to me a wine of good potential: substantial, firm and with a measure of tannin. The intention is that all Riojas from La Primicia will be sold bottled.

Bodegas Nuestra Señora de la Antigua (Arenzana de Abajo)

The large Spanish table wine firm Capel is the owner of this bodega. It is situated in the Rioja Alta and buys wines only, from cooperatives and individual *cosecheros*. An export licence was obtained in 1984. I have only tasted the Viña Lambilla 1981. It was a very pleasant Rioja: a wine with a good colour, a fine vanilla perfume, and is satisfactorily firm and pure. This bodega seems worth following.

Glossary

Abocado Term used on labels of semi-dry white Riojas with generally a somewhat lower sugar content than *semi-dulce*.
Alambrado Characteristic metallic mesh many bodegas fit over their bottles of older wines. Devised long ago to guarantee the authenticity of Rioja wines.
Almacenista Wine wholesaler who holds stocks of Rioja to sell to the large bodegas.
Año Year.
Autopista Spanish motorway; tolls are payable on the one through Rioja.

Barrica (*bordelesa*) Oak cask of 225-litre (about 50-gallon) capacity, identical to the French *barrique bordelaise*. Mostly American oak is used in Rioja.
Barrio District, quarter.
Blanco White.
Bocoy Large cask, usually of about 600 litres (132 gallons). Comparable with the French *demi–muid*.
Bodega Literally a wine cellar, but used here in its extended sense of a place where wine is made as well as matured.
Bota Wineskin.
Botella Bottle.

Calle Street.
Cantara Measure of capacity — 16 litres (3 gallons) — frequently used in the Rioja.
Cartilla Form on which all the particulars of a wine are recorded; it enables the Consejo Regulador to follow and check up on every Rioja from the picking of the grapes to its consumption.
Casa House.
Castillo Castle.
Cementerio Literally a graveyard; most bodegas use the word to refer to the cellar holding their oldest wines. Herederos del Marqués de Riscal, however, uses *catedral* for this.
Cesto Basket of 15 to 20 kg capacity (33 to 44 lb) used by grape pickers.
Champagne Method Way of making sparkling wine. A secondary fermentation takes place in the bottle (as in Champagne itself). The carbon dioxide released by this process is held in the wine under pressure and produces bubbles. Wines are made by

this method in the region but are not entitled to the Rioja name.
Clarete Originally synonymous with Rioja, the word is now used of the lighter type of red wine, or sometimes of a rosé. Not a legally protected term.
Cold stabilization, treatment Drastic reduction of the temperature of a wine for a short period to induce the precipitation of tartaric acid crystals. These small, neutral and completely harmless crystals might otherwise be produced in the bottle.
Comporta Large wooden tub into which from 80 to 120 kg (176 to 265 lb) of grapes can be tipped.
Consejo Regulador (*de la Denominación de Origen Rioja*) Council that regulates, administers and checks the working of the Rioja wine region as well as giving advice and protection, and undertaking publicity.
Corquete Grape picker's implement, like a small sickle.
Cosecha Harvest, vintage.
Cosechero Wine grower, usually on a small scale, who vinifies his own wine.
Crianza see *vino de crianza*

Degustación (Wine) tasting.
Degustador (Wine) taster.
Denominación de origen Qualification applied to wine of approved type and standard from a defined district.
Deposito Tank, or closed wooden vat, for fermenting or storing wine.
Dulce Sweet.

Enología Science of wine and wine making; oenology.
Enologico Wine technician, oenologist, usually with a university-level qualification.
Espumoso Sparkling.
Estación Station.
Etiqueta Label.

Fermentation Process by which the sugar present in grape juice is converted into alcohol and carbon dioxide.
Fining The removal of any remaining solids in the wine by the addition of a coagulant, nearly always albuminous. Called *la clarificación* in Spanish.

Frontón Marked-up bare wall where the Basque game of pelota is played.

Gerente Person in a bodega, usually the manager or managing director, who represents the owners.
Gran reserva Rioja matured for at least two years in cask and three in bottle.
Grupo de Exportadores de Vinos Rioja Group to which all exporting bodegas have to belong.
Iglesia Church.

Lago Rectangular, open fermentation vat, usually of concrete. Used for centuries in the Rioja.

Macération carbonique Method in which intercellular fermentation occurs inside the skins of intact grapes under a 'blanket' of carbon dioxide. The Rioja has its own, very traditional variant of this process. The resulting wines are generally rich in fruit, supple and low in tannin.
Malolactic fermentation Secondary, non-alcoholic fermentation that converts the malic acid in the wine into lactic acid (and carbon dioxide). It reduces the acidity and makes the wine more stable. Essential for all red wines but hardly ever applied to white and rosé Riojas.
Must Unfermented grape juice.

Parador (*Nacionál*) Spanish state-owned hotel, usually in an old, historic building.
Pelota Basque game played against a wall.
Phylloxera vastatrix Parasite that destroyed practically all the European vineyards at the end of the last century and the beginning of this.
Porrón Carafe shaped so that a jet of wine can be aimed into the mouth without the need for any intervening glass.
Prensa Press.
Probador Wine-tasting room.

Reserva Wine matured for at least three years, with a minimum one year in cask.
Río River.
Rosado Rosé.

Seco Dry.

Left:
Cenicero at grape harvest time.

Glossary

Semi-dulce Semi-sweet.
Sierra Mountain range.
Sin crianza see *vino sin crianza*.
Sociedad Anónima Public limited company.
Socio Member of a wine-growing cooperative.

Tannin Substance that has a preservative effect in wine.
Terroir Term indicating a slightly earthy taste.
Tinto The red colour of a wine, or the red wine itself.
Tonelero Cooper.
Trasiega Transfer of wine to a clean cask.

Vendimia Grape harvest, vintage.
Viña, viñedo Vineyard.
Vinification The processing of grapes into wine.
Vino de cosechero A *vino del año* (and therefore also a *vino sin crianza*) obtained by the traditional Riojan fermentation method with uncrushed grapes. Many large bodegas use this term (especially in the Rioja Alavesa) as well as the *cosecheros*.
Vino de crianza Wine that has had at least one year's ageing in cask.
Vino del año Rioja that has had no ageing in cask and as a rule must be drunk young. Officially this type belongs in the *vino sin crianza* category.

Vino sin crianza Wine that has had no ageing in cask.
Viticultor, viticultura Wine grower, wine growing.
Yield Usually expressed in hectolitres per hectare per year.

Bibliography

Actos conmemorativos del VI centenario de la fundación de la villa de Cuzcurrita de Río Tirón, Cuzcurrita de Río Tirón 1969.
Adventures in Taste: The Wines and Folk Food of Spain, D.E. Pohren, Morón de la Frontera 1972.
Bouquet, la guía de los vinos y de la buena mesa, Barcelona, various numbers.
Catastro vitícola y vinícola denominacion de origen Rioja, Instituto Nacionál de Denominaciones de Origen, Madrid 1982
Decanter Magazine, London.
Discovering Spanish Wine, John Reay-Smith, London 1976
Estudios sobre el vino de Rioja, Manuel Ruiz Hernandez, Haro 1978.
Guía de los vino y bodegas de España, Antonio Larreau Redondo and others, Barcelona 1984
Haro '84, various authors Haro 1984
Haro vinos e historia, Antonio Larrea Redondo, Haro 1983
Laguardia, Vitoria 1983.
Manuel de los vinos de Rioja, José Penin, Madrid 1982
The Noble Wines from the Rioja Alavesa, Casa del Vino (Laguardia), Bilbao 1983
Nuestros vinos Rioja Alavesa, José Maria Busca Isusi, Vitoria 1979
La Rioja Alavesa, Salvadir Velilla, Vitoria
Rioja Alta et Alavesa, suite de deux vinifications, Inigo Manso de Zuniga y Ugartechea, Bordeaux 1984
La Rioja, Art Treasures and Wine-Growing Resources, Barcelona 1981
Los suelos de las viñas de Rioja, Manuel Ruiz Hernandez 1982
Le systéme viti-vinicole de la Rioja, C. Béringuier, A. Boudou, H. Castella, J. Pilleboue, Toulouse 1983
Un vaso de bon vino, Manuel Llano Gorostiza, Bilbao 1979.
Vendimia (La Rioja Alta, S.A. edition, Josée Maria de Soroa y Pineda, Haro
De las vides y de las tierras de Rioja, Antonio Larrea Redondo, Haro 1982
Viniferas de Rioja, Manul Ruiz Hernandez, Haro 1982.
Wine Companion Hugh Johnson, London 1983
Wines of Rioja, Jan Read, London 1984.
World Atlas of Wine Hugh Johnson, London 1978.

Index

Index

Left:
Staves from old casks (left) and for new ones at La Rioja Alta, Haro.

Right:
Cooper's tools at Bodegas Martínez Lacusta, also in Haro.

Index

Left:
Old cask under repair at
Martínez Lacuesta.

Right:
As well as making and repairing
casks, the cooper's workshop at
Bodegas Martínez Lacuesta
turns out wooden bungs for them
(see Bodegas Martínez Lacuesta,
pages 69-71).

Index

Left:
Waving to friends, pickers go home after a day in the vineyards.

Index

Picture credits

The great majority of the pictures in this book were taken by the Amsterdam photographer Peter van der Velde, who spent many weeks in Rioja on this assignment.

Acknowledgments of the other photographs:
(the figures 1, 2, 3 etc. following the page numbers refer to the position of the illustration on the page, going from left to right and top to bottom)

Hubrecht Duijker: *6–2/ 11–2, 3, 4/ 13–2/ 14–2/ 15–2/ 16–1, 3/ 17–1/ 19–2/ 22–3/ 26–2/ 27–1/ 30–1, 2/ 48–3/ 55–1/ 60–1/ 63–1, 3/ 64–1/ 65–1/ 69–2, 3/ 70–1/ 75–1, 2/ 76–3/ 77–1/ 78–1/ 79–1/ 81–1/ 85–2/ 87–2/ 106–2/ 108–2/ 109–1/ 110–1/ 116–1/ 120–2/ 133–1/ 137–1, 2/ 141–1/ 152–1/ 155–1/ 156–3/ 159–1, 2/ 167–1/ 188–1, 2, 3/ 193–1.*

The author and publishers are also indebted to the bodegas that so readily made material available:

Herederos del Marqués de Riscal: *14–3/ 35–2/ 110–1/ 111–1, 2.*
Federico Paternina: *66–1, 2.*
Bodegas Rioja Santiago: *73–1.*
Bodegas Montecillo: *149–3.*
Bodegas Franco-Españolas: *165–1.*
Bodegas Olarra: *168–1.*

The producers of this book are also grateful to Casa del Vino in Laguardia for the illustrative material provided: *31–2/ 36–2/ 37–1, 2/ 38–1, 2/ 44–1.*